MEDJUGORJE
THE MISSION

Medjugorje – A Shining Inspiration

Other titles available from Paraclete Press

MEDJUGORJE
THE MISSION

WAYNE WEIBLE

PARACLETE PRESS
Orleans, Massachusetts

To protect the privacy of some individuals involved, names have been changed in certain instances.

Messages and excerpts of messages at the beginning of each segment and chapter, or within the chapters, are taken from those reportedly given by the Blessed Virgin Mary to the visionaries at Medjugorje, over the past thirteen years.

The apparitions of the Blessed Virgin Mary at Medjugorje, have not as of this writing been officially approved by the investigating commission established by the Roman Catholic Church. However, they have not been disapproved or censored, which would have been the case had anything contrary to Church doctrine or Holy Scripture been discovered in the thirteen years they have allegedly occurred. Because of the overwhelming number of pilgrims, it has been designated as an official Marian shrine. The author submits totally to the authority of the Church in its ultimate conclusion of these events.

Library of Congress Cataloging-in-Publication Data

Weible, Wayne.
  Medjugorje the Mission/Wayne Weible.
     p.   cm.
  ISBN 1-55725-127-4

  1. Mary, Blessed Virgin, Saint—Apparitions and miracles—Bosnia and Hercegovina—Medjugorje. 2. Medjugorje (Bosnia and Hercegovina)—Religious life and customs. 3. Christian pilgrims and pilgrimages—Bosnia and Hercegovina—Medjugorje. 4. Weible, Wayne. I. Title.

BT660.M44W46   1994
232.91'7'0949742—dc20   94-25229
                                               CIP

10 9 8 7 6 5 4 3 2

Printed in the United States of America at Paraclete Press.
Cover: Images © PhotoDisc, Inc. 1994

*I dedicate this book to all souls who
have heeded the call of return to the
Gospel message of Jesus, through
the apparitions of Our Lady
at Medjugorje, and have answered
with prayer, fasting and penance.*

*Also to my wife, Terri,
whose encouragement, assistance,
collaboration, persistence and
spiritual acceptance made possible
not just this book,
but the entire mission.*

Table of Contents

Foreword

I met Wayne Weible at the first Medjugorje Peace conference, held at Notre Dame University, in 1988. I was curious to find out more about this Lutheran who had taken up the mission of spreading the Medjugorje message, giving up a lucrative business career to do so.

Having seen him on the national *Sally Jessy Raphael* television show, and being personally familiar with the tabloid containing his articles on Medjugorje, I was pleased to accompany friends to the airport at South Bend, to pick him up for the conference. I had been pronouncing Wayne's last name, "Weeble," but was immediately corrected, as he gently informed me the best way to remember the correct pronunciation was that it rhymed with "Bible." It was the beginning of a long friendship.

Little did I know that one day, I would receive Wayne and his beautiful wife Terri into the Roman Catholic Church, at yet another Medjugorje conference, this one in New Orleans. Just prior to the ceremony, Archbishop

Phillip Hannan asked who was to be his Godparent. Since I had not selected one, I was duly appointed as such by the Archbishop. Thus, Wayne is more than just a friend—he is my Godson!

In these past seven years, we have shared the stage at many conferences throughout the United States; and, we were able to be together for a special visit to Medjugorje with teenagers as our pilgrims.

There is little doubt in my heart that Wayne has been given a special mission, a mission which again, we both share: that is, to evangelize the Gospel message of Jesus Christ, which is at the heart of the messages being given at Medjugorje by the Blessed Virgin Mary.

–Father Kenneth J. Roberts

Prologue:
Miracle at Medjugorje

"My angels, I send you my Son, Jesus, who was tortured for His faith and yet, He endured everything. You also, my angels, will endure everything. . . ."

Just another village among many scattered throughout the mountains and valleys of Yugoslavia's republic of Bosnia-Hercegovina; that was Medjugorje. Small, rural and rather undistinguished except for its large, cement cross atop Krizevic Mountain overlooking the collection of little hamlets. For four decades, the 36-foot-high structure has served as a constant reminder to the predominantly Croatian villagers of their strong Catholic faith and its effect on the daily ebb and flow of life. This, in spite of living under the oppressive rule of atheistic Communism, in a government dominated by their ethnic enemy, Serbia. Still, for the most part, life was quiet and simple.

That changed suddenly on June 24, 1981.

On that day, several teenagers made the astonishing claim that they had seen an apparition of the Blessed Virgin Mary, the mother of Jesus Christ, on the side of Podbrdo Hill near the Bethlehem-like hamlet. The weather-beaten cross would soon serve as a powerful symbol for this supernatural mystical phenomena that would draw millions of spiritually hungry souls from all corners of the earth.

It began as two girls, Ivanka Ivankovic, 16, and Mirjana Dragecevic, 15, set out for an early evening stroll after finishing family chores. Later, as clouds gathered threatening rain, the two friends started home, disappointed that a third companion, Vicka Ivankovic, 17, had not joined them. They had left a note at her home asking that she meet them beyond Podbrdo Hill.

As the two girls approached the edge of the village, Ivanka was startled suddenly by a brilliant flash of light halfway up the hill. She came to a sudden stop, and was astonished to see the image of a beautiful young woman in the light. Immediately she identified the image from her Catholic heritage: it was *Gospa*—the Blessed Virgin Mary!

Ivanka began screaming for Mirjana to look up on the hill at the image. But she refused to look, thinking her friend was pulling a prank, which they regularly played on one another. Continuing toward the village, Mirjana scolded her friend playfully for trying to trick her.

Fixated by the dazzling beauty of the image, Ivanka seemed frozen in her tracks, before breaking into a run after Mirjana, who by this time had met up with another young girl on her way to get the family sheep. It didn't take long for them to see that Ivanka was serious; this was no prank. Quickly, they hurried to the spot, and now they too were able to see the vision in the brilliant light.

As the young girls stared at the image, she beckoned for them to come closer; no one moved. They were too frightened. Vicka, finally coming to join her two friends, turned and fled in fright when her friends shouted for her to come and see Gospa. She returned shortly with two boys whom she had met on the road and told what was happening near Podbrdo. As they joined the others, they also were able to see the image.

Some of the young people began to pray while others cried; one young man who had come with Vicka, ran frightened to his nearby home. But none of the young people answered the beckoning of the image to come to her. Instead, they began to drift home one by one as a light mist of rain began to fall. Once in the security of family and friends, they excitedly related what they had seen. Word spread like wildfire with reactions ranging from wonderment to disbelief.

The following day, June 25, answering an inexplicable urge within them to return to the spot where they had first seen the "beautiful lady in the light," six youngsters scrambled up the side of the hill as the vision again beckoned to them. It was then conversation between the teens and the image commenced, one that would continue daily for years to come.

The four girls and two boys were immediately transformed from ordinary peasant teenagers, to visionaries of the Blessed Virgin Mary. Mirjana, Ivanka and Vicka were joined by Marija Pavlovic, 16, Ivan Dragecevic, 17, and little Jakov Colo, a cousin of Marija, who was only ten years old.

As the children knelt in reverence before the vision and felt the peace and love emanating from the light, they gained enough courage to begin asking questions. She smiled serenely and began to answer. She was the Blessed Virgin Mary, and had come to tell them that "God exists and He loves you."

God had sent her to give this message of love to the village—and to the world. It was a message not just for Catholics, but for everyone. She would lead them in total conversion to her Son, Jesus, by teaching them to pray, to fast, and to do penance. Those who listened and obeyed would find true peace and happiness.

Word quickly spread throughout the region, and thousands came to experience the phenomenon for themselves. Claims of cures from illness and handicaps created even larger crowds. Serb-dominated government authorities became alarmed. Such huge gatherings meant only one thing to them: the Croatians were planning insurrection and overthrow of the government. Hatred between the two ethnic groups had fomented over years from accusations and atrocities.

Local authorities in nearby Citluk sent for the six young people and harshly interrogated them, having them examined by physicians and psychologists; they found nothing wrong medically or mentally. Worse, family, friends, and even the Franciscan priests did not believe their story; they were accused of lying, of being on drugs, of pulling a great hoax. But the children stuck to their story.

The pastor of St. James Catholic Church in Medjugorje, Franciscan priest Jozo Zovko, soon became convinced the children were telling the truth; he would later spend a year and a half in prison for defending their claims and refusing the local government's demands to bring the apparitions to an end. And his bishop, who at first enthusiastically supported the claims of the visionary children, soon bowed to the government threats of jail and became the prime adversary of the apparitions.

The Croatian villagers, beset with endless skirmishes with Serb authorities and the usual variety of generic social problems that plague every community, slowly began to change. Workdays were cut short to attend church services in the evening; long-running feuds between family clans were settled; and, prayers followed by Mass soon formed the foundation for the good fruits that would convince millions from around the world to make the difficult pilgrimage to the village.

This phenomenal event which has transformed millions of lives in the last thirteen years, continues as of this writing. . . .

Introduction:
The Mission

"God has chosen each one of you in order to use you in a great plan for the salvation of mankind."

On first learning about reported apparitions of the Blessed Virgin Mary in the tiny village of Medjugorje, I was not moved spiritually. Nor did I necessarily believe the story. My faith at that time could best be described as lukewarm, but there was interest; as owner and publisher of four weekly newspapers, I was always looking for unique human-interest stories. This qualified.

Personal involvement began as I reviewed a video tape that contained an actual encounter of the six children claiming to see the Virgin Mary. I was stunned with what I was seeing. Then, something happened; like the six teenagers, I suddenly felt the Virgin Mary speaking directly to me.

There was no doubt in my heart—or in my mind. It was as if the entire message was placed in my heart all at once as she said to me: *"You are my son, and I am asking you to do my Son's will. I ask you to write about these events, and if you chose, you will no longer be in the work you are in; the spreading of the messages will become your life mission."*

1

I was being asked to give up everything, including my businesses and career as a newspaper journalist. In place of this, the mother of Jesus was inviting me to become an evangelist of the messages she was giving to the world through these children at Medjugorje.

But how? As a Protestant, I knew little about Mary. And nothing about apparitions. In truth I didn't even know how to pray beyond memorized words.

I was certainly not a "good Christian," sporadic in church attendance and having gone through a horrible divorce from a marriage that included four children. Even though I had remarried, my second wife Terri and I had stayed away from all churches for more than seven years because of my anger at God over the divorce. Only recently had I returned to my family's Lutheran faith, mainly at the insistence of Terri, so that our two-year-old son Kennedy could be baptized. Even then, I went more in the interest of aiding our businesses through social and business contacts. It had little to do with spiritual conviction.

But I knew beyond doubt that the Virgin Mary had spoken to me. I began to study furiously; to learn everything I could about the Virgin Mary and apparitions. I also learned to pray, truly pray with my heart. Six months later, we sold our newspapers leaving us with only a printing company and four employees. It freed me to fulfill what the Madonna was asking. On May 1, 1986, I arrived in Medjugorje for the first of many trips.

In the weeks after receiving this personal, mystical call I wrote a series of articles about the apparitions. Published in newspaper tabloid form, they were later reprinted in dozens of languages, and distributed around the world at the astounding number of more than 50 million copies.

Business interests were soon replaced with a year-round schedule of travel to give talks about this modern-day miracle. Reaction to the story as well as the storyteller was the same: People were fascinated that a Lutheran Protestant would take up a mission to spread the story of these apparitions of the Blessed Virgin Mary.

Later, I wrote two books about the apparitions and my personal conversion story. The first, *Medjugorje: The Message,* continues to be the largest-selling book on the phenomena; the second, *Letters From Medjugorje,* details personal conversion experiences through encounters and letters from thousands of people from all over the world.

This book chronicles the unique mission given in a miraculous way to this lukewarm Protestant that would deeply touch people of all faiths; it is testimony of a soul transformed by the love and peace of the Madonna's messages; and, it is discovery of the wonderful spiritual truths of Christianity through the Roman Catholic Church.

Included is an update of the apparitions and the effects on the people involved, including the horrific war of invasion by Serbia into the former Yugoslavia republics of Croatia and Bosnia-Hercegovina, which began in 1991. The war, which continues as of this writing, threatened to curtail the opportunity for others to find the peace and conversion which has occurred through Mary's daily visits to Medjugorje. But it has failed; people continue to go.

Through these pages that tell of the travels, the miracles, the outreach to souls of every belief and non-belief, the holy messenger at tiny Medjugorje confirms repeatedly her call to this son to do *her* Son's will. It is hoped that through these pages, each reader will hear clearly that same loving call.

1

New Directions

". . . These days are the days when you need to decide for God, for peace and for the good. May every hatred and jealousy disappear from your life and your thoughts, and may there only dwell love for God and for your neighbor. . . ."

The airplane lifted off the runway of the Myrtle Beach airport into the blue, cloud-scattered sky. Suddenly, the significance of the day of departure struck me; it was the 25th, the anniversary day, exactly 11 years and seven months since the Blessed Virgin Mary had first appeared in Medjugorje.

Was it coincidence this day, January 25, 1993, also marked the beginning of my 18th trip in the last six years to this tiny village, trips that had given dramatic, new direction to my life? Hardly, I thought with a half-smile.

I settled into my seat and let out a weary sigh as the airliner banked in a turn over the sparkling oceanfront of my hometown en route to Charlotte, North Carolina; from there I would fly to Frankfurt, Germany, on to Zagreb, Croatia, and then to Split. There, Franciscan priest Svetozar Kraljevic, would meet me and drive us to the village. It was as safe a route as could be expected considering the wartime conditions now prevailing in the republics formerly grouped together as Communist Yugoslavia.

Gazing out the window at the placid sky, I thought of how the outbreak of fighting in the last twelve months had changed the peaceful face of Medjugorje into present-day turmoil. This unfortunate new direction of events had reduced eleven years of continuous good fruits to a sparse crop. No longer were thousands of pilgrims coming from every continent to experience spiritual conversion. Now, only a handful were making the dangerous trip. Many were returnees, coming out of gratitude with food, money, medicine, and prayers.

War had kindled following mid-1991 declarations of independence through democratic elections following the dramatic fall of Communism in Eastern Europe; first by Slovenia, then Croatia and finally in the Spring of 1992, Bosnia-Hercegovina, the republic that was home to Medjugorje. That was half of the six republics that formed this post-World War II federation; it was also the half that provided Yugoslavia much of its food and industry.

Serbia, the dominant republic, along with little Montenegro, were all that remained of the Federation of Yugoslavia. Although its constitution clearly stated that any republic within the Federation could choose to leave at any time, Serbia was not about to let it happen and lose the resources of these nations.

Jubilant but premature celebration by the people of the newly-declared freed republics was abruptly halted by swift invasion and occupation by federal troops. They came under the guise of protection and support of Serbian nationals living in these republics; the Serb "irregulars" as they were called, refused to accept the majority vote for independence by the people of Croatia, and Bosnia-Hercegovina. As a result, fierce fighting throughout the two republics, stoked by the evil hand of Satan, had all but shut down pilgrimages to Medjugorje.

The victims of this unholy change of direction were the predominantly Catholic Croatians, and the Moslems. Separated by wide variances in religious beliefs, they found themselves as uncomfortable allies against the abuses of the Serbs. Both were being systematically annihilated and driven from their homes and lands by "ethnic cleansing," a cold, calculated eviction of native Croats and Moslems from their property and villages, replacing them with Serbs; thus, in the eyes of the Serbians the lands became part of "Greater Serbia."

Now, there were new problems. Moslem refugees, driven from their homes, were converging into traditional Croat territory, taking from Croats as Serbs had taken from them. The former allies were now fighting each other as well as Serbs.

It was a horrendous war, a dark paradox to the messages of love and peace asked by the Virgin Mary through the apparitions at Medjugorje, reinforcing the need for urgency in her recent messages for prayer, fasting and penance. She had asked repeatedly that we do these things "as never before" in order not to allow Satan to destroy what heaven had worked so hard to establish in the last twelve years.

Tilting my seat back to a more comfortable position, I tried to block out thoughts of the war surrounding this little oasis of peace. I wanted to think only of my seventeen previous visits. They had been times of great peace and grace, each special in its own right; I had always gone with high anticipation and left with great regret that it was not for a longer period of time. This trip was different. I was going into a war zone. The invaders gave little thought to the nationality of those in the way of their single-minded goal of conquest. I was apprehensive.

Deep down though, I was happy to be going. Father Svetozar had persuaded me to come and see for myself these new changes of direction. This Catholic priest who had now turned full attention to providing relief funds for food and medicine, and creating awareness of the situation in his native Bosnia-Hercegovina, had become a close friend. He had asked me repeatedly to make another trip during these wartime conditions.

At an October Medjugorje conference in Denver, Colorado he took up the offensive again as we shared a few moments together in the speakers' lounge. "But why, Father?" I had answered, "I've been there enough times; I know what's going on with the war. Besides, my traveling schedule is already too full."

Quietly, my priest-friend pointed out that I did not know Medjugorje after the last two years of war; I did not know firsthand the suffering penance of the people. It was true. I hadn't been there since August, 1991, just before the war began in earnest.

"Come and see," he said, pausing for emphasis. "Just come and see."

"Okay, Father," I relented, "I'll pray about it, but the only time I have open is the week after Christmas and that's usually family time. Terri would be upset if I took that week away from being with her and the kids."

Father Svet reached over and squeezed my shoulder and said with a little smile, "You pray about it. And then we shall see what happens!"

Not wasting any time, I had gone straight to a little prayer chapel that had been set up near the lounge, adding to the prayers something that through past Medjugorje experiences I had learned to reserve for special matters. I asked for a sign. Let me receive or see a red rose as a sign that I was to come back to Medjugorje. A real red rose. With that, I went back to the speakers' lounge.

The prayer received quick response. Within the hour,

a conference volunteer came into the lounge looking for me. "Here's a little gift for you," and she handed me a single, long-stemmed red rose!

"Thank you," I laughed, "I've kind of been expecting this!"

The lady looked at me puzzled. "Well, I was simply asked by one of the conference attendees to give you this and to tell you thank you for all you're doing."

Okay, I thought after thanking the woman again, there's the sign; I guess I'm supposed to return to Medjugorje—that is, if I can convince my wife.

I was now sure I needed to go again. How could I speak knowledgeably about the messages of the Queen of Peace, as the Virgin Mary had titled herself at Medjugorje, without seeing personally how the enemy of God and man was attempting to destroy what had taken so long to establish? I wondered why I hadn't thought of that before. Seeing Father Svet across the room, I told him what had happened. "But you're still going to have to convince Terri."

He assured me he would speak to her when he came to our home the following week. I had invited him to come for a few days of rest before the next conference in California, where we were again scheduled as speakers; it was an invitation intended to give him a break from a demanding schedule, but also to allow Terri and the children to spend a few days with him. Since meeting Father Svet during her first trip to Medjugorje, he had become her favorite person of all her Medjugorje experiences.

Father Svet spoke to Terri, giving her his reasons for wanting me to come. She agreed, but I could see the disappointment in her eyes at the lost chance of a quiet week of family time.

I later thanked Father Svet for convincing Terri. "Oh, no," he answered with a slight smile, "There is no need to thank me. But, you can do me a small favor. I have been given many things to take back with me and I do not have the capability to do this, and I was wondering if you would bring some of these things with you when you come?"

"Of course. What do you want me to bring?"

Father Svet started upstairs to his room. "Come. I must show you."

In the corner of the room was a package wrapped in brown, wrinkled paper. He carefully unwrapped it to reveal a large crucifix, with the figure of Jesus broken in several places. A hand and foot were missing. "Do you remember this cross?" he asked, holding it up for my closer inspection.

"Yes, it's the cross you had at the Denver conference."

"That is correct. It is a cross from our church in Mostar. I have carried it throughout the United States to show the people what has happened to the Church in Croatia, and Bosnia. Like Jesus, it has suffered—it has been crucified."

As always, his words were simple and direct. "I would now ask you if you could bring this cross with you. I do not have room in my small bag, and I cannot pack it for fear it will be completely destroyed in the luggage compartment."

The cross was at least three feet long and almost as wide. I hesitated before answering, feeling a little uneasy about having to carry a cross through several airports. "Well, uh, yes, I'll bring it for you."

"Are you sure?" Father Svet sensed my hesitation.

"Of course, it's no problem. Terri can wrap it up in padding to protect it." I quickly realized that by wrapping it, no one would recognize it as a cross.

Taking a cold drink offered by the flight attendant as the plane leveled off at its altitude for the short hop to Charlotte, I smiled ruefully as I thought of what happened next.

Lugging two carry-on bags and Father Svet's cross well

wrapped in bubble packaging, I left for Medjugorje on the Monday after Christmas, bound for New York's Kennedy Airport. From there, I was scheduled for a Lufthansa flight to Frankfort, and then on to Split, for a two-hour auto ride into Medjugorje. I would arrive on Tuesday and stay through Friday, allowing me just enough time to return home for a few days with the kids before they started school.

Problems popped up immediately. Sending the cross through the X-ray machine, the attendant looked at me rather strangely. "Is that a cross?"

I had to admit it was, right there in the midst of a crowd of people waiting to get through the security check. So much for being discreet about carrying a cross! I was beginning to feel guilty about my reluctance in wanting to carry it in public. Having gone through so many spiritual experiences in the last six years, I was dismayed that I was still so worldly, as to be embarrassed by outward signs of spirituality.

Little problems at the Myrtle Beach airport turned into larger problems at Charlotte; because of weather conditions and holiday overbookings, the connection into New York was 45 minutes late. I missed my international flight by twenty minutes!

"Well," I replied in disgust when told the flight had just left, "Then book me on the next one out of here; I've got to get to Bosnia-Hercegovina!" I was not in a good mood, having run through traffic and light rain to reach the international terminal. And now the cross was beginning to poke through at the corners of the rain-soaked wrapping.

"I'm sorry, sir, but there are no flights until tomorrow, and even then, I can't get you on Croatian Airlines. They're completely booked for the rest of the week due to the holiday crowds," the agent said, staring at the tattered package I was now holding tightly under by arm. "Is that a cross? Are you a missionary?"

"Yes, it's a cross! And no, I'm not a missionary—I'm a journalist." I was trying not to lose my composure. Desperate now, I pleaded with the agent to exhaust every possible avenue that might possibly get me into Bosnia-Hercegovina. After a futile ten minutes of computer keyboard queries, he apologized again. "I'm sorry, there's absolutely nothing available." And then pausing, he added with a quizzical smile, "Isn't there a war going on there? Why are you going to such a dangerous place?"

All I could do was limply smile. "I told you, I'm a journalist." There was no way to explain that the Blessed Virgin Mary had given me a sure sign to return, and that I knew I was supposed to be able to get there.

Finally accepting that I could not get there anytime in the next five days, I trudged wearily back through the rain to the terminal from which I had just come. By now the cross was clearly visible through the torn wrapping. I was frustrated. Hadn't the Blessed Virgin given me a sure sign that I was to make another trip to Medjugorje? How could it be that I had come all the way to New York and was now having to return home?

During the flight back to Charlotte where I would have to stay overnight before returning to Myrtle Beach the next morning, I suddenly "felt" the discernment of the day's events: yes, I was to return to Medjugorje, but not at this time! This post-Christmas week was family time and that came first. Although it would crowd my January itinerary, I did have the last week of that month open.

And then I felt another voice speaking to me: *"How did it feel to carry My cross today?"*

The exhaustion and frustration of running through airports and missing connections suddenly vanished. I closed my eyes and whispered, "Oh, Jesus, please forgive me for . . ." I couldn't even think of the right words.

Why did I still have to learn these lessons of letting go and letting God direct everything? My contriteness began to fade. In its place came the satisfaction of knowing that as always, God was in charge. It would be done His way. Such lessons in humility had occurred rather frequently through the first years of the mission.

And so, here I was a month later on my way to Medjugorje again, dead tired, having arrived home a few days before from a full week's speaking engagements. It had been the third such tour during this first month of 1993. I wondered if it might be the start of yet another new direction for the mission.

I reclined my seat to the maximum and closed my eyes, hoping to catch a little sleep between stops on the long 15-hour flight to Split. Drifting off, I smiled as I thought of the last dramatic change of direction my mission had received. I was tired then as well.

Once again, a beautiful message from the Madonna of Medjugorje had been the catalyst for the new direction the mission would take. My thoughts wandered back to that time in June, 1988, during an exhaustive ten-day speaking tour in the little Caribbean island nations of Trinidad and Grenada. There was plenty of time before arrival in Split to reminisce. . . .

2
You are my son

". . . I have given you my love so that you may give it to others. . . ."

There was a gentle but persistent knock at the door.

"Are you up yet, Wayne? I have some hot coffee for you. I'm sorry to push you but we need to be on the road in forty-five minutes." It was Ronald Grosberg, organizer and host for my speaking tour in Trinidad.

I rolled over and squinted at the alarm clock; the blurred figures read 6:15 A.M. Reluctantly leaving the soft down of the bed and heading for the door, I wondered how this man could be so cheery and energetic after seven straight days of an early-morning to late-night schedule. We had been in about every village, town, and city of Trinidad. Each day had been a frenetic crisscrossing of the land along jammed, fume-filled roads to give talks on the messages of the Blessed Virgin Mary at Medjugorje. Mixed in with the talks were numerous media interviews; after seven days, I was worn out.

"Morning, Ronald, thanks," I mumbled as I opened the door and took the cup of steaming coffee. "Are you

14

sure this isn't the day for me to go home?"

His hearty laugh filled the air. "Just a few more days, you can make it," he said in his pleasant singsong Trinidadian accent.

"I'm not sure," I answered wryly.

Ronald laughed again. He was a stocky man who moved with surprising quickness. His features were dominated by short-clipped, salt-and-pepper colored hair and a well-groomed beard that softened rather fierce eyes. His exterior belied the warm demeanor I had come to know so well these last seven days. He was also rigidly punctual. "Come on, now; we've got to be at the school by eight o'clock," he said over his shoulder, hurrying down the hallway of his home to prepare for the day.

Wearily, I began to get dressed. At least at this hectic pace we had accomplished far more than expected in the beginning. Events had been added along the way due to the highly receptive response to a Lutheran Protestant who spoke about apparitions of the Blessed Virgin Mary. Being a journalist only added to the fervor. It was unique and delightful to the people of this overwhelmingly Catholic, multiracial population. Spiced also with a large variety of Protestant faiths, Trinidad was affectionately called the "Rainbow Nation."

On arriving, I was greeted by a throng of happy faces singing a welcoming song. Among them were the members of Ronald's family; his wife Charla, oldest son Mark, teenage daughter Braunia, and two little ones, Greer and Jaimi. We quickly traveled to the Grosberg home and were soon engrossed in a crammed and minutely-detailed schedule worked out on a large calendar hanging on a wall in the kitchen.

I sat in dazed silence as Ronald went over the events; there were already more than 40 listed, including radio, television, and newspapers interviews, all planned in a period of only eight days. Halfway through the briefing, the telephone rang. It was the archbishop of Grenada; he had heard of my tour in Trinidad and insisted that I take at least one day to come to Grenada. How could I say no to an archbishop? With Ronald's marathon schedule there was no room in the already allotted days. Another day and another event was added to the calendar.

"Ronald, this poor man is not superman, you know," Charla softly chided her husband.

"Oh, he'll survive all right, he's got the Blessed Mother watching after things!" And with a chuckle and a quick pat on my back, Ronald continued his intense briefing of the schedule.

But Charla proved to be right. After a week of non-stop events, I was still filled with spiritual fervor, but the flesh was not very willing. I usually managed to squeeze in a morning run during travel but had only been able to do so a couple of times in Trinidad. All I could think about now was, "Thank God, it's almost over!"

Following a quick breakfast of sweet rolls and more coffee—and another lecture from Charla to her husband, charging him to see that I got some rest during the day—we were on our way to the last talk to be given at a school.

"You'll enjoy this," Ronald stated as he darted in and out of the congested traffic of the city. "It's an all-girl public school with more than 1,600 students."

"As long as it's the last one, I'm sure I'll enjoy it," I answered wryly, more to myself than to Ronald.

Speaking to young people was one of the most difficult tasks of my mission; yet it was extremely rewarding, and I truly enjoyed being around them. Throughout the first year of speaking, I was never intimidated by huge crowds or media. Except when I was face-to-face with groups of youth. I could never gauge their thoughts or how they were accepting my story of conversion and apparitions.

Yet everywhere I traveled for the tours, the planners would inevitably throw in several schools during the daytime. Knowing it was extremely important to reach the youth with this message, I would just grit my teeth and do it.

"Think of what we've accomplished in these seven days," Ronald said enthusiastically, making a sweeping gesture with one hand while steering his car through precarious near-entanglements along the highway with the other. He was not about to be deterred by my unenthusiastic attitude this morning, or the chiding of his wife.

"You've spoken to thousands, to thousands and many of them have been students of every age and grade. And who knows how many more you have reached through the television and radio shows?"

"You're right," I sighed. "It's been tremendous, but I hope somehow we can get to Mass since we haven't been able to work it in for three days now. It would be nice to sit quietly in a church for an hour."

Ronald looked at me and smiled, shaking his head. "I never thought I'd see the day a Protestant would love the Catholic Mass so, not to mention the praying of the rosary!" He paused after taking a quick glance at his watch, "We can possibly make the noon Mass in the city if we finish at our second stop at Emmanuel Community in time."

Ronald was right. I did love the Catholic Mass; but I also still loved attending my Lutheran church when I was home on the weekends. However, because of frequent travel mainly on weekends in the last year, my attendance there had been infrequent. That was a major difference; I could attend Mass every day, while the Lutheran church was only open on Sundays. Ironically, before Medjugorje, I could hardly stand to be in a church for more than an hour. Now I saw it as a wonderful way to begin the day.

The most difficult part of going to Catholic Mass was not being able to fully participate. As a Protestant, I was not supposed to receive Communion out of obedience and respect for Catholic doctrine. This is a holy sacrament for Catholics who believe fully that Jesus is present as living flesh and blood in the Eucharist. I believed it too, and it was this belief that now had me wanting to become a member of the Catholic Church.

I was still a Lutheran, though, and it was through the Lutheran Church that I had first learned about the apparitions at Medjugorje. And the messages being given by the Virgin Mary were definitely directed at people of all faiths, and even those with no faith. She asked that we love and respect people who sincerely sought after God; that did not mean that all faiths were the same and were acceptable to God as was so misinterpreted by some critics of Medjugorje. It was in effect asking us to respect and tolerate people without regard to belief or life-style.

One of the highlights of this tour had been a large, outdoor ecumenical prayer service in Port-of-Spain, the largest city in Trinidad. The archbishop of Trinidad, as well as leaders of most of the Protestant churches participated. Thousands came and shared and for those few precious hours, there were no denominational walls dividing the children of God. We were one family under His care. It was evident to me from the beginning of the mission that I was called to represent that message of all-faiths unity, physically as well as verbally.

"We're here." Ronald's words brought me quickly back to the present as he wheeled his vehicle into a long gravel driveway that led to a large school building. As usual my heart began to pound as I saw a large vista of students massed together outside in a tree-shaded area with a make-shift platform near the front of the gathering. "Come on now, do your best. It's the last one," Ronald said with his now-familiar quick pat on the back as I got out of the car.

After several chaotic moments as the school principal tried to quiet the chatter and constant movement of the young girls, I began to speak. As always, the intimidation quickly vanished as I began to tell of the beautiful events taking place in Medjugorje. I never planned my talks in advance. There were no notes. I simply began, and felt that whatever came was meant for this particular group at this time. It was pure Holy Spirit and I was merely an instrument, a microphone for a personalized message to each of the young people directly from the mother of Jesus.

On this day, I compared the young visionaries to the listening students. I pointed out that at Medjugorje as well as other reported apparition sites, the Virgin Mary did not appear to a priest, or the mayor of the village, but to young people. She chose those young in spirit and age to give this all-important message to the people of the world.

"Who would have ever thought," I asked them, "that six teenagers living in an isolated village in a rather unknown country would be chosen by heaven to relay messages that would have such a tremendous effect on millions of people from every continent in the world?"

For just under an hour they listened raptly. Drawing the talk to a close, I told them about Tanya, a 16-year-old girl from Australia whom I'd met at Medjugorje on my second trip. I related to them how this young girl had become hooked on drugs at the tender age of 13; how she had somehow heard of Medjugorje and feeling drawn to go, begged her mother to take her in place of having to go into a hospital for the eighth time to "dry out" from drugs after nearly overdosing.

There was now a near-impossible stillness from the 1,600 students as they listened to the story of one of their peers. I continued, pointing out that Tanya, like many young people who had come to Medjugorje with a drug problem, had received special attention from the priests, had met and befriended all of the visionaries and had been allowed to go into the apparition room many times during the actual time of Mary's mystical appearances. Yet, this girl was not healed; shortly after I left, she departed Medjugorje and went to Italy with some young friends and sadly, became immersed in the drug scene again.

"Going to Medjugorje, meeting the visionaries, getting into the apparition room—none of these incredible gifts can bring Tanya, or you, into conversion to the ways of God unless you accept it." I paused a moment for effect. "Unless you say yes to Jesus as Mary said yes to God!"

As the girls remained in a state of unmoving silence, I did something that I had done with young people in Ireland on a tour there two months earlier. It was inspired by what I felt was a special request by the Virgin Mary. I took from my pocket five medals that had been blessed by the Madonna at Medjugorje during the time of an apparition, and holding them up I told them I was going to pass them out to five students selected at random.

As I moved through the now highly-charged crowd of girls, I told them that it was Mary, and not myself that decided who was to receive a medal. I began to pass them out to excited and surprised squeals from the recipients, pointing out that receiving a medal did not mean the person was good or bad, and that they were to pray for the entire student body of the school.

After handing the last of the five medals to a girl in the very back of the crowd, I started to make my way back to the platform. After a few steps a girl stopped me and exclaimed excitedly, "You gave that last medal to a girl who is a Pentecostal! She won't know what to do with it!"

"I'm sorry but Our Lady does the selecting, not me," I answered smiling, as I kept moving towards the platform. Still, I could not help but wonder what the reaction of the

Pentecostal girl would be.

As we closed the meeting to thunderous applause, a rarity for visiting speakers according to a somewhat dazed principal, many of the girls immediately surrounded us and began firing questions at us from all directions. It took a good fifteen minutes to finally make our way to the car. As I opened the car door, two young girls came running toward us, one of them in tears but smiling broadly.

"Oh, thank you, thank you so much for the medal," she gushed. "I don't know anything about the Virgin Mary, but I'm going to find out because I believe these messages are real!"

It was the Pentecostal student! Her face radiant with happiness, she continued to thank me over and over. We were finally able to drive slowly through the throng of waving girls and onto the road back to the city.

I looked at Ronald who was filled with emotion. "How can you possibly be afraid to speak to young people when you have such a thing as that happen?" he said, slowly shaking his head.

"I don't know, Ronald. I simply don't know." I was as happily stunned as he was. In my heart I knew that speaking to youth, no matter how uncomfortable it was, would always be a strong part of this mission.

It wasn't the only happy event of the morning. As we arrived at the Emmanuel Community Center, a charismatic community, we were surprised to discover that there would be a Mass before my talk! For the next hour and a half, we shared in a joyful and emotional celebration of love with song and prayer in a packed auditorium. By the time I was to speak, I had long forgotten the weariness of the start of the day.

As I finished, a woman named Violet, who was co-leader of the Emmanuel Community and had served as emcee for the morning's events took to the stage and

began to lead us in the song, "Battle Hymn of the Republic." I was delighted! This was the "theme song" of
Medjugorje; at least, its tune was, even though the words
in Croatian were different.

Suddenly Violet raised her hand and the singing
stopped. The auditorium became quiet. In a soft and gentle
voice and with eyes closed, she began to speak in prophecy; it was a message from the Virgin Mary for me!

I sat stone still, hardly afraid to breathe as the words
poured forth from her, slowly and clearly:

*"And you, my little son, whom I have picked up like a little
seed, you have been blown by the breath of the Holy Spirit. And
I have said to you that I shall speak through you. I now say to
you, a new anointing is upon your life. The way you have walked,
looking back and concerned; now a new way shall be opened for
you. Your family shall be united with you in the work you are to
do. I say to you, my son, you shall go from place to place and as
you speak, a new ministry of love shall be poured upon my people
through you. It shall be a special and unique gift, one deeper
than you have received before.*

*"I say to you, my son, stand ready, stand ready! For the
breath of the Holy Spirit shall blow you into great, great palaces,
and into little hovels. I say to you, stand ready, for you are only
on the threshold of the work you have offered me. Your little
heart, offered to me, I have accepted and placed in my own. I say
to you now, as stated in Scripture, behold, greater things than
Jesus did, you will do. For behold, today, with the media, with
the way the message can be carried, you shall touch millions.*

*"A new ministry of love, healing love, a renewing love, love
that will touch the hardened hearts of sinners and cause them to
fall on their knees right then and there. As you go, notice that
love shall follow and flow to each human being that you speak
to.*

*"Go now with a new anointing, go now with a new commis-
sion, my little seed. For truly, you have been planted. And yet,*

even though you were like a mustard seed bringing forth a shrub, now I shall make you into an acorn, bringing forth a stately oak.

"Fear not, you are my delight. You are my son!"

As the woman spoke the last words, her voice trailed off. There was what seemed like an eternity of silence; then a few of the people began to quietly sing again the song that had been interrupted a few minutes before. Soon others joined in and the session ended in a spirited rendition that would be hard-matched in Medjugorje itself.

I sat there for a few moments trying to take in all that had happened, trying to remember the words the woman had spoken. One thing was explicitly clear: The mission had just taken a quantum leap forward.

3

"Become as little children . . ."

"Dear children, you know this time is a time of special graces; that is why I ask you to renew in you the messages I give. Live those messages with the heart."

I sat there for several minutes, stunned by the depth and length of the prophecy message. People stopped to offer thanks and ask questions, but I was there in body only; my spirit was floating, filled with a warm mixture of joy, humility and awe.

Suddenly, it occurred to me to get the message and write it down. I looked around, thinking that the woman with the soft voice might already have left; I did not know her name or that she was co-leader of the community. "Wayne, we must go. They are waiting for us downstairs for lunch." It was Ronald.

"But I've got to find that woman, I need to talk to her!"

Ronald gave me a reassuring pat on the shoulder. "Don't worry, that was Violet, and she's downstairs with the others." I finished with the few remaining well-wishers and hurried down the stairs with Ronald, relieved to see the woman at a table with other members of the charismatic community.

"Oh, there you are. Please come, we have a place for the both of you here with us." It was the other co-leader of the community.

After introductions, I went directly to the woman named Violet who had given the prophecy, and dropping to one knee I asked in a low voice, "Look, can you give me that message again. Can you write it down for me?"

"Oh, I'm sorry but I can't remember it all," she answered, shaking her head. "That is the way it is with this gift; the Holy Spirit uses me to say what needs to be said, but I am only a small instrument and I am not always aware of what is being said."

I felt a sudden sinking feeling. "Well, thank you anyway; it was so beautiful!" Resigned that the precious words were lost beyond faint memory, I took my seat at the table.

Violet smiled and said softly, "You really needn't thank me. It is the work of the Holy Spirit through the Blessed Mother."

I could only nod in agreement.

Listening to the different conversations, I remained distracted by the prophecy; was this startlingly personal message given through this woman really . . . authentic? Such doubts had filled my mind many times since the beginning of this spiritual experience. At times I even doubted the original message given to me. It was the opposite of hard, journalistic training, a stark contrast to the parallel development of a childlike faith. However, I was quickly filled with a warm sense of reassurance as I thought of the only answer that fittingly described these mystical messages; or for that matter, the many other phenomena I had read, heard about, and experienced during the activity of this mission: For those with faith, no proof is necessary; for those without faith, no proof is sufficient.

The undeniable fact was, I did receive the first message; and part of the proof was the very fact that I was traveling throughout the world, and was now here in Trinidad, carrying out what I felt had been asked of me.

It really boiled down to acceptance of a simple but profound scriptural truth found in the words of Jesus in the book of Matthew (18:3): "I tell you the truth, unless you become like little children, you will never enter the kingdom of heaven."

It certainly took the faith of a little child to accept at face value such direct communications with heaven.

"Excuse me, Mr. Weible." My thoughts were interrupted by a lady at the next table. "I apologize for eavesdropping but I couldn't help but overhear you, and I think I might be of some help."

I waited intently to hear how she could help.

"I taped your talk and it includes the prophecy that was given at the end and—"

"Great!" I interrupted. "Can you play it for me? Can I copy it? Does someone have a paper and pencil?"

"Oh, that won't be necessary," she said. "You can have the tape; my friend also taped the morning's events and she will be glad to give me a copy."

"Thank you, thank you, so much!" I happily accepted the tape. Here was proof of believing with childlike faith; I was sure the Virgin Mother wanted me to have a copy of the message! It was a morning of surprises. This was the best.

As we began the long drive back to Ronald's home to catch a short rest and prepare for the evening's talk, Ronald reached over and poked me kiddingly in the ribs. "Well now, are you still weary? Are you still anxious to go home?"

I laughed. "No, I'm exhilarated and doubt if I could rest even if I wanted to; and no, I'm not quite ready to go home!"

We rode along in silence for a few minutes, each lost

in thought. "Well, one thing's certain; your mission seems to have taken a great leap forward. That was a powerful message!"

I nodded in agreement, thinking of all the ways the mission had developed. "This whole experience has been like—" I groped for the right words. "Like a huge mosaic forming a new picture of my life's work. And now, this message with all of its new implications."

"I would say that it's a major piece of your 'mosaic' as you describe it!"

"Yes, and without Terri's part in all this, none of it could have happened. That's definitely been a major piece." I thought about that for a moment, wondering if that is what was meant by the family getting more involved. I hoped that was the case.

"I can understand that," Ronald said. "My own little mission here in Trinidad is totally dependent on Charla's support and help."

We drove in silence for awhile. I recalled that in the weeks after receiving the initial message from the Blessed Virgin, in the fall of 1985, Terri soon accepted the new direction of our lives. And Kennedy, whose baptism had led us back to church, was now an altar boy on a regular basis, as he prepared for religious instruction into the Catholic faith while attending the Catholic school in Myrtle Beach.

Still, in the beginning I was worried; I had not yet learned to place it all before God and let Him take care of the details. All I could think about was that my travels around the country and the world would place nearly all of the home responsibilities on Terri.

She refused my pleadings to visit the village. It was a reluctance centering totally on not wanting to leave her children to go into a Communist country. Refusing to take no for an answer, I all but shoved her on an airplane in

September of 1986, for a pilgrimage with the same group with whom I had gone, assuring her that I could take care of the children.

Like others, Terri came home changed. Her transformation was quiet; no spiritual flashes of lightning or booms of thunder, no drama. But the change was definitely there unfolding day by day as she meditated on all that had happened. It would strongly affect and assist us both in the mission to spread the messages.

And while Terri was away for her first pilgrimage to Medjugorje, another piece of the mosaic began to form. Almost as if on cue, Ronald interrupted my thoughts. "If I remember correctly, it was my wife who first brought home your little tabloid newspaper. That's what prompted our interest to the point of finally going there ourselves— not to mention our inviting you to come to Trinidad to speak!"

"Yes, the articles." I mused, "They're another major part of all this."

"Major is right! They are all over the world. How did you ever arrange for such distribution?"

I grinned at Ronald. "You'll never believe how they got started."

"Well, we've still got plenty of driving time; tell me!"

Settling in the seat, I told Ronald the story of how the columns came into being, ironically, during the week Terri was away on her pilgrimage.

The spark that set things into motion emanated from a complaining secretary who worked for us at our printing company. She was tired of making copies of my Medjugorje articles, she stated to me in a huff one morning. Swamped with mail and telephone requests for sets of the columns, she had to copy, collate, and prepare them for mailing; the number of requests was increasing dramatically. My solution was to publish the columns in an eight-page tabloid, with a lead story that for the first time revealed the fact that I felt the Virgin Mary had spoken directly to me, giving me this special mission to spread the messages of Medjugorje. I convinced my secretary this would make distribution easier and relieve her of the extra hassle. Also, they would be good pass-outs at the talks I was now giving locally, mostly in Protestant churches.

Astonishingly, requests for the tabloids exceeded 100,000 copies in just a few months; the figure jumped even more dramatically with my appearance on the *Sally Jessy Raphael* national television talk show in February, 1987. The initial interest for the show was three professional journalists; a practicing but lukewarm Lutheran, a Baptist who claimed to be an agnostic, and a fallen-away Catholic who hadn't been to church for years. All had become not only believers but strong, active promoters of Medjugorje.

The show was a great success. Especially for me. Hundreds of calls came to the station in the following weeks requesting copies of the articles. With requests for the articles came invitations to lecture on the apparitions. In effect, the mission was launched nationally and then internationally as the columns swiftly made their way over seas.

"And of course I wouldn't be here in Trinidad now without the spreading of the articles, or the visit to Medjugorje by Terri," I concluded, as we turned off the highway onto the final leg of the trip to Ronald's home.

The discussion of these two events reinforced for me an important premise in the initial message given to me by the Virgin Mary: She asked me to write about the events of Medjugorje, and she asked me to make the spreading of its messages my life's work. Through the gift of free will, I made the decision to say yes. That voluntary yes thus becomes the cornerstone of all conversions.

"Home at last," Ronald said as he wheeled the car through the iron gate leading into the driveway of his spacious house. "How about a cup of tea?"

"That sounds wonderful." It took a few seconds to answer; my thoughts were still focused on the good fruits of the morning's work. The words of Jesus kept echoing through my mind: "Unless you become like little children. . . ."

That evening's talk was the last in Trinidad. Hundreds came and listened with rapt attention; there was hardly any movement except for the slow, silent whisk of hand-held fans working to bring relief from the humid heat of the Trinidad night. On scale, the evening was a spiritual ten, ending a day which would be long remembered.

I promised those in attendance I would continue to pray for them and all of Trinidad. In response the overflow audience stood and applauded; no one, including me, wanted the evening or the tour to end. In a hectic, nonstop eight days, I had given 48 talks and media interviews, reached millions by television and radio, and personally had spoken in front of more than 28,000 people throughout Trinidad and Tobago. That figure included over 6,000 schoolchildren of all grades.

As we huddled together at the airport, Ronald was the last to say good-bye. There were tears in the eyes of this man with the fierce demeanor. "Well now, you must come back soon," he said with exaggerated sternness, trying to hide his feelings.

"I will, Ronald, but next time, just rent the sports stadium for one large talk; I don't think I could survive another of your eight-day tours!"

"That's a promise!" he said, hitting his fist in his hand,

"You come back and we'll fill that stadium!" With that we all laughed and said our final farewells.

I hurried down the ramp onto the plane that would carry me to the tiny island nation of Grenada, the final stop on the tour. What in the beginning of the trip had been an unimaginable addition to an already overbooked schedule was now seen as one more opportunity to share the fruits of the mission.

Of course, the reason for my revitalization was the prophecy message. It contained so much! I had listened to the tape several times, thanking God each time that I was able to have a copy of the precious words. They clearly indicated that new spiritual gifts and anointing—not to mention challenges—were being added: . . . *your family will be more involved . . . a new anointing is given that will change the hardest of hearts . . . you will be blown into great palaces and into small hovels . . .*

The next thing I knew the plane was landing and I was stepping out onto the stairway, overwhelmed with the stifling heat and suffocating humidity that seemed to hang in the air; it was worse than Trinidad.

Passing through customs, I was warmly greeted by a beautiful black woman. "Welcome to our country, Mr. Weible, my name is Margaret and I am happy to greet you in the name of Archbishop Sidney Charles."

Her quiet charm and warm smile were evident from the outset, and in minutes we felt like we'd known each other a long time. It was a comfortable feeling experienced often in the months of travel as I met those who had been called to help spread the Medjugorje messages. I learned early on that everyone involved soon becomes like a brother or sister.

We wound our way through thick, jungle foliage along a narrow paved road as Margaret gave me a quick background on the short history of the Center for Peace. She and several others from Grenada, had gone to Medjugorje with one of Ronald Grosberg's pilgrimages. Now, they were working fervently to spread the messages and renew faith in God throughout the tiny country. "And now, you're here!" She added, "Everyone's very excited about tonight!"

Driving through an area of hills covered with lush growth and a few small homes scattered throughout the hills, Margaret suddenly asked, "I wonder if I might ask a special favor of you?"

"Yes, of course. What is it?"

"This is really unplanned," she said hesitantly, "but since your flight came in early and we've some spare time, would you be willing to make a very old and disabled woman extremely happy?"

Margaret looked at me with pleading eyes and optimistic smile, slowly pulling the car to the side of the road in anticipation of a positive response. It worked.

"I guess so," I answered with a little laugh. "What do you want me to do?"

"There is a lady who lives there," She pointed to a tiny shack approximately 50 yards from the roadway. "Her name is Mary, and she loves the Blessed Mother dearly! After reading your tabloid and knowing you were coming to the island for this evening's talk, she wanted in the worst way to meet you. Unfortunately, she is unable to get around on her own due to failing health and no transportation. I was wondering if you would mind stopping for a moment or two—?"

I felt chills along my spine, knowing this was clearly a graphic example of the "small hovel" mentioned in the prophecy message! "Yes, let's go, I'd be happy to visit with her!" I said excitedly, motioning Margaret toward the shack.

We drove off the paved road onto a dirt pathway and into a sparse but clean clearing around the little house. "Hello, Mary, it's Margaret and I have a special guest with me," my guide called out as she knocked on a fragile wooden screen door.

Standing behind Margaret on the rickety porch, I peered into the dim interior of the little house in time to see a small, frail woman making her way slowly to the door. She was smiling broadly, giving special radiance to her dark, wrinkled face.

"Come in, come in, you're more than welcome!" she said in a raspy voice. Mary was so thin it seemed her thread-bare dress might fall off her stooped, rounded shoulders at any moment. She was a small woman and her bent posture made her appear even smaller. But she had an inner beauty that could only be described as spiritual beauty; the way Mother Theresa is beautiful.

Giving her a light kiss on the cheek, Margaret said, "I've a surprise for you, Mary! This is Wayne Weible, all the way from the United States, to talk about the apparitions of Our Lady in Yugoslavia tonight. You said you wanted to meet him, and he was kind enough to agree to stop for a quick chat with you."

"Oh, yes, I know," she answered softly as her eyes, locked on me, began to moisten. "I've been praying to the Blessed Virgin all morning, asking her if she would send him to me, so I've been expecting you." She clasped her hands together, as though in prayer and continuing to stare at me added, "She is so good to me!"

Margaret and I looked at each other. We knew her suggestion to visit this woman was a spur-of-the moment thing; yet, we also knew that indeed, Our Lady had given this little gift to an old and faithful child of God. "I'm very glad to meet you, Mary," I said, embracing her lightly as I fought the emotion of the moment.

We shared conversation for a solid hour, mainly about the good gifts of heaven. Mary told me in rather matter-of-fact terms of her "conversations" with the Blessed

Mother, and of other gifts she had received in her long
life. She expressed how happy she was to be living in this
particular place and time, fully satisfied with the scant life-
style, completely happy and at peace. She was living testimony of what the Blessed Virgin Mary was asking of all of
us at Medjugorje: to live simply and in faith that God will
always provide for those who turn to Him.

I knew this unscheduled stop was meant to reinforce
within me that through the mission, I would be called on
to visit many such "small hovels," and many "Marys" of
the world. We left the elderly woman, sharing in her joy
and the mystical wonderment that comes from such un-
wavering faith, as we motored on to the home of the people
with whom I would be staying the night.

Walter and Vilma Coard were an integral part of
Margaret's prayer group and were delighted to serve as
hosts for my brief stopover. For forty-plus years, they had
lived at the top of a small hill in their quaint, colonial style
home overlooking the harbor. It was a beautiful view that
had afforded many evenings of quiet time together on the
front porch, watching the doings of the little hamlet.

"We've seen people come and go, witnessed all the
good times and the bad times," Walter related to me during a lengthy discourse as we sat on the porch sipping
cold drinks. "And the best of the good times was having a
front row seat to watch the splendid liberation of our country by your wonderful president!"

I was surprised. Most media reports following the "invasion" of Grenada by United States armed forces was
strongly critical of a superpower nation mounting such
an assault on a helpless and tiny republic. "Oh, no, on the
contrary," Walter responded when I queried him about
these reports. "If the United States hadn't come to our
rescue, we would definitely be under Communist rule. And

you," he said, raising his eyebrows and pointing at me, "you wouldn't be here to speak because a major aim of the rebels was to shut down the Church!"

I could sense Walter was just warming to the subject as he pulled his chair closer. And so could Vilma and Margaret. Both interrupted simultaneously to remind him that I had an appointment with the governor of Grenada in less than an hour. "You ask the governor about it; he'll confirm what I'm saying," Walter persisted. "When you return this evening after the talk, I'll show you a special video that gives the entire story."

"You must begin getting ready if we're to be on time." Margaret interrupted a second time. Actually, in the excitement of stopping to see Mary, I had forgotten the appointment until this moment. Margaret had told me of this special honor as we had left the airport. The governor had personally asked for the appointment.

"By the way," she said as I started for my guest room, "The governor is somewhat of an expert on the life of Martin Luther; he looks forward to discussing him with you."

Now in an uncomfortable formally required coat and tie, I was taken to another colonial-style house on a hill; this one large, surrounded by gardens and tall iron fences. There were guards to open the car doors, and a butler to answer the door. I laughed as we pulled into the driveway; first, there was the small hovel of Mary's house. And now this "grand palace"!

Margaret looked at me in puzzlement. "I'll explain later," I whispered with a smile as we approached the door of the governor's mansion.

The visit with the governor of Grenada, Sir Paul Scoon, and his wife, lasted nearly an hour with much of the time spent discussing Luther, and the modern-day Lutheran Church. I was able to give him an important piece of in-

formation of which he was not aware; I pointed out that
Martin Luther, to his dying day, never lost his strong devotion to the Blessed Virgin Mary. "And neither did John
Calvin, the other major leader in the Protestant movement," I added.

As for Medjugorje, he and his wife had little trouble
believing in the apparitions and the work of Our Lady.
"If it were not for the strong faith and prayers during
the uprising, with I believe, more than a little aid from the
Blessed Virgin, we would definitely have fallen under
the rule of Communism." He spoke with conviction and
evident gratitude in his voice. Of course this did indeed
confirm Walter's earlier statements about the uprising.

I sat spellbound as Governor Scoon told of the har-
rowing hours when the rebellion began and the Communist rebels actually came and placed him under house
arrest, threatening him and his family. And then the dramatic rescue by U.S. forces. Like Walter, he was thoroughly
convinced that Our Lady had protected this tiny nation
because of its deep devotion to her.

Pressed for time due to the early evening start of the
talk, we bade the governor and his wife a hasty good-bye,
receiving a warm invitation to return to Grenada in the
near future when "we could visit and speak more about
Martin Luther and the apparitions at Medjugorje." They
would attend my talk, but would have to leave immediately afterwards.

In a short time we were at the church which was literally overflowing with people. "Oh my goodness, this is
wonderful!" Margaret was obviously surprised at the turnout and as if anticipating a question from me concerning
their preparation for the event, added with a wide smile,
"I felt we would fill the church but this is far beyond our
wildest expectations! You should feel very welcome, Mr.
Wayne Weible!"

Shaking my head I answered in a low voice, "I feel totally overwhelmed."

Parking the car, immediately surrounded by people peering curiously inside, Margaret put into words the singular thought that had dwelled in my heart like a burning piece of coal since early involvement in Medjugorje: "Well, we know who's really responsible for this. Our Lord chooses, waits for a yes, and then gives what is needed by way of the Holy Spirit. The rest is up to us."

"Yes, and to make sure we know it is He who does the choosing," I added as we got out of the car, "He seems to always pick the least likely people—like me!"

Taking a seat next to the podium, I looked around the interior of the church as the music began to play. It was a large, beautiful structure with huge, open windows along both walls. Faces were peering in from every window as crowds gathered at each opening, swelling the attendance to more than two thousand. As if to add a final touch to an already spectacular scene, streams of sunlight filtered over the heads of the people crowded into the window openings on the right side of the church, as the warm Caribbean sun began to set.

After a warm welcome and introduction, I began to speak. The words poured easily from me as I felt myself immersed in the spiritual enchantment of so many souls gathered to hear about Our Lady's appearances. I told my story, of receiving the message from Mary at my home, and of going to Medjugorje for the first time eight months later. As I was describing the phenomena of the spinning and dancing sun seen so often by pilgrims at the little village, a strong confirmation that the mother of Jesus was truly present, I was startled as suddenly the full force of the setting sun's rays came streaming through one of the windows, falling directly on me. It was as if someone had hit a switch and turned on a spotlight.

After a slight hesitation, I tried to continue but my voice trailed off; there, before me occurring at that very moment, was the miracle of which I was speaking! The sun began to do its dance, throwing off brilliant streams of colors and pulsating erratically, framed in the small window opening! I stood there and stared until the growing buzz of the crowd caught my attention. They sensed something unusual was happening.

I looked at them for a moment and then pointing to the sun said, "The miracle of the sun I've just described to you, is happening right now, as I stand here. All I can say is thank you to Our Lady for she is truly letting us know that she is here in Grenada, just as she is in Medjugorje!"

Heads turned and dozens rushed to the windows. There were shouts of excitement as others were able to see the phenomena; soon the place was bedlam.

It took several minutes to restore order before I was able to resume speaking. By then, words were secondary. Many of the people in attendance had actually experienced the miracle of Medjugorje through the phenomena of the sun. Others were deeply affected by what was taking place around them. It was pure high-energy spirituality.

Conversion truly occurred in many hearts that evening. Long after the talk, many were still there, not wanting the magic of the moment to dissipate. People wanted to know more. They asked me to pray over them, something new to me. But I did it. I was just as caught up as the audience in the emotion of such a strong presence of God.

Late that evening, I enjoyed a Caribbean meal—and viewed the video on the rebellion Walter promised to show. Later, in the wee hours of the morning, I lay in a small bed soaked in perspiration. I didn't mind. Nor was there concern that sleep was near impossible. The evening's dramatic conclusion of the tour, and the phenomena of the sun during the talk were like huge exclamation points at the end of a ten-day story.

So many people in these small Caribbean island nations had been reached by the love of God. So much more had been given to the mission with this new prophecy message. I did indeed feel like a little child of God.

At the moment, nothing else mattered.

4
Conversion

*" . . . I would like you to pray in your families with your
children. I would like you to talk with your children. I would
like you to exchange your experiences and help them to solve
all their problems."*

"You can't imagine how beautiful . . . how awesome it was
to have the miracle of the sun occur right in the middle of
my talk!"

Terri listened intently. She smiled softly, her elbow
resting on the table, chin on her hand. After a quick
catch-up on the happenings of their little world, Kennedy
and Rebecca had left the breakfast table in favor of Saturday morning cartoons, giving us this quiet time together.

"One thing's for sure," Terri said, "life has been anything but boring since this all began." The smile turned
slowly into a slight frown. "But we really miss you when
you're gone on these long trips, especially in the summer
months."

"I know. The only thing that kept me from getting
homesick was the schedule. I didn't have time to dwell too
long on thoughts of you and the kids."

"At least we won't have to worry about that for Alaska,"
Terri said brightly, getting up and reaching for a pile of

papers on a nearby cabinet. "Look what I've got!"

Quickly moving the dishes aside, she spread out an assortment of brochures, maps and papers, all about Alaska, my next tour destination. I would be leaving in a few days for an eight-day speaking tour in and around Juneau. Terri and the kids were flying to Anchorage the following week where we would rendezvous for a week's vacation, touring Alaska in a rented RV camper. It was a dream come true for her as she had always wanted to visit this beautiful state.

"I've got everything worked out, including the different parks we want to see," she said as she flipped open a notebook containing a schedule for the entire trip.

Such meticulous planning and attention to the smallest detail eased my concerns while on tour, and enabled Terri to handle all of the home responsibilities. As I listened to my wife go over details of the upcoming trip, I couldn't help thinking how much she had grown spiritually in the last two years.

When Medjugorje first came into our lives in such an overwhelming way, she had hoped it would pass; when it didn't, her concern deepened. Until then our spiritual life had been low key—not the most important thing in family life. Medjugorje threatened to change things.

Disappointed in her reaction, I could not let it deter my response to the call. In the following weeks, I devoured every book I could find concerning apparitions, the Virgin Mary, and early church history. While searching through them for information, I also discovered saints. And one saint in particular. For reasons not understood at the time, this saint would become extremely important to us. It was Saint Therese of Lisieux, known among Catholics as the most popular and powerful saint of modern times.

Known affectionately by her followers as "The Little

Flower," Saint Therese convinced authorities of the church to allow her to enter the convent in 1888, at the tender age of fifteen. She simply wanted to live totally dedicated to God. And for nine years she did so in a way that has since touched the lives of millions of people.

Death came at age 24, but Therese had accomplished her all-consuming goal: she became a saint. And she did so by daily living her "little way" of love. This young saint represented exactly what the Virgin Mary was asking of each person touched by her apparitions at Medjugorje.

In learning about St. Therese, I sensed she was special; she was the Virgin Mary's "first lieutenant." And appropriately, she was named Therese, the same as my wife. I asked St. Therese to intercede for Terri, to assist her in spiritual growth so that we could accomplish this mission together. Giving Terri several books about her, I told her since I couldn't convince her that our Medjugorje mission was authentic, I was turning her over to someone who could.

Terri laughed, taking it lightly, thinking it to be but one more example of how far I had gone off the deep end with Medjugorje. However, she began to change. My wife became as dedicated to St. Therese as I was. She began to understand and accept what had actually been given to us as a family. It was the strongest of the early signs given me that our involvement was real.

". . . And we then return to Anchorage on Friday, staying over the weekend before flying home on Monday," Terri smiled and let out a long sigh as she pushed away from the table. She was pleased with her plans. "It'll be a great trip for the kids."

"Well," I said, standing up and stretching, "I've still got a few days before I leave, so let's enjoy it; let's go to the beach!"

"Sorry, but we need to go to the mall first while I have

you here," Terri said as she moved down the hallway. "There are lots of little things we need before going!"

I let out a loud groan in mock anguish. Shopping was not one of my favorite things. But I really didn't care. It was good just to be home doing the routine chores that made family life so warm and comfortable.

Three days later, I left for Juneau, Alaska. It was easier than usual knowing we would soon be together in Anchorage.

Settling in for the long flight, I basked in the warm glow of how graced we, as a family, were through involvement in spreading the Medjugorje message. It had affected not only the immediate family, but was finally beginning to reach my four older children.

For Terri and our two little children, the daily exposure of what was happening to us created a family environment that almost naturally led to spiritual conversion. But with Lisa, Angela, Steve, and Michael, the job of conversion was filled with frustration for me and indifference from them. I met solid resistance to my efforts, which were now constant. Ranging in age from 18 to 24, they were well into their own little worlds; it was a world that didn't include religion and its morally-suffocating rules.

And why not? We had become geographically, emotionally and spiritually divided due to the traumatic divorce that had shattered their childhood and any pretense at a home life. Even though we sporadically went to the Baptist church of my former wife, there was no family spiritual nucleus, no prayer, nothing that had to do with religion. My children had become classic products of a broken home. They were now living in a contemporary world that said anything goes that feels good. As far as they were concerned, their father had become a religious fanatic.

I was frustrated to the point of total exasperation, until

one day Terri pointed out I would have far more success in reaching them if I stopped beating them with words and simply did what Our Lady was asking: Live the messages and let them find it through my example. Never one for patience, I reluctantly agreed since everything else had failed.

Terri was right. After more than a year of traveling the world to witness and tell my story, it finally began to register that this was something special. Steve and Michael, more impressed by the national attention I was receiving than by the actual fruits of Medjugorje, began to ask questions. Still, my claim to have received a message direct from heaven was far less impressive to them than my having been on the *Sally Jessy Raphael* show.

Angela, barely 18 years of age, married her high school sweetheart Roy, right after graduation. They had suffered through stormy years of fighting and separations, caused mainly by mutual immaturity. She was desperate for anything that might help her and Roy. With the birth of their first child, a baby girl, there was a renewed sense of urgency to find peace and happiness in their marriage. She, too, began asking questions.

But not Lisa, my first-born.

As a twelve year old, Lisa had experienced the full crisis of a child of a broken marriage. She was old enough to understand fully that her family was being destroyed. The constant tugging for support from both parents, as well as having to be the big sister and cope with the needs and fears of her brothers and sister, had developed in her a sense of bitterness and insecurity. That soon turned to hard cynicism.

After graduating from college in 1984 and obtaining a good job, she was determined to live the good life to fill the emptiness of lost family love; she was open to anything that might make up for it.

Blessed with good looks and personality Lisa was popular and loved to have a good time. She had more than her share during and after college, until finally settling into an all-too-intimate relationship with a young man she had met at school. And then one day in May of 1985, the cold reality of her life-style hit without warning. She discovered she was pregnant.

Lisa was shocked since she had been on birth control pills. Life at the time was looking pretty good. She had a great job, wore fashionable clothes and knew how to live in the material world. Her boyfriend David was a nice enough young man, but without a lot of ambition. The pregnancy threatened to ruin everything.

Frightened and ashamed, my cosmopolitan daughter, suddenly a desperate little girl again, called and tearfully gave me the grim news. I was glad that despite the soap-opera turmoil of ongoing family trials caused by the divorce, we had become close as father and daughter. More important, we were friends.

I went to her immediately, my mind racing during the long drive to her apartment in Columbia. What should I say or do to help her? She hadn't told her mother and didn't plan to. She just couldn't, she tearfully told me as we sat in her apartment tightly gripping hands. The doctors had said chances were good that she would miscarry due to medical problems they had discovered during the examination, and that . . . she should have an abortion.

David, as shocked as Lisa by this sudden intrusion into their relationship, was willing to get married right away— and he didn't want her to have the abortion. But she felt he offered only out of guilt. With life just beginning to take a positive turn, my daughter did not know what to do with so many life-affecting decisions to make.

Even though my own spiritual life at this time was only

lukewarm, I knew abortion was morally wrong. I tried to talk her out it and attempted to convince her to accept David's proposal of marriage—and to have the child. But she had made up her mind to go through with the abortion, rationalizing that based on the doctor's opinion she might lose it anyway.

The unspoken truth was, to give birth to a baby as a single mother at this particular time would totally disrupt Lisa's life-style—and bring with it shame she could never live down.

I was devastated with her decision. But she was my daughter. I loved her and would support her as best I could even though I was repulsed by what she was going to do.

Lisa had the abortion and began the struggle to return to a normal life. Less than a year later, she further complicated her struggles by accepting David's proposal. They were married in March, 1986. It was her way of covering up one mistake by making another.

On the surface, everything seemed fine. They appeared to be a happy, newlywed couple. But too much trauma, guilt and unspoken blame between them began to quietly eat away at their marriage. I encouraged Lisa and David to at least start going to church. But trying to convince them about the authenticity of heaven, using Medjugorje's apparitions as proof, had just the opposite effect. They would just look at me, roll their eyes upward, and shake their heads. But I knew why Lisa wouldn't listen; it was too painful a reminder of what she had done, and what she felt was beyond forgiveness.

At least some progress was being made with the other children, I thought as I gathered my bags and began making my way down the aisle as the plane arrived in Juneau.

My constant prayer was that Lisa and David would open their hearts to the healing love of God; that one day, they might want to go to Medjugorje to find that healing.

5
Medjugorje Fever

"I thank you for the love which you are showing me. You know, dear children, that I love you immeasurably, and daily I pray the Lord to help you to understand the love which I am showing you. . . ."

Paul Arnoldt, chief proponent of the prayer group that had asked me to come to Alaska, met me at the airport filled with special excitement and eagerness. I had come to recognize and describe this as "Medjugorje fever."

"Boy, do we need you here," he said as we pulled out of the airport parking lot and headed for his home. "We've been spreading your tabloids all over the place. You've got four talks in Juneau, plus a couple of stops way out in the middle of nowhere; you'll have to go there by small plane. You should enjoy that."

The "fever" raged on at a rapid-fire pace throughout the drive to Paul's house, letting up temporarily as he unlocked the door and deposited my bags in the hallway. "How about a cup of coffee? You hungry?"

"Yes to both!" I laughed. "That is, if you can stop long enough to get it!"

"Oh, sorry. You probably go through this everywhere you go."

"Yes, but I never get tired of it. I love seeing the change in people and listening to the stories of conversion through Medjugorje." I hesitated before adding with mock sternness, "Well, almost never!"

Over coffee and sandwiches, Paul explained the schedule. "I've even penciled in Friday daytime for a special treat if you agree. We thought we'd take you salmon fishing. You'll be back in plenty of time for the evening talk."

He looked at me inquiringly as I hesitated. "Well, I don't know; it's a fast day and I usually try to keep things quiet."

"Okay, if you'd rather not do anything we can always scratch—"

"No, don't do that yet," I answered quickly. "We'll just see how things go."

He dropped the subject and we were soon were sharing stories of our visits to Medjugorje. It was a favorite pastime of those who had become infected with the fever. Its major symptom was total devotion to the living, spreading and sharing of the messages, mystical experiences, and personal stories of conversion.

It was this feeling that made me hesitate about the fishing trip. I didn't want anything to interfere with the spreading of the messages. It would take time and experience for me to learn that we are not being asked to give up all of life's little enjoyments, but to put God first and then let everything else fall into place. Many converts who were far away from God, would swing to the other extreme in the beginning days of conversion. It took time to find the proper balance.

My host was a good example of how Marian apparitions not only convert the lukewarm and unbelievers, but also reinforce those who have faith. For them, the extremes were not quite as wide. A cradle Catholic, Paul had always had a devotion to Mary, having been raised in a family atmosphere that stressed the basic messages of belief just as the mother of Jesus was giving in the little village. But like so many other devotees of Medjugorje, Paul, now in his early forties, had also absorbed his share of faith-threatening crises. They had come with the swiftness and crush of a tidal wave in the last couple of years.

He told me of his devastation by what he felt was a near-perfect marriage that ended in perplexing divorce after three years. And recently, through no fault of his own, he lost an apparently secure state government job due to political changes of administration. It was a gut-wrenching emotional and spiritual storm in his life that threatened to drown out years of steady faith.

Medjugorje's apparitions served as a lifesaver for Paul. Because of its impact, he was able to rise above personal tragedies and go on with life, now filled with promises of hope because of Mary's appearances in the little village. "I've been fascinated by Our Lady's apparitions at Fatima, since I was a kid," Paul said softly. "I always wished that I could have been there, that it had happened to me. When I heard that she was appearing in Yugoslavia, well, I had to go. I mean, to think that she was coming to these kids *every day*! I just had to go!"

I glanced at the clock on the wall, noting that it was after midnight. "Well, as pleasant as this has been," I said standing up and stretching, "I've got to go to bed. I think I've been up about 26 hours and I'm ready to fall asleep standing here!"

"Oh, gosh, I didn't realize—"

I held up my hand. "Don't worry about it, it's been an exciting evening."

That excitement carried over to the next day as I spoke at two different locations and managed to work in a special visit at the hospital to a 92-year-old Episcopalian nun named Sister Trinity. Cathy, a member of Paul's prayer group, had met her while doing volunteer work at the hospital. She was ecstatic that I was taking time to visit with this elderly nun.

Although frail and weakened by her present condition, Sister Trinity greeted me with enthusiasm. Her small room was filled with flowers from well-wishers. I knew in my heart that her time on this earth was fast running out, as the pain and intensity of her illness was clear on her thin, angular face. But as with so many others of great faith facing the inevitable, there was peace and full acceptance in her eyes.

"It's wonderful that you, a Lutheran, would be chosen to spread these messages," she said weakly as I took her hand. And of course she fully believed that Our Lady was appearing in Medjugorje.

"She loves us all, no matter what faith we claim," she added when I mentioned my surprise that first of all the Episcopalian Church had nuns; and secondly, that she believed in apparitions so readily.

"Oh, yes," Sister Trinity answered when I questioned her about the order, "we have a great devotion to the Blessed Mother." This ethereal woman who was so near death now, had served God in her Protestant order for more than fifty years. I quickly recognized her as another "Mary," like my Mary of Grenada.

I was happy to respond when she asked me if I would pray over her. I prayed for a peaceful death. Later, after returning home from the tour, I would learn from Paul that Sister Trinity died on August 15, the Feast of the Assumption of Our Lady. I knew her departure for heaven on this particular day was no coincidence.

In the early morning hours, I boarded a small, four-seater plane for an exhilarating journey over seemingly endless miles of barren, ice-covered mountains and valleys. It was breathtaking. Flying in and out, and around the towering mountain peaks of Alaska, gave a whole new meaning to the word grandeur. I felt we were just a little dot in the sky against this mammoth backdrop of nature.

After a precarious, wind-blown approach to a tiny landing strip in which I was convinced we were going to land sideways, we finally touched down on the outskirts of the settlement called Haines, the only inhabited outpost for hundreds of miles around.

Thirty-five hearty souls representing several different denominations, along with non-believers and some who were simply curious, came to a large assembly hall used by various groups of the town. I gave my story the same as I would if there were 3,500 present. They were still wanting to ask questions as I literally had to be led away by the local hosts to the airport for the return flight to Juneau. Two days later, I made a similar trip to another outpost, Sitka, for about 50 people to hear the message. The reaction was the same. It was clear Our Lady was making sure I understood that I would be going to many "small hovels" in the coming years!

The days flew by as we squeezed in every possible opportunity to reach the population of Juneau, with the Medjugorje message. As we were driving to the site of the next talk on a Thursday evening, Cathy suddenly asked somewhat timidly from the back seat, "Since you have a little time tomorrow, would you be willing to go to the docks where the tourist ships arrive and stand on the corner and talk about Medjugorje?"

Paul looked over at me with a pained expression. "Cathy suggested this at one of our planning meetings. We talked about it, and then decided to leave it up to you."

I could tell he wasn't too crazy about the idea. Neither was I. Shifting uncomfortably in the car seat, I started to answer when the young woman cut me off, taking my hesitation as a yes. "I think it would be a great way to teach people about Medjugorje. We could pass out your articles and—"

"Wait a minute!" I interjected. "I'm afraid I have to decline on that one. Besides, I think Paul has plans for us." All of a sudden, the fishing trip Paul had proposed earlier sounded like a great idea.

Her facial expression changed from stimulated fervor to disappointment and embarrassment. "Look," I began, trying to salvage her enthusiasm, "It's not a bad idea, but I'm not comfortable doing that. I think I need to keep the image of a businessman, or a journalist who has been given a special grace to witness through Medjugorje's apparitions in as professional a manner as possible."

"I'm sorry, I just thought it would be a good way to reach people who aren't aware of what is happening in Medjugorje."

I reached over and squeezed her hand. "Hey, don't change! Maybe you and some of the others could meet the cruise ships sometime and simply hand out the articles. But don't stop thinking of ways to spread the messages."

Her smile indicated that everything was right again, especially as Paul added that maybe the entire prayer group would try that sometime in the future.

Cathy's request reminded me of an incident that had taken place in a shopping mall in Myrtle Beach. I was in the food court section grabbing a quick meal and the place was filled with people. Suddenly a young man and woman abruptly entered the area carrying a large, wooden cross. I could tell they were both very nervous. And scared. Setting the cross upright, the young man began preaching in a quavering but loud voice. It was a strong message of the need for repentance. And it was very blunt.

Within minutes security personnel were on the scene and brusquely escorted the young couple out of the mall.

I admired the courage of these young people, but it generated more negativity and criticism than good. I remembered thinking at the time whatever I did with this mission, I would try to do it with the dignity of Jesus.

Friday morning arrived with cooler temperatures and cloudy skies, not what we wanted on this particular day. It was strange to feel chill in the air in the middle of July! I had agreed to go salmon fishing with Paul and another member of the prayer group, Homer Beedle. "Look, I'll make you two promises," Paul had said. "First, that the three of us will fast on good, homemade bread and fruit juices; second, that you will catch the biggest fish in your life!"

"So you've never been salmon fishing?" Homer asked as the two of us helped Paul launch the boat into the harbor waters. He was a tall, lanky man in his middle sixties, whose weathered face seemed always to wear a broad smile. He had been our constant companion, beginning with breakfast the morning after my arrival in Juneau. It was while sharing meals and stories at these breakfast get-togethers following early-morning Mass, that I learned of his own personal little mission. He was totally dedicated to taking the gospel of Jesus into a large prison in Juneau. I had promised him I would go with him into the prison on Saturday afternoon to talk about Medjugorje.

Dressed in a yellow slicker and knee-high rubber boots, Homer tossed a similar set and pair of boots at me. "Better put these on; it gets a little cold out on the water." As he hoisted the last of the gear to Paul in the boat, he added as an aside, "Everything's set for our talk at the prison tomorrow afternoon. The guys are excited about you coming. And it's not until after 3 P.M. so if you want, we can fish again in the morning and be back in plenty of time for the talk."

I grinned at him. "I guess that depends on if we catch any today!"

"Oh, don't worry, you'll catch more than your share," Paul yelled above the roar of the boat's engine as we headed for open waters.

Less than an hour later, with our fishing lines trolling at the back of the boat, I suddenly felt a hard tug. "I got one! I got one!" I shouted, as the largest fish I had ever hooked jumped high into the air from the end of my line. I began reeling as fast and hard as I could. About ten minutes later, just as I was ready to bring the fish to where Homer could net it and bring it into the boat, he suddenly grabbed my line as Paul snapped his knife open—and then cut the line! As I stood gasping in disbelief, my huge, beautiful Alaska salmon swam off with a last splash of its tail. "What are you doing?" I screamed, as both men roared with laughter.

"This is what we do to all rookies with their first salmon," Paul explained still convulsed in laughter, as he slipped an arm around my shoulders. "Welcome to Alaska salmon fishing, and don't worry, you'll catch a lot more even bigger than that one!"

I smiled ruefully, feeling every bit the rookie fisherman. But their little joke backfired. I didn't catch another fish the rest of the day, and they only caught a couple, including a large halibut. Homer felt so guilty, he let me finish hauling it in! Paul and I cooked it at midnight as an end-of-fast meal. It was absolutely delicious and marked a super ending to a great day of fun and relaxation from the grind of the tour. I was glad I had agreed to a little recreation with these two new friends.

But I didn't let either of them forget what they had done to my one and only opportunity at catching an Alaska salmon. For the remainder of the tour, especially since we did go out again the next morning and I still didn't hook another fish, it became the fuel for friendly teasing banter at every opportunity.

Saturday afternoon proved to be the most dramatic stop of the tour. As Homer led me into the prison, I felt uneasy. I had never done this before. It was exciting to have the opportunity to take the message of Medjugorje to those who needed it. Yet it was disturbing to hear the clank of large, electronically controlled gates as they slammed shut, to see the heavy barbed wire strung along high metal fences.

Prisoners stared as we walked across an exercise yard and into a separate building where church services were normally held. Homer waved and spoke to several of the inmates and invited them to come in for the talk. I could see a beautiful peace and sense of accomplishment on his face as we crossed the yard. This was his mission of caring for the poor of heart.

As we entered the building, I was a little disappointed; there were only about 25 prisoners in attendance. They didn't look too friendly or receptive to the impending talk. One in particular, a large Alaska native sitting near the front of the room began staring at me from the moment I entered.

Feeling a bit intimidated, I prayed that the right words would come and that my fear would not show. I told them that they in particular were the reason for Our Lady coming in apparition. They had sinned and were now paying the price. She loved them, Jesus loved them, and they had this time to make their lives right. "Amens" were emphatically given throughout the talk.

As Homer and a prison official passed out my articles, many of the prisoners came forward for autographs and questions. It was just like any other talk and I was filled with happiness and relief when it was over.

The room began to empty as the inmates left. Homer and the official started carrying out the boxes with the remaining materials. Suddenly, I found myself alone in the room with the Alaska native. He hadn't moved throughout the talk; he didn't ask any questions and never changed the expression on his face. He just kept staring at me.

Slowly, he got up and came toward me. My heart jumped and I tried not to let the fear show. He stood there, looking first at me, then at a copy of the articles he held in his large hands. For the first time, his expression softened. "I was going to ask you for your autograph," he began in a deep, slow voice, "But now, I don't think I need to. You have written it across my heart." With that, a slight smile creased his face as he thanked me for coming and then slowly turned and left the room.

I stood there stunned, wanting to say thank you, but nothing came out. When Homer returned, I asked him, "Homer, who was that last guy, that big guy that just left?"

"Oh, that's Joe," Homer said, looking back toward the door at the departing inmate. "He's become a good friend, a real good friend. Frankly, I think he was framed by members of his own family, and shouldn't be in here. Something about some insurance money."

As we left the prison, Homer told me more about Joe, and several other prisoners. I could detect a real sense of the personal responsibility he had taken on for these men. His mission wasn't limited to just visiting them in the prison—he also visited with the men's families. His Medjugorje Fever was just as intense as Paul's but expressed a little differently in his dedication to serving these men who lived behind bars.

Sunday evening's talk was the last as planned, but there had been an addition. A prayer group from Anchorage found out I was in Juneau and was coming to Anchorage; they wanted to know if I would give just one talk there, knowing that I was there specifically to vacation with family. I had agreed, and the talk was to be held in the auditorium of a hospital on Monday evening. We weren't leaving Anchorage for our vacation until Tuesday anyway and I was pleased that Terri and the children would be able to attend.

As always it was difficult to leave the many new friends in Juneau. Each tour became a mini-mission within itself. Paul was pleased with our accomplishments and his prayer group was filled with a renewal of that beautiful "Medjugorje fever."

"Daddy!" The cries of Kennedy and Rebecca were sweet music as I exited the gate at the Anchorage air terminal. They and their mother had arrived the day before and were more than ready to start our week of touring Alaska.

"I'm glad we'll have the chance to be at your talk this evening, especially since we can't rent the RV until tomorrow," Terri said as we drove into Anchorage.

"Yeah, but I look forward to getting on the road and seeing this beautiful state." I was more than ready for a few days off, and half-wished I hadn't agreed to the impromptu talk. But as always, there was an underlying reason for this particular event not seen by me or those who planned it. It was Our Lady's quiet way of speaking to those who accepted her call of conversion to her Son.

The crowd was small but it readily filled the little auditorium of Providence Hospital. One family in particular was pleased that I was there. Sharon McMichael and her two teenage daughters sought me out afterwards to tell me about Doctor Richard McMichael, her husband, a surgeon at the hospital who specialized in cancer treatment.

"He really wanted to be here tonight, but he is in surgery right now operating on a patient," she told me in a quiet voice. "All of us, especially my husband, have been strongly affected by the apparitions of the Virgin Mary at Medjugorje. We want to go because Richard is himself seriously ill with cancer, but we're not sure he could physically make the trip."

Marie, one of Sharon's daughters spoke up. "We'd like to ask you to pray for our dad, that we get him to Medjugorje for a healing."

With that tears flowed from the eyes of all three women. Sharon went on to tell me that her husband, despite his illness, was continuing to treat other cancer patients. "Of course, he knows how sick he is but feels it's important to treat others as long as he is physically able. Thanks to your articles, Medjugorje has given Richard the strength to accept whatever God has in store for him. He's not a bit afraid."

I left the hospital auditorium knowing that meeting the McMichaels was the reason for my acceptance of this last-minute speaking invitation.

Our vacation was everything we hoped it would be, leaving me refreshed and ready for the next assignment: a return to my native state and birthplace: Los Angeles, California.

6
Dark Memories

"Dear children, today I am calling you to the way of holiness. Pray that you may comprehend the beauty and the greatness of this way . . ."

Dark memories stirred within me as the plane began its descent into the Los Angeles airport. I was returning to the city of my birth and home for the first eight years of life, nightmarish years of family turmoil and upheaval.

As the plane taxied along the runway, the memories became distinct and clear; it had been living hell for me and my younger brother and sister, a time I wanted to blot out. I had pretty much done so until now, surprised at the intensity of discomfort I felt.

Most of our problems stemmed from my mother, who suffered a long history of social ills caused by a dysfunctional family background. Filled with insecurity and a constant need to be loved, she was unable to cope with my father's long periods of absence due to naval service in the Pacific during World War II.

My mother had been previously married, divorced and had a son. She met my father, who after joining the Navy had come to the Long Beach Naval station near Los Angeles. Coming straight off the family farm in Oshkosh, Nebraska, he knew little about the outside world and within a few months my mother became pregnant with me. They were hastily married, and in the next three years two more children were born.

It was too much for my mother to handle. Her escape from responsibility and reality was found in partying with equally irresponsible acquaintances for days at a time, leaving her four children to fend for themselves. Jimmy, my older half-brother would also disappear; that left me as the next oldest to care for my little sister Lola, and infant brother Jack. I learned to feed us by taking small food items at the local grocery store, and telling the milkman and other food delivery services that my mother instructed me to have them to leave an order at the doorstep. By the time I was seven, I could lie and steal with proficiency, having swiftly grown up the wrong way out of a need for survival.

It didn't take long for neighbors to discover a pattern of abandonment and neglect, and to call the authorities. The next year and a half became a blur of mostly uncaring and cruel surrogate parents in foster homes and juvenile centers, with separation from my brothers and sister for long periods of time as we were usually placed with different families.

Finally, my father's brother Fritz and his wife June, came to our rescue and took the three of us to their home in Lewellen, Nebraska. We would live with them and their three children of similar ages until my father returned from the war. They really couldn't afford to take us but they felt there was no choice; we were family. We would somehow manage. Fritz was a hard man, and while he was strict and brusque, his goal was to make sure we grew up the right way. Aunt June was a perfect balance, offsetting Uncle Fritz's stern discipline with her constant care and genuine love for us, the same for us as for her own children.

As a family, we didn't attend church very often. Uncle Fritz worked extremely hard six days a week and Sunday was his day of relaxation. But there was a tremendous amount of love in our new family. It was the best medicine possible to erase the horror of my early years in California.

There was warmth in recalling those five years of family stability. And I had long ago forgiven my mother. It had been years since I had heard from or about her, but I knew she was still in California. With some apprehension, I held hopes that during this trip I might by some small miracle find her. Maybe she had heard about her son and would come to one of the talks. . . .

Contemplating those early years in California, I also recalled a wonderful and mysterious presence within which helped me survive. Throughout the trials of abandonment, separation, cruelty and unloving foster homes, I always felt a sense of protection. It was a soothing sense that I was being watched over and that everything would be okay. Even later in South Carolina, when reunited with my father who remarried, the feeling was there.

As I grew older, it never left and I knew that at some point in my life, I had a special mission. I also knew that one day I would write a book. Now, both were underway. The book was originally going to be a great work of fiction. Now, that book was turning out to be a real-life story of spiritual conversion through the unlikely events of Medjugorje. And the special task was the mission of spreading its messages.

Today, I know that presence in the early years was the love and protection of the Blessed Virgin Mary through her role as spiritual mother. God was waiting for his child to say yes and accept the task. He had given me His mother to replace mine. Without that gift, I would not have survived the trauma of those early years.

These thoughts were still with me as I was met at the flight gate by three women: Kay Sentovich, who had first contacted me about coming to Southern California, Elaine Starbuck, and Janine Moran, the core group that had planned my tour.

"We thought you might like a little touch of Hollywood so we planned lunch at the Polo Club in Beverly Hills," Elaine said as we loaded my bags into the trunk of her car.

"Sounds good to me. Maybe we'll even see a movie star," I laughed.

That seemed to break the formality as the women began talking excitedly about the events planned over the next seven days. We drove around for fifteen minutes before Elaine finally pulled over to the side of the road; she was lost and didn't know which road to take next. That brought on an animated discussion amidst some embarrassment as they tried to figure out how to get to the Polo Club.

"I know it's in this area but I'm a little turned around," Elaine said with some exasperation.

As the car moved into traffic again, I suggested we pray a rosary as we looked for the club. "Oh, that's a good idea!" Janine exclaimed as we pulled rosaries out of pockets and purses.

Twenty minutes later, as we finished the final prayer of the last mystery, Kay shouted, "There it is!"

Amid laughter and relief, we were seated in the restaurant and soon were busy going over details of the day and the rest of the tour. It was an amusing start to the tour which temporarily pushed aside concerns of returning to the city of so many traumatic memories. I was glad to be here and I liked these women.

Following lunch I was going to the home of Loretta Young, one of Hollywood's legendary movie and television stars, whose durable career had delighted millions of fans for years. She had journeyed to Medjugorje with her son several months before and had been spiritually renewed by the pilgrimage even though severely spraining her ankle on the pathway up Podbrdo on the first day. Despite this annoyance, she had become an advocate of Medjugorje, and hearing of my coming to Los Angeles, she wanted to meet me.

As we drove into the heart of Beverly Hills, I could hardly believe this woman whom I had admired for so long had read my articles and was open to meeting me to discuss Medjugorje. My admiration stemmed not only because of her acting ability, but the fact that she always ended her popular weekly television show with a moral message based on Scripture.

At a church near Loretta's home, we met two other people who would join us that afternoon. Karen Kopins was a rising young starlet who also had been to Medjugorje, creating a change of perspective in her budding television and movie career. With her was a priest, Father Susa, who worked in Calcutta, India, with Mother Teresa. He had known Loretta for years and had a deep interest in finding out more about Medjugorje. We quickly got to know each other and hastily arranged with my escorts to meet at the church in a couple of hours.

At the door of a spacious but modest home by Hollywood standards, we were greeted by Loretta herself. The conversation immediately turned to Medjugorje; stories flowed as we sipped hot tea.

It was apparent that Loretta was indeed what she appeared to be on stage and screen. Here was a woman whose life as well as career revolved around her faith. Just as any other pilgrim to the little village, she told of its effects not only on her but also on her son.

I was mesmerized as she related the story of going to Lourdes at a critical point in her career to do a show about the shrine. "Things were not going well at all at that time, but I wanted to do something special for my faith and the Lourdes show was it."

She had just received cancellation from her long-time sponsor who had requested repeatedly that she stop doing her trademark moral and scriptural references at the end of each show. "There was no way I was going to do that," she added with emphasis, "so they cancelled."

Things became worse once they arrived on location at Lourdes. Heavy rains caused long overruns and extended expenses, which she was forced to assume personally when her insurance company balked at paying for the extra time.

"But it wasn't all bad," she continued. "One of the executives with the production company was an alcoholic and with nothing to do and nowhere to find a drink, he went out one evening walking up the hill where the stations of the cross were located. Suddenly, there is this deluge of rain with fierce thunder and lightning. As he struggled up the pathway in the dark, a bolt of lightning struck and he found himself staring directly up at the huge cross at the top of the hill—and there was Jesus, staring down at him!"

Loretta laughed at the memory. "Needless to say, he was converted—and cured of alcoholism. On the flight home, I'm happy for him but I'm thinking, that was a mighty expensive conversion!"

"That's quite a story," I said.

Loretta held up her hand. "Wait a minute, that's not all. We arrive home and my agent is waiting for me at the airport with a big smile on his face. He informs me that we already have a new sponsor for the show. And, the insurance company has decided to cover all costs of the production overrun! All this and a conversion too!"

As Loretta finished her story, I knew I wanted to see that show. Hesitantly, I asked, "Loretta, would you happen to have a copy of that show? I'd love to see it."

"Well, I have the original which as far as I know is the only copy," she answered after a few moments of thought. Suddenly, she clapped her hands. "Oh, I have an idea, why don't all of you come back later this week for lunch and you can watch it here!"

I was overwhelmed. Being with her was a tremendous gift in itself; now, she was inviting us back. "I think I have Friday afternoon open, but maybe you have something scheduled—"

"That would be ideal," Loretta answered quickly. "I have an appointment that morning but I'll be home before noon."

With that, arrangements were made to return Friday to view the show on Lourdes. Karen, just as excited as I was to be with Loretta, would also be able to return but Father Susa would not. His stories of times with Mother Teresa were as readily received as those of Medjugorje. Throughout the visit, I felt like a kid turned loose in a candy store.

Glancing at my watch I was shocked to see that we had been talking for nearly four hours. I jumped to my feet apologizing, "I can't believe we've been talking this long. Please forgive us for taking so much of your time."

"Nonsense!" Loretta responded. "I've enjoyed every minute of it."

My concern was also for Kay, Elaine, and Janine whom I had left waiting at the church; we were more than two hours late and time for the evening's talk was near. Good-byes were quickly exchanged with assurances that we would meet again on Friday. A swift trip to the church found my escorts nervously waiting, and after quick apologies we departed for the site of the first evening's talk.

It was a small but enthusiastic crowd, a disappointment to the sponsoring prayer group. "I was hoping we would fill the church," Elaine said dejectedly.

"It's still a nice turnout," I assured her. "Besides, I've come to accept that whoever is meant to be here will come." Even though I forgot it at times, that lesson had been learned the hard way. In some of the smallest crowds, the most unique conversions occurred.

I remembered earlier in the year finally receiving an invitation to speak in my own Lutheran church in Myrtle Beach. The scheduled time was just two days after returning from Ireland, but it didn't matter; I had waited a long time to be able to share the story of Medjugorje with my home congregation and I wasn't going to let a little jet lag slow me down.

That evening as I arrived at the church, there were few cars in the parking lot. Inside, there were only 13 people. Of that, four were from the Catholic church where I attended daily Mass. The total was less than were normally at our Sunday school class. My heart was broken. How I longed for my sisters and brothers of the Lutheran faith, especially here at my local church, to know of this miracle and how it had changed my life.

I plunged ahead trying to give as strong a talk as though there were hundreds present. And afterwards, two young women who only recently had joined the church came forward, and the "look" was in their eyes. They kept thanking me and asking questions, and I knew they had been deeply touched. I vowed to try harder to not question where I was sent to speak or how many attended.

Prior to the start of the talk, I met other members of the prayer group including John Sentovich, Don Moran, and Bob Starbuck, the husbands of my three escorts. I could see immediately they were as dedicated as their wives to the task of spreading the Medjugorje message.

During Kay's introduction, I glanced over the crowd wondering if possibly my mother might be there, not sure I would recognize her if she was. Within a few moments, I was speaking on the motherhood of Our Lady, and how she was coming to Medjugorje to gather together her children. "You might picture Mary's coming to Medjugorje as a mother standing in the door of a burning building beckoning her children toward the way to safety," I stated, again glancing over the crowd. "She is very much the human mother trying to take care of us and to lead us to the safety of her Son, Jesus."

As I later lay in the darkness of the guest room at John and Kay Sentovich's home, I couldn't stop thinking about my mother. I still hoped she might somehow know about me and come to one of the talks in the next week. There was an intense desire within to see her face-to-face and tell her personally that I forgave her for the early years and still loved her.

The morning found us gathered at Janine and Don Moran's home for a brunch with the prayer group. It was a good time to get acquainted with the entire prayer group. I was especially drawn to Bob Starbuck, Elaine's husband. Bob and I had much in common beyond interest in Medjugorje. I soon found myself telling him about my mother, something I rarely discussed, much less with someone I had just met. In turn, he told me about concerns for his children. "Especially my son Kevin," Bob added.

Kevin, his only son, had married at an early age. He and his wife Mary had lived a stormy seven years of marriage that had seen the birth of three boys and two girls, the oldest being only six.

"Kevin and Mary are good kids, but the pressure of trying to get ahead and handle the stress of such a large and young family has taken its toll. They don't attend Mass regularly and we haven't been able to get them to accept anything about Medjugorje at this point." Bob sighed and shook his head. "I just don't know what else we can do."

I laughed softly, assuring Bob that I fully understood. "We share problems, believe me," I told him, relating my problems with my older children, especially Lisa, including her having had an abortion. "We'll just have to pray for each other." I then purposely changed the subject. "Hey, I'm really looking forward to our golf outing Saturday."

Bob had planned a Saturday morning match for John, Don, and the two of us. "I'm glad you mentioned that," Bob interjected, "I was wondering if you would mind if Kevin joins us, and—you know, maybe you could talk to him about Medjugorje?"

"That's fine. We'll see if the opportunity presents itself." I was hesitant, remembering the problems of trying to convince my own children.

Janine suggested we pray a rosary for the success of the tour before the meal. I reached into my pocket, discovering that I had left my rosary in the coat I had worn the previous evening. "That's okay with me if you can find me a rosary," I answered, a little embarrassed. "It seems I've come without one this morning."

Immediately a lady sitting nearby handed me a rosary with silver wire and bright pink beads. "This is an extra one I have, if you don't mind using it because of its color."

Don, sitting across from me at the same table, grinned teasingly, noting my slight discomfort at having to use what was definitely a feminine-looking rosary. His jaw dropped and his eyes widened a few minutes later as he stared at the rosary in my hands as we prayed. Continuing the prayers, I looked down to see what was affecting him about the rosary and was taken aback to see the silver chain links between the beads were changing to a golden color as I prayed!

On completion of the prayers, Don suddenly shouted, "Look at this! It's changed to gold!" And with that everyone crowded around. I was delighted, having had several rosaries of silver turn to a gold color, but never as I was praying them. The lady who had lent me the rosary was in a state of pure happiness. Later, I found she was struggling spiritually with private problems and this was a much-needed sign of heaven's presence. And of course that was the purpose of little miracles like this: to reveal that gifts of grace happen today just as they did in Biblical times, and always as proof that God exists and that He loves us individually as well as collectively.

It would continue to be a day of mini-miracles. We arrived at the site of the talk that evening almost a full hour early only to discover a wedding rehearsal in progress, causing us to have to wait outside in the parking lot. As we stood around talking, someone suddenly shouted, "Look at the sun!"

I looked up to see the phenomena of pulsating, dazzling light coming from the setting sun, creating an extraordinary golden hue that seemed to cover everything in view. The silence of those present in the parking lot was broken only by muffled exclamations as almost everyone was able to see the phenomena. Like at Grenada, when it had occurred during my talk, it was magnificent.

In the midst of all this, a young woman approached me with tears flowing. "I came to hear you tonight because I have so many problems and my faith is so weak. I wanted to ask you to pray for me and my family." She paused, overcome with emotion. "But this is beyond belief! I've never seen anything like it and I have such peace!" She was laughing and crying at the same time as I hugged her and assured her I would pray for her. She told me her name was Monica, and that she was going to attend all of the remaining talks.

"Well, that's up to you, Monica," I laughed. "But I think you've already received strong confirmation that your prayers are being heard!"

I explained to her and the others that the gifts of rosaries turning gold and the miracle of the spinning, pulsating sun were signs of the reality of the miracle of apparitions. "They are like the colorful, shiny banners that car dealers sometimes drape around their lots to attract customers," I said, pointing to a used car lot down the street. "Once Our Lady gets our attention, she points us to her Son through the messages she gives at Medjugorje."

Saturday morning's golf game brought welcomed relief from the grind of the tour. But I was also reminded about talking to Kevin about Medjugorje. I wanted to just relax, and felt a little uncertain about how to handle it. As we pulled into the Starbuck's driveway, Kevin was there with Mary and the children. He was a stocky, energetic young man with flashing eyes that seemed to be trying to see everything at once. "How you doin'," he said with a wide grin, grabbing my hand in a firm handshake. "Dad told me a lot about you and what you're doing. How's your golf game?"

Great, I thought before answering Kevin, how am I going to talk about Medjugorje to this guy? I could feel the usual reluctance of talking to young people setting in early. Mary, busily trying to keep her kids together to meet me, seemed high-strung and nervous. It was evident at first glance that the mantle of motherhood weighed heavily on her. Who wouldn't struggle, I wondered, trying to handle so many little ones? I remembered my own family difficulties magnified by having four children in a short time frame.

As we began play at a nearby public course, I kept receiving eye contact messages from Bob, reminding me about talking to Kevin; but Kevin was a gamer. Once play began, he was thinking only about golf—and winning. He also knew why his father had asked him to play with us. At the end of the first half of the match, we stopped for refreshments. Bob rather obviously, made sure that Kevin was seated next to me. "What can I get you?" Kevin stated. "I'm buying."

"Well, okay, I'll have a beer."

Kevin looked at me questioningly, "You want a beer?"

"Yes, if that's all right."

"Oh—yeah, it's all right. That's what I'm going to have. I just thought—"

I began to laugh. "You thought that since I'm involved with Medjugorje, religion, and all that, I couldn't possibly want a beer—right?"

Now Kevin was embarrassed. Flushed, he stammered, "Well. . ." And then the disarming grin returned. "Yeah, that's right. I guess I had this mental picture of you being, you know, holy!"

I laughed. "Listen, I'm no different personality-wise than I was before my conversion. It's just that now I put God first and everything else second." I pointed at the score card of our match. "In case you hadn't noticed, I'm doing my best to beat you!"

Kevin's grin grew wider. "Yeah, I noticed you're awfully competitive—like me!"

It was an opening I hadn't expected. All barriers came down as we talked animatedly about Medjugorje and the many miracles. I tried to answer Kevin's questions which were coming like machine gun fire, relating a couple of quick stories of other young people and how Medjugorje had affected them. Pulling out my rosary, I told him that it went everywhere with me. As we got up from the table and headed for the golf carts I concluded by telling him that even though we were here to relax and have fun, I was constantly reminded by things around me that God was my number one priority.

Before teeing off on the next hole, I suddenly grabbed Kevin's arm. "Kevin, I've never done this before, but I'm going to ask the Blessed Virgin Mary to turn this rosary chain from its silver color to gold, and then I'm going to give it to you."

It was the topper, definitely cementing Kevin's interest. He was stunned. "Wow, are you sure? What if it don't change?"

"I'll let Our Lady worry about that. Now, let's play golf!" I uttered a silent prayer of thanks, shaking my head in awe that even on a golf course I could witness about Medjugorje. Bob was ecstatic. This was beyond his wildest hopes.

Kevin's wife Mary was waiting for us at the Starbucks, and he could hardly contain himself telling her about the afternoon, especially about the rosary I was planning to give him. She listened with only slight interest.

Later, as we were standing around in the kitchen having cold drinks, I began a conversation with Mary, talking about parenting and interspersing bits of Medjugorje's messages on the importance of families and their praying together. Just as had happened with Kevin concerning the rosary, I suddenly said to Mary in a calm deliberate manner: "Mary, you're going to have another child; it's going to be a little girl. She will be extra special because she will bring your family very close together. She will be the apple of your eye, and you will name her Mary."

There was stunned silence. Mary vigorously shook her head. She heard only the part of having another child and none of the good that would come of it. "No way! No way!" she said laughing nervously. "I can't handle what I have now!" I assured her quickly that it would happen when she would be able to not only handle it but enjoy it. That didn't matter. It just wasn't going to happen, she repeated as she moved away from me.

The awkward silence was broken as Elaine reminded us we needed to get ready for the evening's talk, which was at a cathedral some distance away. We were due to arrive there in less than two hours for dinner with the people who had handled the arrangements. We made it in time to relax at a restaurant close to the cathedral.

"There is one small problem," one of organizers stated as we talked. "The archbishop has refused permission to hold the talk in the sanctuary of the church, so we will be in our activities hall. But it's a large hall and there should be no problems with seating."

I was disappointed, preferring to give talks in churches rather than halls and auditoriums. "What's the problem?"

The organizers looked at each other uneasily. "The archbishop isn't really a firm believer in Medjugorje. It was all we could do to obtain his permission to even let you speak in the activities hall."

I wasn't angry—just perturbed; and didn't mean to sound that way. "Well, I'm going to pray to Our Lady that so many people come tonight, it will have to be moved from the hall to the sanctuary!"

Little did I realize the power of that prayer! Arriving at the cathedral about forty-five minutes before the talk, the activities hall was filled. A young associate priest, left in charge in the absence of the archbishop, didn't know what to do. "He explicitly stated that the talk could not be held in the church," he kept saying to the pleadings of members of the organizing group.

"Father," I asked, "what about the fire laws? It's unsafe to squeeze more people inside the hall. You wouldn't be in disobedience to the archbishop if the fire department told you this was a violation." By now there were almost as many people outside of the hall as inside!

"I can't. I just can't do it!" He threw his arms up and hurried inside the hall.

As the evening's program began with a short fifteen-minute video introducing Medjugorje, there was hardly room to even stand. Throughout the video, I prayed to the Virgin Mary to do something to help the associate priest make the move to the church. As the video ended, the young priest gingerly picked his way through the throng of people to the front of the hall, finally standing in the only open space available. "Okay, I give up!" he said in humorous resignation. "Our Lady wins. We're moving inside the cathedral!"

There was a roar of approval and thunderous applause as the huge crowd surged toward the door leading to the sanctuary. Amazingly, it was just large enough to fill every seat and accommodate the largest crowd of the tour.

Sunday evening I spoke in the mission church at Capistrano, in one of the most beautiful settings I had seen in California. Kevin and Mary were in attendance, having been able to get Kevin's sister to baby-sit. Afterward I answered questions as the attendees enjoyed light refreshments. Finding myself momentarily alone, Mary approached. "That was beautiful," she began. And then she gripped my arm. "I'm beginning to believe the Virgin Mary is appearing there, but please, tell me what you said yesterday about me having another baby is, well, you know, not true. I couldn't survive that!" She began to cry.

I wondered why I had said that to her, but swiftly felt confirmation that it was meant to be said. "Mary, Our Lady is there for you," I began softly. "Believe me, you won't have this child until you are able to accept it as a grace. Didn't you hear what I said tonight? God never gives us more than we can handle."

Kevin, who had been standing nearby placed his arms around her. "Hey, don't worry. We've managed this far and if it happens, we'll handle it!" I knew they would.

The next week continued to bring good fruits, ending

with the return to Loretta Young's home to watch the hour-long show on Lourdes. It was truly a classic and a fitting end to a week of wonders.

Good-byes were said after the last talk that evening since I would be catching an early flight home in the morning. Everyone was exhausted. Yet there they all were at the airport as we arrived. I knew I would see these newfound friends many times over in the coming years.

I instinctively reached in my pocket and pulled out my rosary as I started toward the boarding ramp. The chain links had turned to a golden color! I turned around and returned to the group. "Here," I said with a smile as I handed Bob my rosary. "Give this to Kevin, and tell him Our Lady was listening!"

As the airplane swept into the clouds I felt that warm feeling that comes from knowing the grace of heaven had been poured out in so many ways on this tour. The only regret was in not locating or seeing my mother. Maybe someday . . .

But the dark memories of early days in California had been exorcised. Too many good things had happened.

7
The Good Fruits

*"Dear children, thank God, the Creator, even for little things.
I would like you to thank God for your family, for the place
where you work, and for the people God puts in your way."*

There wasn't a lot of time to savor the fruits of California's
trip. I still had several speaking engagements before a trip
to Medjugorje in late October to complete research for
my book.

Although I was already at work on the early chapters
of the manuscript, David Manuel, my editor, felt we needed
to return to the village for final updates with the priests
and visionaries. That was fine with me; I jumped at any
chance to return to Medjugorje. And since David was also
Protestant, he needed more exposure to Medjugorje, in
order to properly assist me.

Thanks to an offer by a Medjugorje tour director in
Chicago under whose guidance David and I had gone in
June, I would also serve as spiritual leader. Many people
throughout the country, including several in Myrtle Beach,
had stated a desire to go if I were to lead a group; thus, it
became an opportunity to accomplish both tasks on the
same trip.

I only wished my older children had a desire to go—especially Lisa.

Pausing from work on the manuscript a couple of evenings after returning, I thought about the remarkable things that had happened to Kevin and Mary in California, hoping the same would happen to Lisa someday. Just then, the telephone rang. It was my daughter.

Lisa had heard I was going to be speaking in Spartanburg, South Carolina, only a two-hour drive from her home in Columbia. She and Angela had decided they would come and listen; what did I think of that? "Great," I answered, trying not to let the surge of emotion show in my voice. "It will give us time to catch up on things."

I felt a warmth and a tingling sensation as I thanked God for this opportunity to possibly reach my daughters with the message. Fully aware they were coming only to appease me, I recounted Terri's advice to live the messages and not preach to them; now they were curious.

Lisa had settled into marriage with David, and for the moment everything seemed to be fine. Yet, every time I saw her, even for the briefest of moments, her eyes reflected the anguish of knowing what she had done. I drove to Spartanburg filled with all kinds of thoughts. Would this finally be the turning point? Was my firstborn at last coming to grips with the never-ending pangs of guilt from having had an abortion? Would it help her sister Angie and Roy in their marriage? So many questions. And so many doubts to dull my optimism.

The auditorium in Spartanburg was filled to overflowing; it was a good mix of Catholics and Protestants, as this northern South Carolina city was located in the heart of the "Bible Belt." Some had come out of curiosity, some to challenge. But that was okay; I relished every opportunity to involve Protestants in Medjugorje, to assure them that Our Lady was coming for everyone.

I didn't see Lisa and Angela until the talk began, wryly noting they had taken seats in the rear of the auditorium. It seemed to confirm my apprehensions that they had come only out of family obligation. Then as usual, everything but the message was blocked out. No longer was I thinking about them—or about the denominations of those present.

It was a special evening for unity. The talk focused on Our Lady's messages stating she was appearing there for all of her children. I could sense the deep spirituality of the audience as they listened in rapt silence.

Afterward, people came to the podium thanking me and asking questions. As a crowd formed, a man grabbed my hand. "I'm a Baptist and I read a lot of Scripture. I've always wondered what it meant in Luke's Gospel where the Virgin Mary says, 'I will be called blessed by all generations.' Maybe that's what this Medjugorje business is all about!"

There were other comments and inquiries from Protestants, one wanting to debate, quoting Scripture and asking for biblical proof of apparitions. "The Bible doesn't speak of apparitions or Mary as a messenger," he stated holding his Bible open and pointing to it. "Where is your proof this is from God?"

"Well, there is no mention in Scripture of Mary coming in apparition," I answered with a smile, trying to maintain the positive grace of the evening and not wanting to get into a debate, "But there is the Transfiguration of Jesus. And Moses and Elijah came in what you might call an apparition." There were nods of approval and a chorus of "that's right" from the crowd. I continued: "It also says that a good tree can only bear good fruit, and a bad tree only gives bad fruit. I assure you from my own experience and that of others in the last seven years, people are returning to the ways of God after going there. The fruits of

Medjugorje have been excellent!"

My debater pressed on. "But you know, the Bible says the devil can come disguised as an angel of light. How do you know it isn't him appearing disguised as the Blessed Virgin?"

I'd heard this one many times. "If this is Satan," I laughed, "it's the worst mistake he has ever made!" Turning serious again, I continued: "Because people from all faiths, all cultures and all walks of life are truly turning to Jesus; my own life is a good example of that, the same as many others here tonight who have made the pilgrimage!"

With that there was a burst of applause. My debater quietly closed his Bible and said softly, "I'm not sure I agree with all that you've said, but I do know you're sincere in what you're doing. God bless you!"

As the man left, the crowd began to thin. I glanced around furtively, looking for Lisa and Angela. Out of the corner of my eye, I spotted my daughters, still in the rear of the auditorium, with Lisa crying on Angela's shoulder. Angela caught my eye, shrugged, and turned up her free hand in an expression that she didn't have a clue as to what was wrong with her older sister.

But I knew what was wrong with Lisa—or rather, what was the beginning of what would make everything right for her: She had been struck by the message!

It took awhile to make my way through the crowd. Lisa had stopped crying, until she saw me. A few moments later with her arms tightly around my neck, she whispered softly, "Daddy, that wasn't you speaking. That was God, and He was talking to me. I really believe that, and . . . I want to go to Medjugorje!"

Now I had to fight back tears. After years of anguish attempting to convince my spiritually-crippled daughter that this was the only solution to erase the sin of abortion from her soul, it had happened in a matter of minutes. I recalled the beautiful words of the Trinidad prophecy, *"your family shall be united with you in the work you are to do. . . ."*

While the talk had struck Lisa a direct spiritual hit, Angela was impressed, but not noticeably moved—until a few days later. She called me at home one evening, filled with awe. "Daddy, I had to call you to tell you about something that happened this evening," she began. "When I was putting Erin to bed, I saw the outline of the Virgin Mary in the blanket that was on her bed. Daddy, I'm not one to look for such things and I know it was just the light and shadows, but I'm telling you, it looked just like the Virgin Mary!"

A few weeks later, Angela began attending a Baptist church with three-month-old daughter Erin. Soon, Roy was going with them and both became involved in church activities on a regular basis. The heavy problems that had plagued their marriage slowly began to dissolve.

The tremendous change in my two daughters brought to mind one of the most important messages given by the Blessed Virgin Mary at Medjugorje, during the week of my first pilgrimage there in May 1986. It would become an anchor message of my mission.

This unique message was given on Podbrdo Hill at the original spot where Mary had first appeared late on a Monday evening to hundreds of pilgrims, including my group. We had gathered to be with several of the visionaries for an impromptu prayer session as requested by Our Lady to Marija earlier in the day.

Huddling together in the darkness, the mother of Jesus asked us to go home from our pilgrimage and to convert our families by living her messages of prayer, fasting, and penance. It was exactly what Terri had told me to do in order to reach my older children!

But the final words of the message from that wondrous evening are what now came to mind. By doing these things, she said, we would grow holy together, "*. . . And then I can present your family as a beautiful flower that unfolds for my Son, Jesus!*"

I left Spartanburg convinced the flower was unfolding.

There was a lot to be done before going to Medjugorje. My schedule still included a five-day trip to Cleveland, Ohio, in late September; and, a four-day tour in Pennsylvania. After being turned down by local clergy, I still needed a Catholic priest to serve as spiritual guide for the pilgrimage since it would be predominantly Catholic pilgrims going. I was determined to find one.

If all else failed, there was a Baptist minister from the state of Washington, and a Lutheran pastor from Pennsylvania who would also be on the trip. Their presence was another story in itself; both had read my articles and written to me expressing a desire to someday go and see for themselves.

I felt this was the someday for them. It afforded an excellent opportunity to expose Protestant clergy to the message. Both were ecstatic when I telephoned them to invite them to go with us.

Lisa also wanted to go, but I knew she needed to go without her father to influence her in order to discover the true spiritual gifts of Medjugorje. After several conversations embellished with tears and disappointment on her part, I arranged for her to go in September. She came home convinced that God was indeed working there, and was soon witnessing to the rest of the family—meeting much the same resistance I had. But her healing had begun.

I arrived in Cleveland uplifted by the dramatic change in my daughters. And when Jack Weiland, my host for the tour, asked if I would take time to meet and talk to a young man whom he was sure would play a powerful and important part in the conversion message of Medjugorje to youth, I readily agreed. "You've got to meet this kid, Wayne," Jack said as we drove to his apartment. "His story is something else."

Tall, lanky, and animated, Jack had been through more than his share of personal suffering and hardship. "I brought most of it on myself," he added in a unique, gravely voice while relating his background as we headed toward the city. "I smoked and drank heavily, went through divorce and alienation from family, and now I got heart problems."

Jack paused a moment and then with a smile added, "But being over sixty, I don't worry about it. My future's in the hands of God. I got turned around by Medjugorje, and I plan to spend the rest of my life, whether it's a day, a year, or ten years, trying to live the messages and getting others involved. And that's why you gotta meet this kid," he added, quickly changing the subject back to the young man. "I really think Our Lady is gonna use him to get to other young people. He's been given a special job—he just don't know it yet!"

Jack related how Michael O'Brien, a 25-year-old native of Cleveland, who was rapidly developing into a talented rock musician, had come to be involved with Medjugorje. Six months earlier a friend showed him a tape about the apparitions. He was immediately convinced it was real, and insisted his parents go to see firsthand what it was about. As good Catholics who had tried their best to raise their kids in the faith, he was sure they would want to make a pilgrimage.

What Michael didn't count on was going with his parents. They asked all of their other children but none had accepted. Michael, acknowledged as the least religious of the family, was the last one they thought would go with them. He was into rock music and all that came with it. Good and bad. And now, their son was on the verge of possibly getting a national contract and an opportunity to be a recording star. For reasons unknown to him or his parents, Michael said yes. A few weeks later, they were on pilgrimage to Medjugorje.

The family spent the first few days doing what everyone else coming to Medjugorje does: climbing the hills and mountains, going to Mass and sharing stories with others. Michael was unimpressed. It was only when their group went to meet visionary Vicka, that his involvement began.

Standing around after Vicka had spoken to their group, watching her sign autographs and having her picture taken with the pilgrims, he pictured himself someday doing the same as a star singer. Suddenly, Vicka looked at him and asked for a pen and paper. She began writing furiously, giving the note to Michael and telling the interpreter that it was a special message for him from Our Lady.

The young man didn't know what to do or say. The message was written in Croatian. He was shocked when the guide said, "Vicka says it is a special message for you from the Blessed Mother; it says: *'With your ability and musical talent, you can lead young people to God.'* "

Michael was stunned. He had never seen Vicka before, and she had no way of knowing he was a musician. He stuck the note in his pocket, convinced that something special was happening, but not willing to accept its consequences or its effect on his rising singing career.

In the course of his remaining days at Medjugorje, Michael experienced several other mystical occurrences that both confirmed the message and frightened him. Struggling to ignore them, he was relieved when they finally left for home and the note was stuck in a dresser drawer and forgotten.

"The thing is, he's done *nothing* about the message. Can you imagine that?" Jack shook his head. "I just got this feeling that if you can spend some time with him, it might jar him into action."

I told Jack I would be glad to help in any way he wished, still filled with the wonderment of change in Kevin and Mary in Los Angeles, and then my daughters. A few days later, he arranged for Michael to join us at a talk. There would be Mass, then the talk. Jack had invited him to dine with us afterward at the rectory as guests of the pastor of the church where I was speaking.

As Mass began, Jack's young protegé had not arrived. Halfway through the liturgy, he came clumping noisily down the side aisle. I turned to see a young man slide into the seat next to me. He had long, black curly hair, an earring in one ear, and was wearing tight-fitting black jeans and a leather jacket. Jack, sitting on my right leaned over and whispered, "Mike, this is Wayne Weible!"

Michael stuck out his hand. "How ya doin'."

"Fine." Brusquely shaking his hand I thought, "This is the guy Jack thinks I can help?" I was totally unimpressed with Michael O'Brien.

As we sang a hymn a few minutes later, I noticed that Michael was not singing. "I thought you were a singer," I said, nudging him.

Michael smiled sheepishly. "Yeah, well, I don't sing hymns."

At the dinner following Mass, I zeroed in on Michael, asking pointed questions. With Jack's urging, Michael related the story of the note for me and the priest. I asked him why he didn't follow up with what had been given to him if he thought it was from the Virgin Mary. He just shrugged his shoulders. Why did he go to Medjugorje in the first place? "Well, it was a good way to see a part of

Europe," he answered with a giggle.

Jack, sensing my hostility, leaned over and whispered, "Hey, take it easy on the kid!" I nodded, but I did not share Jack's enthusiasm about this young man.

During the talk, with Michael squatting on the floor in front of the first pew so that he could videotape parts of the talk, I spoke about the ill effects that rock music had on so many young people, staring directly at him. My young target never flinched; he had heard it all before.

Afterwards, we went to Michael's home for light refreshments and a small gathering of all who had assisted in arranging the tour. Jack had quietly arranged it with Michael's parents, unbeknownst to Michael—or me. He was as surprised on our arrival as I was. I had to give my host credit; he was determined to put me in a position to be with this young musician. Later, we found ourselves sitting alone across from each other at the kitchen table.

"Mike," I suddenly blurted out, no longer able to keep the frustration out of my voice, "I have to ask you again: why didn't you do something about that note? I mean, if it's really from the Virgin Mary, don't you know there are some beautiful religious songs that, well, you could do in a rock style." I adjusted my chair, looking intently at him; he was actually listening. "For instance, there's this song called 'Gentle Woman,' which is beautiful, and there are others like it."

Michael squinted and shrugged. "I don't know any of those songs but, who knows, maybe someday . . ."

We talked about Medjugorje. He had been deeply affected by the trip but had kept his feelings to himself. Just as we began to warm to the subject, several people came to the table and began asking me questions. Within seconds Michael was gone. As I left the O'Brien home that night, I didn't think I would ever see him again.

Several weeks later, I received an audio cassette tape

in the mail. It was from Michael. On it was the most beautiful singing of "Gentle Woman" I had ever heard! I sat there listening to it over and over, with chills—and tears. Once again, despite my resistance, Our Lady had used me to reach one of her beloved young people.

Later, on my trip to Pennsylvania in early October, I found it would include stops in Ohio: Akron, and then at the Shrine of Lebanon, near Youngstown. In Akron, as I prepared to leave for the sanctuary with the priest, the door bell rang. The priest opened the door, and there were Michael and Jack. Michael and I looked at each other, and after a few seconds he stepped forward and hugged me in silence. No words were necessary. That evening, I told the story of Michael O'Brien and his note from Vicka.

Two weeks later, I received another audio cassette tape with *five* religious songs recorded by my new musician friend. Interspersed among the songs were actual sounds of Medjugorje and recorded pieces of interviews and prayers with the visionaries. It was called appropriately, "Sounds of Medjugorje." Michael's name was nowhere on the tape or jacket cover, but he was the one singing the songs. I discovered later that moved by the events during my two trips to Ohio, he had done the entire tape by himself, unknown to the rest of his rock group or his manager.

It was a tremendous two months; I prepared to return to Medjugorje, with only one remaining problem: I *still* did not have a Catholic priest to go with us as spiritual guide.

An opportunity to solve that was presented a few days later when I received a telephone call from a Medjugorje friend who lived in Wilmington, North Carolina. Karen

Stoffel had been to Medjugorje, and her mission on returning was to try to get the priests in Wilmington involved.

Karen was determined to "convert" these priests to belief in the apparitions. She was calling to ask me a favor: would I be willing to come to a luncheon at her home to speak to these priests about my experiences? "They're very reluctant when I try to tell them about my trip, but you being a Protestant, I think they'll listen!"

Karen was ecstatic when I said I would come with the hope that possibly one or more of them would accept my invitation to join our October pilgrimage. "That would be incredible," she gushed. "If one of them actually went there. I know it would influence the rest!"

A few days later I was sitting in her home assessing the possibilities of which of the five priests she had invited would actually accept the invitation to go to Medjugorje. "There is only one that I'm absolutely sure won't accept," she added as we finished discussing each priest. "That's Father Jim Watters. He's into some strange things—New Age things. And he doesn't believe in Medjugorje. The only reason he's coming to the luncheon is because I assist him at his church periodically."

Soon there was a knock at the door; Karen, busy in the kitchen preparing the meal, asked if I would answer it. I opened the door to see a huge man standing there. He was at least six feet, four inches and close to 250 pounds. "Hey, how are ya," he said in a fast-talking New York accent as he mangled my hand. "You must be the guy involved in the apparition thing. Gotta tell ya right off—I don't believe!" With that he clapped me on the back, let out a loud laugh and yelled, "Okay Karen, I'm here—where's the food!"

"Karen's right," I thought, "this guy's not going!"

After the others arrived, I uttered a silent prayer to

Our Lady asking that one of them might say yes. Any of them, that is, except Father Jim Watters!

As we sat over coffee following the lunch, I began speaking about Medjugorje, and answering their few questions. After a noticeable hesitancy, I decided to make my move. "I understand your caution concerning such things as apparitions," I began, "but there is a pilgrimage going over in several weeks. It might be more acceptable if one of you actually went to Medjugorje to see for yourself. Then you could relate your feelings and findings to the others. So—" I hesitated a moment and smiled, "I'm inviting each of you to come with me on this pilgrimage as a spiritual guide."

There was silence before one of the priests thanked me for the "generous offer" but politely declined, citing a busy schedule. Soon the rest chimed in with similar excuses. And then Father Watters: "Well, hey, that's a great offer! I tell you what—I'll go. It should be interesting!"

Karen and the other priests were as stunned as I was. Later, as he was leaving, Father Watters pulled me aside. "Look, since the others declined to go, how about taking a friend of mine from Florida? He's a monsignor and he believes in this stuff."

"Why not?" I answered weakly, "Get me his name and telephone number and I'll call him."

"Oh, don't worry about that—I'll do it; just tell us what we need and where to be and I'll take care of the rest!"

I drove home in a daze. This was *not* at all what I had expected. I was stuck with this odd priest—and now his friend. "That's great," I muttered as I pulled onto the highway heading home, "it's going to be some trip. A Lutheran pastor, a Baptist preacher—and now a strange priest!"

8
Pilgrimage

"Dear children, I have chosen this parish in a special way and I wish to lead it. I am guarding it in love and I want everyone to be mine . . ."

There was the usual organized mass confusion as the pilgrimage came together at O'Hare Airport in Chicago. The travel agency people were busily scurrying along the ticket area of Yugoslav Airlines, passing out tickets and herding arriving pilgrims into the proper lines for boarding passes.

I smiled as I stood near the telephone at the far end of the area watching the proceedings, enjoying the now-familiar process that was part of a Medjugorje pilgrimage. For the third time, I reached into my travel folder to make sure I had passport, tickets and other needed documents.

"Wayne, there you are. All set for the trip?"

David Manuel dropped his bag and extended his hand. "Hi, David, just checking again to make sure I have everything," I said, shaking his hand. "Better take your passport to the agent so she can get your boarding pass."

"No problem, I have it right here." He began foraging through a folder. Suddenly he grew pale. "I can't believe it, I think I've forgotten my passport! How could I have done this?" Stunned, he mumbled the question several times as we sought the travel agent to inform her of the dilemma.

I knew how he could have done it; such things were always happening even to the best prepared of pilgrims. It was part of the annoyances that characterized pilgrimages to Medjugorje, and other holy places—distractions from the dark side that did not want the fount of grace to continue reaching souls. David had become a victim.

Arrangements were hastily made to have his forgotten passport sent to New York; he would fly there and stay with relatives overnight before catching the only other flight to Yugoslavia from the United States that week. While sympathetic to David's predicament, I was at least grateful his delay would allow me a couple of days to spend with the pilgrims before the two of us would have to isolate ourselves to work on the book.

After seeing David off, I joined our group of pilgrims now assembled in the holding area awaiting boarding. Since we had an hour, it was an opportune time to personally meet and talk with the two Protestant ministers who had by this time discovered each other and formed a protective relationship among the predominantly Catholic pilgrims.

"I can't thank you enough for inviting me," David Conrad, the Lutheran minister exclaimed several times between a barrage of questions. "I think the entire Medjugorje phenomena is a major breakthrough in ecumenism; don't you agree?" he added, turning to his newfound associate, Arthur Jacobson, for confirmation.

"Well, that remains to be seen." My Baptist minister was more reserved. Older in years and experience, initial conversations with him concerning Medjugorje had centered on theology rather than the curiosity of most who become interested in the apparitions. Although positively influenced by my articles and appreciative of the opportunity to make the journey, he was reserving final judgment as to the authenticity of the apparitions. "It should be an interesting experience. I'm certain that if it is of God, we will know it by the end of the trip!"

Suddenly we were interrupted. "Hey, Wayne, come over here a sec. I want you to meet Monsignor!"

Not waiting for a reply, Father Jim Watters strode to where we were and, ignoring the other two men, grabbed my arm, pulling me to where a white-haired, older priest was waiting. "This is my friend from Florida, Monsignor Carter."

I was mildly surprised. The monsignor was an elderly man who spoke in a humble, quiet manner—just the opposite of Father Watters. Within minutes, Father Watters interrupted, "Look, I need a few favors; how 'bout getting me a seat in the front of the plane with some legroom? And could you arrange a private room for us in Medjugorje?"

The list of requests continued. My only consolation was that at least he was wearing his priest's collar, which turned out to be my saving grace. Before I could answer his requests a woman from our group came over and grabbed *him* by the arm. "Father, I have to talk to you— now!"

Try as he might, Father Jim could not persuade the woman to wait until we arrived in Medjugorje. She wanted him to hear her confession before we left. Just as we began boarding, Father Jim returned, shaken and pale. "That's the most difficult—and beautiful—confession I have ever heard!" There was a definite change in his demeanor. Hours after takeoff, I saw Father Jim sitting next to the Monsignor, his long legs cramped against the seat, unusually quiet and remaining that way throughout the flight.

Nearly twenty-two hours later, our two chartered buses turned onto the short, narrow road leading to Medjugorje. Everyone became excited, including the priests and the two Protestant ministers. Fatigue of the journey was momentarily forgotten. Someone suggested we pray the rosary as we entered the village and immediately everyone was in deep prayer, again, including the Protestants. I smiled as I noticed they had been given rosaries by members of the group.

But my thoughts did not stay on the rosary. The happiness of being back in Medjugorje was tempered by the fact that I would not be receiving the Holy Eucharist in the church where I had first received it. It was the one negative aspect in returning to Medjugorje the last couple of trips. The sacrament of the Eucharist had most influenced my desire to become a Roman Catholic, a desire that was not fully realized until the last day of my first trip to Medjugorje, in May of 1986.

That day had been an emotional one. I didn't want to go home and leave the indescribable peace and love I felt during those six days of pilgrimage, much of it due to receiving Jesus in the Eucharist. Throughout the pilgrimage I watched the long lines of people going through another beautiful Catholic ritual, that of confession. Talking to many in my group of the positive results, it seemed to be the final piece of their pilgrimage; I wanted to experience it as well.

But there was a complication. My last-minute urge to suddenly want to go to confession was clouded by despondency at having to leave Medjugorje. Again, one of those "interventions" from heaven occurred; arriving at St. James Church early that afternoon for the final evening Mass before departing for home the next morning, I found a spot in the back, sitting on the end of the last pew on the right side of the church. The wall was lined with little confessional booths, each having a small sign on the floor in front identifying the language of the priest hearing confession.

After the apparition and completion of the rosary, I decided to forgo confession; I would wait until I returned home so that I might go to my own Lutheran pastor. After all, I reasoned, it was all the same.

As I stood up to leave the church and return to my room in Citluk, my pathway was blocked by a rotund priest, standing in front of one of the confessionals. For some reason I glanced down at the sign and noted it was Italian. Pointing at me now, he whispered, "Italiano?"

"No, no, English," I answered as I tried to move past him.

"Oh, *Englaise*—si!" With that, he virtually shoved me into the next booth—which was for English confessions!

It was during that unexpected experience in the confessional that I heard myself saying to the priest, that I wanted to become . . . a Catholic. Never in the eight months since first receiving the interior message from the Blessed Virgin Mary, had I considered converting to the Catholic faith. Medjugorje's messages were for all faiths; conversion meant turning to God, and not necessarily to Catholic doctrine. But in this wondrous week, a week in which I literally fell in love with Jesus through receiving Him in the Holy Eucharist, I had never experienced such a closeness to Him.

Like the Catholics, I believed the Eucharist was the actual body and blood of Jesus, and after this week of constant church and prayer, I couldn't imagine not being able to receive Him. Even though Our Lady's message was an all-faiths message, I knew it was no accident that she chose this predominantly Catholic village as a place to bring renewal of the Gospel message of her Son.

Before coming here, I was ignorant of the fact that

Protestants were not supposed to participate in the Catholic Eucharist, and I joined the throngs in sharing Holy Communion. Later in the week after I was told it was improper, I continued to receive. Surely, I rationalized, this was meant for everyone. I was so centered on *self* that the thought that I was being disobedient and disrespectful never entered my mind. This beautiful sacrament represented my *entire* Medjugorje experience and I didn't want to lose it.

On returning home from that first pilgrimage, I prayed to the Blessed Virgin for guidance to do what her Son wanted. I was going to daily Mass at the Catholic church to receive the Eucharist—and also going to my Lutheran church on Sundays. Several days later, I contacted a priest outside of the Myrtle Beach parish, as the local priest did not believe in Medjugorje. Or, for that matter, any apparitions past or present.

I began to depend on this new priest, Father Mike, as my spiritual guide, asking him to help me enter into the Catholic faith. He quickly pointed out that because of my divorce it might not be possible, and that it would take considerable time. "How long?" I asked.

"Anywhere from six months to a year and a half or more."

I only heard six months.

Several evenings later as I was praying in thanksgiving for the developments to this point, I suddenly felt the Madonna speaking to my heart again; she was saying that I would not become Catholic "*at this time . . .*"

Shock and alarm filled my heart. "Why not?" I asked out loud. There was no answer.

I immediately rationalized that it must be because of my divorce, and that it would have to be clarified by the Catholic Church Tribunal process before proceeding. That meant going through a trial process to determine if there were grounds for a Church-recognized annulment of my first marriage. There was no guarantee it would be positive. But in spite of this new message from the Blessed Virgin and the uncertain chances of success, I was determined to continue the process.

Then something happened that began to bring into focus the reason for the "not yet" message. One morning at Mass in Myrtle Beach, as I went forward to receive, the priest whispered, "See me after Mass." I knew something was wrong. As I approached him a few minutes later in the sacristy, he shoved a copy of the local diocesan newspaper at me and said, "Read this." It was an article about bishops warning priests to crack down on non-Catholics receiving Communion in the Catholic Church. As I looked up dazed after reading the article, the priest clapped me on the back and said, "I knew you would understand—see you around." With that he walked away leaving me standing there in numb disbelief.

I was devastated. How was I going to get through the day without receiving Jesus in the Holy Eucharist? I didn't know what to do. I went see Father Mike, and as I entered his office I prayed for direction through his words.

"Wayne," he began smiling sympathetically as I related to him what had happened, "what do you imagine people are thinking when you say you are a Lutheran and yet you are coming to Mass regularly and receiving the sacraments of the Catholic Church? And since you are speaking about Medjugorje, and about obedience to God, how do you think this looks to them?"

I didn't have an answer.

Father Mike related that he had received complaints about my receiving Holy Communion from some of his parishioners; "But, I will allow you to receive here," he added quickly, "if you feel that is what you must do."

As he waited for a response, I knew what I had to do; my heart was suddenly filled with understanding. Quietly,

I said to him: "Father, I will not receive Jesus in the Eucharist again . . . until I become a Catholic in name the right way, through the tribunal process."

"Good, that's exactly what I wanted to hear you say," Father Mike replied as he hugged me.

It was an important beginning lesson in true submission to God. Without obedience, true child-of-God obedience, there can be no real conversion.

It had been two years since I had made that decision, and paperwork for the annulment process for both Terri and myself had long ago been completed. Yet we were still awaiting a hopefully positive ruling that would allow us to enter the Church. Attending Mass had become bittersweet. It was the spiritual elixir needed to fully carry out my mission. But the spiritual pain of not being able to receive the Holy Eucharist had become nearly unbearable—especially in Medjugorje.

As the rosary ended, the bus pulled to a stop in front of a large home where the group would be housed for the week. There was just enough time to settle into quarters before hurrying to the evening Mass, with the promise of a good Croatian meal afterwards.

Following the Mass, I caught a taxi and headed for Marija's home. Even though I had stayed there the last three trips to Medjugorje, I still had difficulty accepting the reality of not only personally knowing this deeply spiritual visionary, but of staying with her family.

It had occurred a little more than a year ago when I related my story to her in a private meeting, with Father Svet serving as interpreter. As we were leaving, she had stared at me intently for a moment before responding in halting English, "From now on when you come to Medjugorje, you stay here. You are family."

A special bond developed that enabled me to see her

not primarily as a visionary, but as a sister in Christ. I knew that Our Lady wanted me to pray for her in a special way, just as she seemed to know that I was supposed to stay there.

"Oh, you are here!" As I entered the tiny courtyard of her home, Marija came bounding down the steps to greet me with a hug and the customary kiss on each cheek. "Come, I have food for you."

Soon we were at the kitchen table enjoying the simple but delicious fare, with steaming, thick expresso coffee to wash it down. It amazed me that I could drink this stuff and still sleep, even after 30 hours of travel. But there was a special peace in Medjugorje that went beyond the norm of everyday habits.

Marija's brother Antonio, his wife Macha, and their five-year-old son Philipe, were also staying at the house as they worked on completing the construction of their own home. And while only Marija understood a limited amount of English, the conversation was lively.

"Yes, Medjugorje has changed very much," Marija answered in reply to my question about the surge of construction going on throughout the village. Everyone was building additional rooms, including Antonio and Macha, to house the literally thousands of pilgrims now surging steadily into the village. I remembered on my first visit that Antonio owned and operated one of only three restaurants in the township. Now they were everywhere, including at the base of both Podbrdo Hill and Mt. Krizevic. Souvenir stands dotted the narrow roadways, the pathway through the fields, and were even along the rocky trail up Podbrdo.

"Many changes, some not good," Marija said, clearing away the dishes, and then with a beautiful smile added, "But also, many conversions!"

I nodded in agreement and admiration of her perception, thinking of the many accounts I had read about how the Blessed Virgin Mary had come to six young "uneducated" peasant children in Medjugorje. I had discovered they were bright, intelligent young people blessed with an abundance of common sense. Marija spoke fluent Italian and was good enough with English to carry on lengthy, understandable conversations. She hardly fit the description of uneducated.

Our conversation ran into the night as I forgot my weariness of the long journey. I wanted to know everything that was happening. Indeed, commercialism had wrapped its tentacles of greed around the village. Many villagers who in the beginning held fast to evening Mass, prayer, and fasting, were now too busy taking care of pilgrims. The government had also jumped into the fray. No longer harassing the villagers and pilgrims, they were furiously building hotels and bungalows to grab the lion's share of the pilgrim dollar. To corner the market they were attempting to force the villagers to pay extra taxes on each pilgrim staying with them so that pilgrims would fill their rooms instead.

And of course, the ethnic hatred was still there. Already dominating most available jobs, Serbs now came from the cities to serve as tour guides, and to corner local tour services. They were still the dominant figures in the schools and governments, making it easy for entry into this new source of income.

But as Marija had stated, spiritual conversion was strong. People from surrounding villages and cities, and from other Eastern European countries, streamed into Medjugorje every weekend, many making the difficult trek on crowded buses or by foot. They would enter St. James Church on their knees as special penance of thanksgiving, circling the statue of the Blessed Virgin Mary. Large groups would climb the hill and mountain barefoot and in fervent prayer.

"And groups come all day for me to speak and pray with them," Marija added. "It is difficult but I am happy they come."

Changing the subject, I asked Marija about the health of her other brother Andrija, who was suffering from a kidney disease. I had met Andrija on previous trips and was disturbed at the rapid deterioration of his physical appearance. "He is not well," she answered solemnly. "He must have a kidney transplant." She smiled, adding, "From me!"

I was shocked. Andrija was a happy-go-lucky individual who would rather fish than work—or go to church. Married, and the father of a four-year-old daughter, he was building a large home to house pilgrims when it was discovered he had a terminal kidney disease. And even though his sister was blessed to be a visionary, Andrija had not fully embraced the grace coming from the apparitions. His spiritual life, at best, lacked intensity. I had given him a Croatian-language Bible hoping that this would spur him on.

Marija talked about the urgency of Andrija having the operation, adding that she was the only family member who matched Andrija's need. They were looking for a place and time that the operation could take place. Offers of help had come from England and Germany, but nothing definite had been arranged. Sensing her deep concern, I wanted to help. "Marija, if I can arrange a medical appointment in the United States, would you and Andrija come?" Immediately thinking of Duke University Hospital, in Durham, North Carolina, just a few hours drive from Myrtle Beach, I felt certain we could make the arrangements.

After a momentary hesitation, Marija said, "Yes, we will come."

My mind was in overdrive with details of how to get

Marija and Andrija to the States as I set out the following morning on the pathway through the fields to attend Mass. There were visa's to worry about, finances, and a hundred other details. But soon such thoughts were lost in prayer, enhanced by the sheer, natural beauty that was Medjugorje. Fields once filled with tobacco plants were now cut into smaller garden plots to raise vegetables needed to feed the pilgrims. The change in crops had come as a special request of the Blessed Virgin through the visionaries. A few villagers who chose to continue to plant tobacco soon found their new plantings ruined by a strange disease, mysterious in that tobacco had been the major crop here for years. They were soon converted to Gospa's request.

The garden plots now made up a pretty patchwork of different shades of greens and browns as the final vestiges of autumn played out. All of this, surrounded by majestic snow-capped mountains ringing the valley, seemed to separate it from the world and its problems.

I completed the near-mile walk to St. James Church, unconscious of time, entering just as the Mass was beginning. Squeezing through the crowded front of the church, I made my way slowly to the front right side near the statue of Our Lady. I could not help but feel the recognizing stares and soft touches on the shoulder of fellow pilgrims as I settled in for the service. It was the last thing I wanted this morning; my entire being was focused on worship— and the harsh reality of still not being able to receive the Holy Eucharist.

And then a mild shock; Father Jim Watters was on the altar concelebrating the Mass and was about to do the Gospel reading! He began slowly, deliberately, and with feeling. No machine gun staccato; no pomp or flourish, but with humility.

At the time of the Eucharist, the bonus of Father Watters' moving reading of the Gospel brought the pangs of not being able to share in this sacrament to the surface. I broke into tears, embarrassed and wishing I were invisible, as the priests made their way through the crowd. Suddenly, there were uncontrollable sobs coming from someone next to me. I looked over to see a man hunched over, his face buried in the lap of a woman bending over him and trying to comfort him. As I reached over and placed my hand on his shoulder, he raised his tear-streaked face. "My Gosh," I thought. "It's Professor Robert Stephens!"

His wife hugged me, whispering, "He feels about the Eucharist the same as you do, Wayne. It's been this way since you came to our community."

I had met Robert a few months earlier on a speaking tour through the New England area. He had been assigned to drive me to the site of a talk, and I discovered later he had requested the assignment in order to have time to talk with me. The drive took the better part of an hour and in that time I discovered that he was the head of the Department of Religious Studies at a state university. He and his wife had taken a trip to Ireland earlier in the year for special research on the subject of ancient holy wells. While there, they learned of reports of local apparitions of the Blessed Virgin Mary, and while inquiring about them, learned also about Medjugorje. Amazingly, they were both agnostics!

On returning to the States, this professor of religions began an intense study of Marian apparitions. Part of his research information was my articles, and he was fascinated, he related during the drive, that a Protestant journalist would become involved in this "Catholic thing."

Now, here was my agnostic professor of religion suffering the same hunger for the Eucharist!

As the Mass ended, I was swept out of the church with the crowd as the Italians began flooding the pews for their service. Once outside, I lost sight of Robert Stephens and his wife. Swamped by well-wishers, I attempted to make my way toward the pathway. The weight of my emotions was overwhelming; I just wanted to be alone. But the crowd would have none of it. How long was I going to be there? Would I be speaking? Could I come to their pilgrim home for lunch? Did I have a minute to speak to a youth group?

Evading direct answers and commitments, I gently pushed my way to the edge of the church grounds apologizing and using the excuse of running late for an appointment—which was partly true; Marija had expressly stated I was to be there for lunch at noon sharp. Just as I started down the pathway, two young girls caught up with me. "Wait! Mr. Weible, wait!" Turning around, there was faint recognition of the girls. "Mr. Weible, I don't know if you remember us. From Anchorage, Alaska?"

"Oh, yes, you're the daughters of Dr. Richard McMichael," I said, recognizing them. "How is your father?"

"That's why we stopped you," the older girl replied. "He's here, and he's very sick. He knows you're here also and our mother sent us to find you to see if you would come and see him."

All personal concerns disappeared. "Of course; let's go."

"This way, we have a car," she yelled as they hurried toward the road behind the rectory.

Within minutes we were at the house. Entering a darkened room, the doctor was lying on a bed, his wife Sharon on one side, and a priest sitting on the other holding his hand. They were softly praying the rosary. Sharon gave me a quick glance of gratitude and then whispered to her husband, "Richard, Wayne Weible is here. He's come to see you."

Dr. McMichael weakly turned his head toward me, and with a weak smile, continued to mouth the words of the prayers. He was as white as the sheets. On completion of the rosary, the priest motioned me to take his place at the side of the bed. This was the most difficult part of the mission—having to face situations like this. I just didn't feel worthy to be a strength of any kind to someone who was dying. It wasn't false humility; I knew who I was and what my life had been before Medjugorje.

Fighting the reluctance, I began to talk to Dr. McMichael, keeping it light, yet realizing the seriousness of his illness. I was relieved some ten minutes later when the priest quietly suggested to Richard that he better get some rest. As I started to leave the side of the bed, the doctor gripped my hand with surprising momentary strength. "Thank you for coming. You are the reason I've come here; your story. Don't worry about me. I'll make it."

Sharon rode with me on my return to Marija's house and as we pulled up to the gate, she asked imploringly, "I hope I'm not imposing, but could you ask Marija to come and pray over Richard?"

"Sharon, I don't know, but I'll be glad to ask her. And please know that I'm going to pray for him constantly."

As I entered the kitchen, Marija was standing near the sink with hands on hips and a mock frown on her face. "You are late for lunch!" I hastily explained, telling her about Dr. McMichael, adding that I did not think he would live long enough to leave Medjugorje, and then asked if she would go pray over him. "I will try to go later, and tonight at the apparition, I will recommend him to Gospa."

I hoped "later" would not be too late, but I was grateful for her acceptance. This was Marija's special gift as a visionary: to pray for the sick and handicapped.

Normally shy to the point of not wanting her picture taken and disdaining the signing of autographs, she displayed a special strength when it came to those in need. It was not unusual to find one or more youthful drug addicts staying at her home. And she readily went to those in wheelchairs or otherwise in need, recommending them in a special way during the next apparition with the Blessed Mother. This special penance seen in Marija and the other visionaries served as further evidence that the apparitions were most definitely of God.

Gulping down a quick meal, I hastily excused myself again, much to the chagrin of Marija. "You are leaving again? No, you stay and rest!" Promising to return in time to go with her to the tower in St. James Church, the site of the evening apparition, I backed out the door apologizing, and hurried down the pathway to meet with my group; we were to rendezvous at the church and then proceed to Vicka's house to meet and listen to her story.

As we started down the pathway toward Vicka's house I was pleased to see Art Jacobson in animated conversation with several members of our group. He was enjoying himself and while not committing to personally believing that the apparitions were real, he was impressed with the holiness and focus of the pilgrimages. In stark contrast, David Conrad had returned to his room following morning Mass, extremely disappointed that as a Protestant, he still was not permitted to receive Communion in a Catholic church. He was appalled to find that nothing on that front had changed. And try as they might, the others could not persuade him to join us to go to listen and see Vicka.

"Hey, Wayne, wait a minute." It was Father Watters. "Listen," he began, taking me by the arm to slow me down out of earshot of the others. "I just wanted to thank you for inviting me here. It's absolutely beautiful, everything about it. I'm still not sure I believe these kids are seeing anything but one thing's for sure: this is a Holy Spirit place! Just thought I'd let you know," he said, trotting back to the group. I shook my head in wonder.

Except for the final day in Dubrovnik, the rest of the

pilgrimage was spent in hard work with David Manuel. He had rented a car in Dubrovnik, and had arrived two days into the pilgrimage. Marija had graciously given us her room for sleeping quarters, causing further awe as I related to David that the Blessed Mother had appeared to her in this room often.

One incident in particular brought the reality of this daily, ongoing miracle into David's heart. As we prepared to leave for a special interview with Father Jozo Zovko, in Tihaljina, we found that the temperature had dropped rather dramatically. David returned to the room to get his coat, and upon returning to the car, he just sat there staring straight ahead.

"What's the matter?" I asked.

"Do you know what I just saw," he said in a quivering voice, his eyes beginning to moisten. "You know that little room next to ours? Well, it has three bedrolls on the floor. I saw them as I walked by the door which was slightly ajar." David paused and took a deep breath. "That's where Antonio and his family are sleeping. On that hard, cold floor, because they gave us their room and their beds!"

"I know," I answered. "That's their way of living the messages Our Lady is giving to their sister and the other visionaries."

The final day of the tour was in Dubrovnik, where we would catch an early flight home the following morning. As I walked alone in the back part of the old city, wanting a little private time to gather my thoughts of the trip, I suddenly ran into David Conrad. It was the first time I had seen him since Mass on our first day in the village.

I could see in his expression the tremendous disappointment of his pilgrimage. It was not at all what he had expected. And since he hardly left his room after the first evening Croatian Mass, I could understand why. We made small talk for awhile and after an awkward pause, "Well,

I'll see you back at the hotel. I'm going to walk around–"

"Listen, can we talk a little while? I'm really sorry for not participating more. I know I missed a lot and I do appreciate your bringing me here, but I was sure this had to be the big breakthrough for ecumenism. . . . "

For the next forty minutes we sat in a small sidewalk cafe and talked. I explained to David as best I could that it was up to all of us, Catholics and Protestants alike, to bring true unity to the Church of Jesus. "God isn't going to bring it about by a super miracle like Medjugorje," I concluded. "Medjugorje is simply to make us aware that He is real; that heaven and hell are real. We have to choose by our own free will to follow Jesus, to live His gospel. When we do that, we will unite as one family ."

Several weeks after returning home, I heard from all three clergy who had made the pilgrimage. Arthur Jacobson, back in his Baptist church, was thankful for the experience and wanted to believe in the apparitions. But there were still a lot of theological differences he had to work out.

David Conrad, on the other hand, "blossomed" *after* arriving home. Somewhere in meditation and prayer, he wrote, he discovered the true Medjugorje and what it meant. Already, he had several speaking engagements in churches in his area—both Protestant and Catholic.

As for Father Watters, he now fully believed Mary was appearing in Medjugorje, he told me by telephone. He was "newly born again of the Spirit." Fasting twice a week, Father Jim had already lost 15 pounds. He was now hard at work on a return trip to Medjugorje in several months, with a chartered plane containing at least 300 people, the bishop from his diocese, and a television news crew.

"Well," I thought, hanging up the telephone. "Two out of three—that's pretty good!"

9
Trust

"Why do you not put your trust in me? I know that you have been praying for a long time, but really surrender yourself. Abandon your concerns to Jesus."

The return home brought problems to solve and decisions to be made. Foremost were arrangements to bring Marija and her brother Andrija to the States for the kidney transplant operation.

But that wasn't the only pressing issue; our major printing customer had given notice they were making huge cuts in the circulation of the newspapers they were printing with us, costing us close to half our entire printing business. I was dismayed. It threatened to bring an abrupt halt to my now full-time Medjugorje mission. "What can we do?" I asked Terri as we discussed it after breakfast.

"Well, we have two options: you stop traveling for awhile and come to work full-time to gain back the lost business; or, we shut down the entire business as soon as possible and sell the equipment and stock."

I shook my head. "That doesn't leave a whole lot of choice."

"Not really, but it does present some interesting side

affects." She waited a moment, looking at me with a teasing smile and letting the anticipation build. I wondered what she could find to smile about with such a dilemma facing us. "At least you'd be home with us if you came back to work, which I doubt you'll want to do since Our Lady is making good use of you. But if we shut down the business, I'll be able to stay home and be a full-time mother and wife." It was obvious which option she preferred.

"You're right. I can't quit the mission. Anyway, there's no way we're going to make up that kind of loss. But if we shut down and you stay home, we still need income."

Terri remained calm. She had taken time in my absence to carefully consider the options. It had been a good year for our printing business, but with the cuts beginning the first of the new year, we could lose everything before spring if we attempted to continue the business.

"Besides, your book will be completed soon," she added. "With the income from selling the printing company materials and equipment, we should be okay until the book is out."

"There's just one little problem you're overlooking," I said grimly. "I still don't have a publisher."

Again the bright smile. "Oh, you will. What you've written so far is excellent, and this book is important." While it was gratifying to hear such warm remarks from Terri, I wasn't so sure. It was a strange reversal of personality traits; normally I was the optimist and Terri the pessimist.

My skepticism was based on the fact that David Manuel had contacted several major publishers including one of the largest, Doubleday. There had been little or no significant interest from any of them. I wanted in the worse way to be published by Doubleday, because it would gain tremendous national attention for Medjugorje's apparitions— not to mention the personal prestige it would give me.

However, Doubleday wanted to see more of the book before committing to a contract. Even then, there was no guarantee.

With the draft of the book half-completed, only tiny Paraclete Press, a religious book publishing house operated by the Community of Jesus, a covenant ecumenical community in which David lived, had expressed interest. Their offer was based on the premise that if no one else would do the book, they would. It was the least of my choices since they had never published a book which sold more than ten thousand copies.

Later that evening I headed for the beach; it was my favorite place to think and pray. As I walked alone, I realized for the first time since saying yes to this mission, that I was going to have to truly live one of the basic tenants of spiritual conversion: total trust in Jesus. That was the foundation of faith. With that realization, I knew we had to follow Terri's recommendation and shut down our business. It was time to "walk my talk."

In the midst of these problems, there was one more major trip to be made before the end of the year, to the United Kingdom.

For nine days during the early part of December, a whirlwind of travel by air, train, and automobile, I journeyed from the northern tip of Scotland to the heart of London. It was a difficult tour, in that few people in the UK knew much about the apparitions at Medjugorje; fewer knew me or my story. Fortunately, an audio tape of the talk I gave in the summer of 1987 at St. James Church in Medjugorje had made the rounds. Thousands of copies had been distributed, and I was known as "that Lutheran" who speaks about the Virgin Mary's apparitions.

I arrived home from this last trip of the year, hoping to have time to gather my thoughts and wrap up arrangements on getting Marija and her brother to the States as soon as possible. But there was a surprise awaiting me.

"Guess who is in the United States?" Terri said as she drove me home from the airport. I was shocked when she told me that Marija and Andrija were in Birmingham, Alabama, staying with Terry Colafrancesco, head of a Medjugorje Center called Caritas of Birmingham. They were undergoing medical tests in preparation for the kidney transplant operation.

Terri had gathered most of the information needed to begin actual work on getting Marija and her brother to the states when she heard the news that they were already here. They had come with Terry Colafrancesco on a spur of the moment decision; he had told them there was an excellent kidney transplant center at the University of Alabama at Birmingham Hospital, and was sure this was the place for the operation. After convincing a desperate Marija, he managed to arrange last-minute visas for Marija, Andrija, and two companions.

The companions were American Kathleen Martin, who had been staying with Marija for the last two years to assist her at home and help with the pilgrims; the other was Cyril Abeneau, a Frenchman who had been living in Medjugorje for several years who was close to Marija. Both had come to serve as interpreters, with Kathleen translating for Marija and Cyril for Andrija.

"That's incredible," I said as Terri finished the story, "But I'm glad she's here, and I think we should go and see her."

Several days later, after calling Terry Colafrancesco, I was on my way to Birmingham. Terri had declined to come as the kids were still in school and there was too much to be done with Christmas just a few days away. Terry picked me up at the airport and filled in many of the details on the way to his home. He was sure that the miraculous obtaining of the vital visas on such short notice was sign indeed that Marija's coming was a blessing for America.

Already people were coming to pray for her in a large field close by his home in the countryside. Marija had gone to the field several times and had even had an apparition there; word quickly spread and the field instantly became America's "little Medjugorje" shrine. Although Marija and her brother had only been in the States two weeks, busloads of people were coming regularly to pray in the field, hoping to see or talk to the Medjugorje visionary.

"I don't know how word of her being here got around so fast," Terry said as we turned onto the dirt road leading to his home. "We've tried to keep it quiet so that both of them could rest and prepare for the operation."

But Terry's Medjugorje center had many volunteers and it was easy to imagine how the word got around. Caritas of Birmingham, as he called his center, had begun about the same time as my involvement in Medjugorje. I met Terry in September, 1986, at a hastily-arranged retreat of leaders of centers that were spreading the Medjugorje message. It was held near Boston, Massachusetts, in conjunction with the arrival to the States of the pastor of St. James Church, Franciscan priest Tomislav Pervan, who was coming to give a series of lectures on Medjugorje throughout the country.

Terry was impressed with the tabloid of my articles which I had brought to the retreat and wanted to distribute them through his center. He quickly became the largest distributor of the tabloids outside of our own center. The articles had helped launch Caritas, which now handled many books, tapes and other materials concerning Medjugorje. They also were taking pilgrims over on a regular schedule.

"Wayne! How are you!" It was wonderful to hear Marija's voice and see her warm smile as she came briskly down the pathway from Terry's house to greet me.

As we walked in a wooded area near Terry's home, Marija seemed very much at peace with the decision to come to the United States for the operation. She had reacted out of a gut feeling of urgency that this was the right opportunity to save her brother's life. Andrija had become increasingly worse, losing strength to the point of not being able to work at all. And during the flight to the States, there was great concern that he might not survive the trip to Birmingham. On arrival, he was immediately admitted to the hospital to begin receiving treatment to restore his health enough to undergo the transplant surgery.

"I am sorry I am not able to wait for you to call me, but Andrija became very sick, so I think we need to come quickly for him."

No explanation was necessary. It was wonderful to see Marija again and to know that the procedure would take place as soon as Andrija was able to handle the stress of the operation. The preparatory tests to assure that her kidney was compatible had left her sore and nauseous, but she was living the message of Medjugorje; not just as a sister helping her brother, but as one human giving the precious gift of life to another. The fact that she was a visionary was secondary.

A little while later, we piled into the backseat of the cab of a huge truck, joining Terry, his wife Anna, and their little children, and were soon off to find a Christmas tree for their family. The drive into the countryside gave me time to catch up on news of Medjugorje and the well-being of family members and friends. Suddenly, I remembered Doctor Richard McMichael, and his wife's plea that Marija come and pray over him.

"Marija, do you remember that man, the doctor who was dying of cancer? I asked you to go see and pray over him. Were you able to find him and do you know what happened to him?"

She thought for a moment, then exclaimed with a bright smile, "Oh, yes, Doctor Richard. I go *two* times to see and pray for him. He came to the church for Holy Mass, and then, he and his family left for home in Alaska."

"He went home?"

"Yes, he is able to enjoy Medjugorje for a few days and then go home."

I was stunned. Having seen firsthand how critically ill he was at the time of my visit, I was sure he would never leave Medjugorje alive. His family was convinced of the same. Doctor Richard McMichael's temporary recovery was another of the thousands of miracles involving physical healings and cures of people who had come to Medjugorje on faith. Most of them would never be recorded or known by the public. I would learn later that this courageous doctor who treated so many cancer patients while suffering the extremes of the disease himself, would die peacefully and without pain several weeks after his return home to Anchorage.

Time with Marija and Kathleen was brief. Although Andrija would have to remain in the hospital, they were leaving for Medjugorje in a few days to be in the village on December 8, the Feast of the Immaculate Conception, returning to Birmingham eight days later for the transplant operation. Marija would tell me during a return visit to see her in Birmingham in late January, that Our Lady had appeared to her during the operation, hovering over her in silence but with a beautiful, reassuring smile that indicated everything would be all right. She returned to Medjugorje several days after my last visit, still suffering greatly from the effects of the operation. It was far more difficult for her than for Andrija, who was recovering swiftly.

Andrija received more than a healthy kidney from his visionary sister; the realization of the love it took on the part of Marija to donate her kidney to save his life brought him to a full realization of the love and trust of God. He was suddenly a true convert, enjoying a renewed faith.

By the end of January, we had closed operations at our printing plant. The sale of the press and materials had gone extremely well. Within a few weeks, it had been shipped to Saudi Arabia, and the only thing left in our building was the fledgling Medjugorje center that now required full-time help to handle the increasing requests for materials. We had earned enough income from the closure to take care of needs for the remainder of the year and pay off all business debts. The decision to trust in Jesus was paying dividends.

As if to further confirm the fruits of such trust, I received a telephone call from Father Jim Watters, asking me to come to his parish to give talks on Medjugorje during the coming weekend Masses. He had been on fire since returning from our pilgrimage, and was sure that my coming would help in recruiting others from his area to go to Medjugorje.

"You mean *this* weekend?

"Yeah, this weekend. I've already announced that you'd probably be here."

"Okay, okay," I laughed, "I guess I'd better come since you've already announced it!" Some things never change, I thought, as I hung up the phone. My somewhat eccentric priest had undergone a deeply spiritual conversion through his trip to Medjugorje, but his personality was the same. And of course, that was important for people to understand; God gives us a personality which makes us unique from others. Spiritual change does not mean personality change—just a rearrangement of priorities.

It was good to see Father Jim again. He was still losing weight due to fasting twice a week. "And I've also cut out almost all TV time," he related as we drove to the rectory. "Boy, I'm glad you agreed to come!"

As I took my seat in the front pew of Father Watter's church, I noticed a woman sitting on the opposite end. She was wearing a bright red blouse and shorts, chewing gum and chatting happily with those around her. I shook my head as I knelt for prayers, hoping that maybe my talk this evening might instill in this lady a little more reverence and respect for the Mass.

It was a good evening. Many of the parishioners couldn't believe the tremendous change that had occurred in their priest. They thanked me for having taken Father Jim to Medjugorje. As we drove to the rectory afterwards I noticed that he was unusually quiet. Trying to break the mood, I said, "You know, your people are really happy with you; there's a strong spiritual wave building here."

"Yeah, it's going great, but I gotta tell you a great story about one of my former parishioners I hope will be going with us when we return." He paused a moment. "This is an unbelievable story. I went into a restaurant last week and saw this gal who used to be in my parish a couple of years ago, sitting alone in a corner. She had moved away from here and I was surprised to see her after such a long absence.

"Well, we talked a few minutes catching up on things when suddenly she asks me if I could sit down with her a few minutes and she begins to tell me about how she's now divorced, lost her job—her whole life's a big mess."

Father Jim paused again and then suddenly pulled the car to a stop at the side of the road. "The thing is," he continued now facing me directly, "she suddenly tells me straight out that she plans to commit suicide. She says it with a real calmness that convinces me she means it. Wayne, I spent the next two hours talking to that woman, telling her about Medjugorje and all and the changes it created in me. I made her promise me she wouldn't do anything drastic until we could talk some more. The bottom line is, we met a couple more times, she starts coming to Mass, and she's there tonight to listen to you, sitting in the front row. Isn't that something?"

"Yes, that really is something!" I realized that Father Jim was talking about the woman chewing gum whom I had judged so quickly. The clothes and talking suddenly amounted to nothing in comparison with the fact that if this converted priest hadn't taken the time to talk to her, she might have taken her life. I felt terribly small because of my quick judgment of her, and told Father Jim of my feeling at the time.

There was another long silence as he sat there staring at me. "Wayne, I have to tell you something," he finally said in a low voice. "Before I went with you to Medjugorje . . . I had no real faith. Before Medjugorje, I'd never have taken the time to talk that long to someone like that woman."

"Father—"

He held up his hand. "No, let me finish; I've been a priest for 22 years. Do you have any idea what it's like to stand at that altar day after day, holding up the gifts of the Blessed Sacrament—and not really believe?"

"Father, maybe your faith had just diminished—" I didn't know what else to say, embarrassed by this sudden confession from a priest.

"No!" He shouted, hitting the dash of the car hard with his hand, "I mean *I had no faith!*"

We talked long into the night. The next morning I left for the short drive home, vowing that from now on, I would pray extra hard daily for every priest, nun, religious and other clergy.

There was another important decision made during the early months of 1989; for some time I had felt a strong conviction in my heart to begin speaking out against abortion in my talks. It definitely was part of the message, as were all sins that took away individual peace. The woman at Father Watters' church was despondent enough from such sins that she was ready to take her life. People needed to know that Our Lady was coming to lead us to peace, and away from these things that led to such darkness.

I viewed abortion as the greatest sin of our time. It needed to be addressed directly as the destroyer of God's greatest gift—life. And I knew that somewhere down the road, Lisa's story would have to be told. But it would happen only with her permission and only after she had come to terms with it.

Ironically, I felt Our Lady telling me that in the future, Lisa would be witnessing in public about her conversion, especially the personal experience of having had an abortion. I told my daughter about this message, and she immediately rejected the notion. "No way, Dad," she had answered adamantly, "I still can't even tell Mom or my brothers and sister!"

"But you will; and someday, you'll tell auditoriums filled with people."

Tears welled in Lisa's eyes—as they always did when I broached this subject. "Daddy, I have talked about it with a few people. But that's all I can do. I could never stand in front of a large group and speak about abortion, about what I did."

Putting my arm around Lisa, I let it go at that, having

learned at this stage of the mission that it would happen in God's way and time. Although she was now undergoing conversion, the guilt was still there. In time she would accept God's forgiveness and then forgive herself. I empathized with my daughter and all women who had undergone this new holocaust. The guilt of killing a child in the womb eats away at the soul like a ravenous cancer, as she wonders if it was a boy or a girl. I knew I had to begin including more about this abomination of our age in my talks.

During the next few months, there were plenty of trips to keep me busy, and a fast-approaching deadline to complete the book. The manuscript was coming along nicely thanks to the constant prodding of David Manuel. He had insisted that I include personal background and experiences in telling the Medjugorje story, something I was at first reluctant to do. It soon became the main factor for telling the story, and I was constantly wondering if anyone would read "this hokey stuff."

But to my surprise, Doubleday was warming to the story as we continued to send them finished chapters. Now I was excited and anxious to complete the manuscript by early summer.

Meanwhile the nagging inner conviction to speak against abortion would not go away. I had agreed to be a speaker at a small conference in Virginia Beach, Virginia, scheduled for Mother's Day weekend in May; as it happened, that weekend was also Pentecost Sunday, and as I later discovered, the anniversary of the first apparition in Fatima, Portugal. In fact, the theme of the Virginia Beach conference was to focus on the messages of apparitions at Fatima, Medjugorje, and those reportedly occurring in Lubbock, Texas.

Shortly after agreeing to go to Virginia Beach, I re-

ceived a last-minute invitation to give a short witness of
my conversion at the first international Medjugorje conference, to be held on the campus of Notre Dame University. There was just one problem: it was scheduled for the
same weekend as the Virginia Beach conference. An international conference on Medjugorje was something new,
and I wanted to be a part of it. I called the people in Virginia Beach, asking if they could arrange for me to speak
early Saturday morning so that I could then catch a flight
to Notre Dame in time to speak that evening at their conference. They graciously agreed.

On arriving in Virginia Beach Friday afternoon, I found
that of the expected 300, only about 70 people were registered. But the enthusiasm of the planners and those who
came more than offset the disappointment of a poor turnout. That evening we gathered together at the conference
site for a panel discussion to field questions from the audience concerning details of the three apparitions we represented.

The first question asked was directed to me, and it
concerned abortion: Did the Blessed Mother ever mention abortion in her messages to the six young visionaries? I was taken aback; the Virgin Mary was making sure I
understood abortion was to be part of the message!

The question set the tone for the entire evening as
abortion became the major topic of a discussion that lasted
a little more than two hours. Early Saturday morning I
spoke on Medjugorje and for the first time, included the
fact that abortion and all of the serious sins of our day
were the reasons Our Lady was being sent to us daily to
engage our help to eliminate them through prayer, fasting, and penance. After being rushed to the airport for
my flight to the campus of Notre Dame, I sat in silence
throughout the trip, basking in joyful peace at the reception of my morning talk. It was no mere coincidence that

the Blessed Virgin chose Mother's Day weekend as the time to introduce this new dimension to the mission.

Connie and Rick Bampton, two Medjugorje friends from St. Louis, Missouri, who had arranged a speaking tour for me there several months ago, met me as I exited the ramp at the airport. "What are you doing here?" I asked, as we exchanged hugs.

"We know the people putting on the conference and they asked us to pick you up. We flew Father Ken Roberts in earlier. He's here at the airport with us somewhere," Rick added as he looked around. "He's been wanting to meet you."

Just then he arrived. "Sorry, but someone stopped me to bless some items. God bless you, Wayne, it's good to finally meet you!"

I was delighted. Father Kenneth Roberts, one of the main speakers at the conference, was one of the best-known and most popular priests involved in the Medjugorje movement. An Englishman who at one time had served as a steward for British Airways international flights, he was the author of a popular book called *Playboy to Priest,* an autobiography of his dramatic transformation from world-traveling playboy to dynamic priest. I had first seen him on a tape of a television program on the Eternal Word Television Network (EWTN), in which he was telling the audience about "this Lutheran Protestant" who had been converted by the Blessed Mother at Medjugorje.

"Thank you, Father, I've been looking forward to meeting you—" I was at a loss for words, humbled that this famous priest had come to the airport.

"The pleasure's mine," he answered in his unique English accent as he pumped my hand. His tanned, distinguished features highlighted by the sparkle of steel blue eyes added to the charisma of his personality. I could immediately sense why people were so drawn to him.

"We need to hurry," Rick reminded us. "You're due to speak in just about an hour!"

In the awe of meeting Father Ken, I had momentarily forgotten about my talk. The conversation continued at a steady pace as we drove to the campus of Notre Dame. In that short span of time I felt as though I had known Father Ken a long time. It was easy to see why he was such a strong evangelist of the Catholic faith in addition to his work with youth. I especially wanted to know how he handled his heavy load of travel in giving missions throughout the country. "Rick and Connie are a big help there," he answered. "Rick's a pilot with his own plane and flies me to many of my missions in this region."

Inside the Convocation Center, the site of the conference, there was another pleasant surprise; people were rushing forward to shake my hand or ask for an autograph, much to the amused exasperation of my escorts who were hurrying me through the crowds. It was a tremendous outpouring of love. Suddenly there was the sound of a familiar voice. "Wayne—over here!"

I turned to see my California friends Bob and Elaine Starbuck, and Don and Janine Moran, waving from the back of a small pack of people. "I didn't expect to see you until next week—in California!" I laughed as I pulled away to give quick hugs. They had come for the conference and hoped to spend some time with me if possible. "I'll try," I yelled as we approached the entrance to the stage.

I was lost in happy, chaotic bedlam! All of these people here to listen to testimony of the good fruits of Medjugorje—close to 7,000, a strong contrast to the 70 who had come to Virginia Beach. Yet, both conferences were filled with people who shared the same fervor and hunger to learn more about the contemporary miracles of God. As I was being introduced, I wondered how in the short time allotted I would be able to bring the same fervent message about abortion I had given that morning in two hours; I had less than half an hour here.

Somehow it worked. I told them it was time for those of us involved to "get our hands dirty" by living the messages in daily life. I left the stage to a thundering ovation, feeling as grateful and humble as I had ever felt in my life.

The next morning, Pentecost Sunday *and* Mother's Day, brought the final and most convincing proof yet that abortion would be a strong focal point in all future talks. Rick and Connie were to fly Father Ken back to St. Louis early as he had to prepare for his next mission. I had been invited to share a small, private Mass with them and Father Ken, just before they were to leave. I awoke in a twilight still more asleep than awake.

As I lay there, praying a short prayer to the Holy Spirit to begin this special day, I suddenly had the most beautiful vision. Vividly, I saw the hand of The Blessed Mother—I don't know how I knew it was her hand—and in it was a tiny translucent embryo hand. She gently brought it forward, toward me. No words were spoken. They weren't necessary. I knew this unbelievably beautiful sign to be *total confirmation* that I was to continue to speak out against the evil of abortion.

I managed to find some time to see the Starbucks and Morans that afternoon. I related to them what I had experienced that morning, telling them I could hardly wait for the next speaking engagement the following weekend in Los Angeles. I had agreed to return, buoyed by the tremendous results of the first tour.

The first night in a jammed church located in a Hispanic section of Los Angeles, I began by speaking immediately in the first few minutes on the horrors of abortion. It was probably too much too soon, but I couldn't help it. The vision of that little hand extended to me by the Blessed

Virgin Mary, was burning in my mind. People squirmed. And then something that had never happened before; several people near the back got up and walked out. My heart jumped, but I continued.

Afterwards, as people came to the front of the huge church to greet me, many made it clear that the subject of abortion mixed with the love and peace of Medjugorje bothered them. But many also added that it was needed.

As the crowd began to abate, there was a young woman left standing in front of me. She was visibly shaken as she approached. Looking around to assure no one was within earshot, she said in a quavering voice, tears streaming down her cheeks, "Do you think God will forgive a mother who had an abortion, and didn't know any better at the time?"

I knew she was the mother. It had taken great courage to come forward and ask such a personal, revealing question. I took her by the hands to quiet the trembling. "Yes," I said softly, "a thousand times yes!"

I gave her a medal from Medjugorje, and suggested she find a priest or pastor for further counseling. Hugging her, I promised to pray for her to find peace. She staggered away, hardly able to walk under the emotional release of God's forgiving love.

I stood there awhile, absorbing the dramatic proof of making and accepting hard decisions in the course of shaping the mission. Speaking out against abortion would now be a permanent part of that process.

10
Gospa's Book

"Today, I rejoice with all my angels. The first part of my program has been achieved."

The summer break from school, 1989, began for the kids just as I returned home from California. It was supposed to be a time to relax and regroup, but there were still trips to be made in June and July. Terri was upset.

"I accept the fact that you have to travel in order to fulfill Our Lady's call," she began quietly one evening, "but your children are older now and they need a father around a little more, at least during the summer months when they are home all day. And," she added with emphasis, "you're not a superman, spiritual or otherwise. You're going to burn out!"

She was right and I knew it. But I felt like a spiritual superman, and wanted to do as much as possible as quickly as possible. The warning about the children was another thing; that registered. I resolved to keep travel to a bare minimum in future summer months.

But that wasn't the most pressing time problem at the moment. Deadline for completion of the book was in a couple of weeks. There was an urgency to get it finished and into the hands of the public, an urgency I felt came directly from Our Lady.

Despite the time squeeze, it was a tremendously exciting time as the realization of a lifelong dream was about to come true. Even though we still did not have a commitment of a contract from a publisher outside of Paraclete Press, details of the proposed cover of the book had been worked out by their staff. I had just received in the mail a black and white proof copy for tentative approval.

It was exactly what I envisioned, and what I felt the Blessed Virgin wanted. I was so anxious to see what the book would look like, that I carefully cut the proof to size and taped it to the front of another book, then sat back and just stared at it.

The proposed cover was dominated by a beautiful picture of Our Lady, a special mystical picture reportedly taken during the time of an apparition at Medjugorje. Even though I knew it might generate mild controversy, I felt an inner urging to use this picture on the cover of the book. I was intrigued by the strange phenomena where pictures taken by pilgrims of ordinary things at religious sites would inexplicably contain images of the Blessed Virgin Mary, images that were not there at the time of taking the picture. I had garnered quite a collection, but none struck me more than this particular picture.

According to the story behind it, a nun from the Vatican on pilgrimage to Medjugorje, had been invited to be present in the room during the time of an apparition. She had taken a picture of the crucifix on the wall, above where the young visionaries appeared to be looking during the apparition. When the photograph was developed, a close-up of a beautiful young woman's face appeared on the film. One of the visionaries later stated that it looked very much like Our Lady. "But," he had added, "she is even more beautiful!"

When I showed the picture to one of the Franciscan priests in Medjugorje, he had cautioned me not to put too much stock in such outward signs. I usually didn't. People sent me all sorts of photographs, purportedly of the Madonna's image, in the shadows of tree trunks, clouds and other objects. Most I dismissed as products of over-zealous imaginations.

This picture was different; it had instantly touched my heart. Regardless of its authenticity, it had become my own special image of Mary at Medjugorje. Gazing at it now, I smiled as I thought of another "mystical" incidence that had caused me to change the proposed direction and name of the book.

It had occurred a year earlier, shortly after David began serving as my editor. Up to that point, the limited number of pages I had written focused almost entirely of the factual elements of Medjugorje's reported apparitions. I wanted to keep it as objective as possible and was using a straight newspaper reporting style. My intended title for the book was *Medjugorje: The Edge of Heaven.*

One morning around 2 A.M., I was awakened by the familiar interior calling of Our Lady. I went into the living room where we had set up a small altar for family prayer, and dropped to my knees, waiting expectantly for something further to happen. I remained in that position for what seemed a long time, when suddenly I felt her words in my heart: *"The direction of the book is wrong; it is the message. Write about the message."*

Awed, I returned to my bed, but could not go back to sleep. In trying to wake Terri and tell her what had happened, she just rolled over and mumbled something about telling her in the morning. That was okay; I was content to bask in the warm glow of this mystical gift, and no longer thought of sleep.

In the morning, sitting at my desk and looking over the pitifully small amount of writing accomplished to this point, I knew Our Lady was right. I immediately changed the proposed title to *Medjugorje: The Message*, and trashed most of what had been written, at least in its original form. It would be redone the way Our Lady wanted, using personal experiences of myself and others touched by Medjugorje. This approach, mixed with accurate reporting on the background and history of the phenomena, would hopefully make it the most definitive book on Medjugorje to date.

Now, all but a few loose ends and the final editing of the manuscript was completed. Still, there were no contract offers other than Paraclete Press; it looked as though they were the only choice.

And then, David telephoned.

"I've got some incredible news," he began in subdued tones. "This is so shocking and such a surprise, I can hardly believe it!" There was a long silence.

"Come on, David. Tell me!"

"Doubleday just called—they want the book!"

"Doubleday?" I felt dizzy with excitement. "Are you sure?" This was far more than I could have ever hoped for. My mind began racing with thoughts of the national exposure for Medjugorje offered by this huge publishing house. The promotion alone could make Medjugorje a household name. That was the major reason I had wanted them as the publisher.

"Listen, there's more. Not only do they want to publish the book but they're offering a large cash advance, which is unusual for a first-time author."

I had a hundred questions but the most important was when the book could actually be on the market. There was a pause. "That's the only catch. The date they're setting is April of next year."

"April! That's more than nine months, David, we can't wait that long!"

"I know," David interjected, "and I knew you'd feel that way about the publishing date, but you have to weigh the pros and the cons of the complete package. Paraclete still wants to do the book. They can't come close to Doubleday's offer, but they can have it out in two months, guaranteed. They can't give you a cash advance. In fact, there will be no royalties until early next year. And of course, they aren't big enough to match the promotion and publicity offered by Doubleday. So, you're going to have to do a lot of praying and then make a decision, and both publishers need an answer within two days max."

The surge of excitement and emotion was temporarily throttled. We talked a little while longer, going over options offered by both publishers, but I could sense David wanted me to accept Doubleday's offer. Still, he reminded me again before hanging up, the decision was mine.

By the time I was able to tell Terri of the Doubleday offer, I was subdued by the reality of what was happening. "You know," I said to her as we talked quietly, "all my life, I've dreamed of this moment. I've actually written a book and now I have the best publisher possible offering to do it. But I know in my heart Our Lady wants it out soon, and they won't do it until next year!"

"Well then, go with Paraclete if they can do it in two months." That was my wife, always blunt and to the point.

"But think of the publicity for Medjugorje," I retorted, playing my own devil's advocate.

"I guess you're going to have to pray and ask the Blessed Virgin what to do, then."

I look at her mournfully. "I have, and I felt nothing; it's as if she's leaving it to me."

Terri smiled teasingly. "Well then, do what you always tell me to do. Ask Saint Therese to help you!"

She was having a little good-natured fun with me, but I also knew that was the answer. There had been other times when I felt I needed confirmation or signs from the Blessed Virgin, but like now, there would be no answer; it was in these moments I had turned to St. Therese. "That's exactly what I'm going to do," I answered, suddenly up-lifted.

I shooed Terri out of my office, closed the door and began a "conversational" prayer with St. Therese: "Little Flower, I've got a problem: Which publisher do I go with? I don't like to ask for specific signs, but if it's to be Doubleday, please send or show me a yellow rose; and if it's to be Paraclete, a red rose."

That was it. Very much to the point. I felt a little un-easy asking for such direct signs, always remembering what Our Lady had said in Medjugorje during the early days of the apparitions: *"Let those who cannot see me believe as firmly as those of you who can."* But this was an emergency; I had to have an answer by the next afternoon.

The next morning, having forgotten the request for a sign, I was on my way to Mass when suddenly I saw a patch of yellow flowers up the road on the right. My heart leaped. It was to be Doubleday! But in passing the flowers, I saw they were not roses. I was a little disappointed and felt a tinge of guilt, acknowledging that deep down, I wanted Doubleday to be the publisher.

Arriving at the church, the business of the flowers was again forgotten. I entered the pew, said my usual prayers and then glanced over at the statue of Our Lady in the front right side of the sanctuary. There, in a small white vase standing alone in front of the statue, was one red rose!

I stared in amazement—and then began to quietly laugh. "Okay Blessed Mother, I asked and I received. It's to be Paraclete!"

After a few moments, I went into the sacristy looking for the pastor. I had called him the previous evening and told him of my predicament; his response: "What predicament? Take the money and run!" Now as I told him what had transpired since yesterday, and of the red rose here in the church, he exclaimed, "Are you telling me you're going to make your decision based on this?"

"Yes, Father," I laughed, "I certainly am!"

And I did. All thoughts of "worldly gain" by going with Doubleday were wiped away. This was heaven speaking and doing so in a strong, unmistakable way. Even David was surprised, but after months of working on the book plus two trips to Medjugorje, he readily accepted the sign as a strong enough reason to go with Paraclete.

However, Doubleday did not. They were dismayed that anyone, especially a brand new author, would turn them down. They even telephoned Terri, asking if she knew her husband had rejected their "very generous" offer. "What they really wanted to know," Terri added after telling me of the telephone conversation, "Was if my husband was of sound mind!"

"When it comes to Medjugorje, I sometimes wonder that myself," I muttered, laughing softly.

There were moments of doubt in the aftermath. I signed and mailed the contract to Paraclete, sure in my heart that the right decision had been made. But my mind wasn't quite so sure. How could I have turned down the prestige of being published by Doubleday and the national exposure it would bring, not to mention the money? In the end analysis, it was clearly another opportunity to choose between the material world or the spiritual world and its reward of true peace and happiness. Again, it was learning to truly trust in Jesus in deed and not just in word or intention. Besides, I thought, how could a publishing company named after the Holy Spirit not be the choice!

It also confirmed for me personally that the writing of this book was a vital part of the mission, a fact which would become clearly evident in time. It was, in effect, Our Lady's book. I was simply fortunate to be chosen as its author.

Filled with the euphoria of these events, we left on a beautiful two-week vacation to France, the main purpose being to visit Lourdes. We drove from Paris through the French countryside, stopping for three days in the tiny hamlet of Lisieux, the birthplace and home of Saint Therese. That was worth the trip in itself, and it gave us opportunity to personally thank this beautiful saint for her assistance.

There were other stops at shrines, including little-known Pontmain, where the Virgin Mary appeared one time in the late nineteenth century. And Rue du Bac, the small convent in Paris, where St. Catherine received apparitions from the Blessed Virgin Mary, and was given the design for the miraculous medal.

But by far, Lourdes was the highlight. On our first evening there, thousands of pilgrims streamed through the huge square in front of the basilica, carrying candles and singing Immaculate Mary over and over. I was so filled with emotion that I could never fully complete a verse of the song as I laughed and cried at the same time. Spiritually, it was an exact duplicate of Medjugorje.

The entire trip was one long pilgrimage, ironically, of a "Protestant" family touring Catholic shrines. But by this stage in our spiritual growth, the lines of denominations were blurred; we were slowly learning to center on the spiritual first and the world second. Of course, that isn't to say the kids were totally happy touring shrines. More than once there would be a groan from one of them of "not another church!"

We returned to the States in time to receive another surprise, again through a telephone call from David. "This is truly astonishing," he began. "I've worked with Paraclete for many years and never in that time have they ever accomplished what they have with your book. It's finished!"

"Finished? You mean—"

"I mean finished, printed, ready for the stands!" David could hardly contain himself. "They have never done a book in less than two months. Not only was this one done in a record thirty days but the first copies coming off the presses are near perfect!"

Within a few days we were on our way to Orleans, Massachusetts. It was time to meet the people of Paraclete Press and to receive my first copy of the finished product. On arrival at Boston's airport where David was to meet us, I caught sight of him standing near the entrance of the concourse. Moving swiftly toward him, I took the copy of the book he offered without a word. We just grinned at each other. David could stand it no longer. "Well, come on, what do you think?"

I waited a few seconds before answering. There were no tears. Just a joy that went beyond words as I stared at the cover and the picture of Our Lady in full, glorious color. "It's absolutely magnificent!"

"Whew!" he exclaimed. "I thought so too, but I wasn't sure what your reaction would be."

"It's perfect, just as I envisioned it." Terri felt the same. We were in a state of giddiness for the entire two-hour auto ride to Orleans.

The next two days were two of the happiest of my life. Although Terri and I were shocked at the rather small size of the Paraclete Press facilities (I'm sure if I had seen their plant before signing the contract, I would have had doubts about their ability to do the book), we were impressed with the spiritual atmosphere of the workplace.

All of the employees were members of the Community of Jesus, an ecumenical community of Christians of all walks of life, living together in covenant. One of the foremen assured me that they had "prayed" this book through production, knowing of the urgency to get it out to the public. Incredibly, as David had stated, the very first copies came off the press in almost perfect condition. Under normal printing conditions there were usually a large number of copies known as "throwaways" generated until final adjustments of printing were made for actual production.

While at Orleans, there was another first: a book-signing for the employees of Paraclete, and members of the Community. Two hours later, 165 books had been signed.

Final details in preparation for marketing were worked out with David before leaving for home. We compiled a list of people to send complimentary copies for promotion, or simply as gifts. One such copy went to Father Svet. I had given him a copy of the finished manuscript but wanted him to have it in book form.

A couple of weeks later, I called him in Medjugorje. "The book is excellent," Father said, "but . . . I am not comfortable with the picture on the cover." That was not surprising. The Franciscans wanted the followers of Medjugorje's message to concentrate on the elements of what Our Lady was saying and not on the little signs of confirmation. Father Svet saw this picture as simply that.

I laughed. "Father, I just knew you were going to say that about the picture. But I have to tell you, I really feel Our Lady wanted me to use it."

Now he laughed. "And I knew that you would tell me that!"

The next few weeks became a blur. A second printing of the book was rushed to press less than a month from the original because of overwhelming demand; by September, *Medjugorje: The Message* was well on its way to becoming the largest-selling book on the apparitions. And by the time Doubleday would have been able to publish it, in April of 1990, more than 90,000 copies had been sold in the United States alone.

There was one other little coincidence I later noticed: the final draft of the book was completed on June 25; I received my first copy in the Boston airport on July 25; and, the official publication release date by Paraclete, was August 25. These dates, the 25th of the month, all fell on the anniversary day of the Medjugorje apparitions. None were planned that way.

It was simply one more sign that the book was indeed Gospa's book.

11

"When I say 'pray' "

"When I say 'pray, pray, pray,' I do not only want to say to increase the number of hours of prayer, but also to reinforce the desire for prayer, and to be in contact with God."

The book definitely changed things. Now, after each talk there was an obligatory book signing session. It also gave followers of Medjugorje a unique and much-needed tool to help convince hesitant or stubborn family members and friends of the reality of Medjugorje. I was beginning to understand why Our Lady wanted it out as soon as possible. Now, people of all faiths were open to the story of Medjugorje. If a Protestant journalist could believe and then write about such an experience . . .

The remainder of the summer flew by and I was soon preparing for a crammed September schedule that would take me to the Far East for tours in Singapore, Australia, and the Fiji Islands. Close on its heels was a journey to Ireland to serve as a spiritual guide for a large Irish contingent headed for Medjugorje.

In the midst of preparations, I received devastating news that Father Jim Watters had been critically injured in a head-on automobile accident, causing severe brain damage. He had only recently returned from a second pilgrimage to Medjugorje with more than 175 people from throughout North Carolina, that included a television news crew and a representative from the bishop's office. Although he would survive, defying insurmountable odds created by his injuries, it would take months of rehabilitation to return to normal life, not only physically but mentally, as he lost almost all motor functions due to brain damage.

This man, once so far away from his priestly call and now beautifully transformed by Medjugorje, did not even remember going there. It was doubtful that he would ever function again as a priest.

I immediately began praying with great intensity for Father Jim. I knew in my heart that he had become a victim of the evil one. Satan pays no attention until a soul transforms into a child of God. Then, he will do anything to stop the conversion and resulting fruits. But I also knew God was still in charge. Our Lady had told us often through her messages to 'pray, pray pray,' adding, ". . . *with prayer you can stop wars and alter the laws of nature.*"

There were also gnawing family problems coming to a head. Lisa was doing great spiritually but having difficulties with her marriage. David was not of the same mind spiritually. Nothing of her experience with Medjugorje had touched him. He did not object to her newfound devotion, but he wanted nothing to do with it. It was the beginning of the end and a frustrating time for Lisa.

Adding to the frustration, Lisa's change had hardly touched her two brothers. Michael and Steve continued to live a life of entanglement in the clutter of small problems, caused mostly by their focusing only on themselves. There was no time in their busy young lives for anything related to faith beyond a cursory acknowledgment that God existed.

Michael was working as a pressman at the local newspaper in a small town in upstate South Carolina, while Steve had recently been discharged from the Air Force. It was a mutual parting of the ways, with him being unable to adjust to military life. Since his discharge, he had been in and out of several jobs. I felt helpless in reaching him, more so than Mike, because of his penchant for creating problems for himself that eventually became mine to solve. It would take tons of prayer for him. Still, all I could do for both sons was what I was telling other parents: Pray and have trust in Jesus.

Always in the forefront of my mind concerning my children was a dramatic encounter that had occurred at one of my recent talks. A woman had come to me weeping and pleading that I pray and intercede for her son. She had prayed for years but he was into drugs and all of its related social problems. Before I could answer, another young man stepped forward and said, "Lady, don't you stop your prayers for your son. My mom prayed for me for over ten years when I was addicted to drugs. And now look, I'm here tonight!" I didn't need to say another thing. Remembrance of this story was soothing salve as my sons struggled with life.

At least the latest news from Medjugorje was positive. Mirjana was planning marriage in September, the second of the visionaries to enter into this sacrament. Ivanka, married a year earlier, was now a mother. The other visionaries were growing spiritually, with Ivan becoming active in traveling to various countries and attending conferences to speak of Our Lady's messages, especially concerning youth and family.

Pilgrims were coming by the thousands from all countries, and Medjugorje conferences were springing up everywhere. It was by far the height of Medjugorje popularity.

But there was still a thorn among the roses. Bishop Pavao Zanic of Mostar, who now vigorously opposed and questioned the authenticity of the apparitions, after supporting them fully the first four months of their occurrence, had ordered the visionaries to cease using the choir loft in St. James Church for their daily encounter with Gospa. It was the latest thrust in his ongoing quest to disrupt the burgeoning popularity of pilgrimages.

How could this bishop, who in the early months could hardly be kept from coming to Medjugorje every day with zeal and complete belief in the apparitions, now be its major adversary? Only heaven could know for certain, but growing evidence indicated it to be more a matter of human pride and stubbornness. After years of tremendous spiritual fruits, this bishop would not change his position. Not even after a investigative commission, in which he appointed himself as head, had seen its negative report on the apparitions overruled by the Vatican because of the biased slant of the report. The Church now requested a new commission be formed by the Yugoslav Bishops Conference to continue the investigation. Never in the history of Marian apparitions investigations had this occurred.

Bishop Zanic was also ordered by the Vatican not to comment on, or take action on his own concerning the investigation. Yet, he plunged ahead with an order to the pastor of St. James to bar the visionaries from the church. That order would also ban them from attending Holy Mass, which, according to the canon law of the Church, was illegal. The pastor was delaying enforcement of the order, using every proper means available, but it was a complicated and delicate situation in desperate need of prayer.

It seemed all of these problems, including family, were attempts by Satan to counter the good fruits generated by Medjugorje; they were meant to derail our mission. The only solution was to pray, pray, pray as Our Lady constantly requested.

"I'm sorry, sir, but we cannot book you for a flight to Singapore until Sunday." The agent for Singapore Airlines in Los Angeles informed me that I would be unable to make my connection due to a bizarre computer glitch that had occurred in Myrtle Beach. Somehow during the check-in, the local agent had inadvertently cancelled my entire international itinerary. There was no choice except to stay in Los Angeles for two days and take the Sunday opening. For the first time in the entire mission, I would miss a scheduled speaking engagement.

I called Bob and Elaine Starbuck who readily invited me to spend the two days with them. "You're stuck and you might as well enjoy it," Bob had commented after hearing of my predicament. "And since tomorrow's Saturday, I'll bet we can even arrange a few holes of golf!"

"Sure, why not?" I was consoled that at least there were Medjugorje friends here.

"Oh, there's one other little surprise; we were going to attend tonight's session of the Southern California Renewal Conference. Maybe you'd like to go, especially since Father Ken Roberts will be speaking."

I was delighted. After calls to Singapore to inform them of the situation, we left for the conference. This was an annual gathering of Southern California charismatics, with more than 10,000 in attendance this year. As we walked through the display booths, it was surprising to see so much material on the Blessed Virgin, especially pertaining to Medjugorje. Ironically, Catholic charismatics become so focused on the gifts of the Holy Spirit, that in many instances, Mary, the greatest of those gifts, was forgotten or downplayed. She became seen as taking away the focus on Jesus. Medjugorje was changing that.

We settled into our seats fairly close to the front of the assembly hall where Father Ken would be speaking. As always, I was enraptured. Father Ken definitely had a special calling to evangelization of the Catholic faith, always giving emphasis to the role of the Blessed Virgin. He made good use of common sense to explain theology and church doctrine, using stories with which people could easily identify.

Near the end of his talk, Father Ken suddenly looked straight at me and said, "We have a special guest with us this evening, a man many of you will recognize from his work in spreading Our Lady's message from Medjugorje—Wayne Weible."

And with that he asked me to join him on stage. Caught completely off guard, I numbly made my way to the stage. After a few more remarks pointing out to the audience the uniqueness of a Protestant proclaiming Our Lady's messages, he asked me to lead the closing prayer. I was so taken by the audience's response and the honor of being with Father Ken, I could barely remember the words of the Hail Mary.

"Boy, what a beautiful day for golf!" Bob said as we loaded our clubs onto the golf cart the following morning.

"It sure is, but I feel a little guilty about being here and not in Singapore."

"Hey, there's nothing you can do about that," Don Moran interjected, "so sit back and enjoy!"

He was right. And it was good to be with these special friends. Don would be playing with us, as well as Bob's son Kevin, who though still full of life, had dramatically changed. Mass was now important to him and he took his children regularly, even though his wife Mary still had questions and doubts. And the rosary I had given him that had turned gold in color was never off his person.

"Listen, there's another reason I'm glad you're here." Don suddenly turned serious. "You remember my brother Larry?"

"Sure. As a matter of fact, why isn't he playing with us today?" Larry, who was a scratch golfer, had played with us on my last visit, entertaining us throughout the match with his happy-go-lucky attitude, and a dazzling variety of impromptu trick shots.

"He has cancer and the outlook isn't good." Don paused and took a deep breath before continuing. "I'd like to ask a big favor. Would you mind taking a few minutes to stop by and see him on your way to the airport tomorrow?"

It seemed as if this summer was filled with tests as to Our Lady's messages on the power of prayer. Severe tests. I assured Don that I would be glad to stop and see Larry. It was hard to believe that this large, robust, fun-loving man was now seriously ill with cancer.

As we sat in the golf cart waiting for Bob and Kevin, Don hugged me. "Thanks," he said quietly and then slowly shook his head. "You know Larry, like so many, never took his faith seriously. That is," he paused again, "until you gave him that picture and he came to your talks. He's always enjoyed life to the hilt, and try as I might, I was never able to reach him with Medjugorje."

Don told how Larry had been struck by the unusual picture of the Blessed Virgin Mary that was now on the cover of my book, a copy of which I had given him through Don on my last visit to the area. Something about the picture touched his heart, and for the first time in years had him thinking about God. Larry had come to the talks and like so many others, was now undergoing the changes brought on by spiritual conversion. As was the case with Kevin, Don had invited him to play golf with us during that visit hoping that the time together would reinforce his newfound commitment. It did. Without his recent spiritual change, Don felt Larry could not have handled this devastating change in his life. "Even as sick as he is," Don said as we left the first tee, "he's maintained high spirits and really looks forward to seeing you again."

I thought of Larry throughout the day and was shocked the following morning to see how the cancer had reduced him to a thin, frail shell of his former physical appearance. He had aged well beyond his 40 years and was barely able to speak. We gathered around him making small talk, telling him of our game the previous day. His fiancée, who now spent all of her time taking care of him, could not hold back the tears.

I knew he did not have long to live and as I suggested to him and the others that we pray a special rosary for his healing, I concentrated on his spiritual healing, remembering reading once that sometimes God called home those who had found His peace and happiness before they could lose it again.

As we completed the prayer, there was not a dry eye in the room. It was the most emotional rosary I had ever prayed. I gently took Larry's hand and placed my rosary in it. "Please take this rosary Larry, so that you'll know I'm praying for you every day."

Tears flowed from his pain-filled eyes as he weakly thanked me over and over. I knew he was scared; but I also knew he now had the spiritual strength to accept his fate. Long after the airplane had departed Los Angeles, Larry was still on my mind.

Eighteen hours later I landed in Singapore, met by an enthusiastic group, led by a slender, youthful Chinese man. He stepped forward and took my hand. "Welcome to Singapore, Wayne—finally! I am Victor Wee and this is my wife Vivian." He turned and motioned a woman forward. "I know you are tired but these people are so excited about your coming, they wanted to greet you in a special way. I hope you don't mind."

"Not at all. I'm just a little overwhelmed."

Victor's wife, Vivian, carrying a small, sleeping baby chimed in. "And This is Vincent, our newest addition." Laughing, she added quickly, "I'm afraid he couldn't stay awake for you!"

"That's okay. I'm just glad to finally make it. Sorry for the delay and any problem it caused."

"No need to worry," Victor said with a wave of his hand. "As it turned out, we didn't have enough time to cancel, so we turned it into a large prayer service for the success of your tour. They all promised to come back tonight!"

I immediately liked this man and his wife. After taking time to personally introduce me to each person who had come to the airport, we left for their home. It was only after arriving there I noticed that Vincent, who was now awake, was a Downs Syndrome baby.

"Vincent is our special baby," Vivian said. She then related that Vincent was adopted. Both of the Wee's were doctors and had discovered Vincent at the hospital when his mother refused to accept him. She would not even touch him. For several months, they had taken the baby to personally care for him while trying to find someone to adopt him. When that failed, they decided to adopt him themselves, even though they both had extremely busy schedules. Vivian had curtailed her medical work to care for Vincent. "But I don't mind," she added. "He is a pure delight and we take him with us everywhere."

There was more to the story of the Wee family. Although actively involved in Marriage Encounter, a program to assist marriages, they had also taken on the added duty of helping to spread the Medjugorje messages. Victor began a center for distribution of materials in Singapore, and the entire Indonesian area. Between his extremely busy duties as a physician, he also traveled frequently to give lectures on the apparitions, just as I did. "When we first heard of the apparitions, we had to go," he told me. "It had changed our lives and the center just seemed to come about naturally after our return. Fortunately, we have a large prayer group that assists us."

I was awed. "How do you keep up with all of this?"

Victor laughed heartily. "I don't really know, but it certainly keeps life interesting! But enough talk. You need some rest before the conference tonight."

That evening, more than twice the number of people showed up than had been there for the scheduled first talk. As always I was pumped up by the numbers and by the enthusiasm and intensity of their prayers and singing. I concentrated on the all-faiths aspect of the messages, knowing that there was great diversity of faith in Singapore. Afterward, as I stood near the back of the stage waiting for the last of the huge crowd to leave, I was approached by a man flanked by two security guards. "Excuse me, sir, may I speak with you a moment?"

I wasn't sure what was going on. "Yes, of course."

"These are my sons. They were assigned here this evening, and have listened to your story on the appearances of the Virgin Mary. And they believe." Putting his hand on the shoulder of each he smiled. "This son is a Muslim, and the other is Hindu. I am Catholic. Even though we have taken different paths to God, we are grateful to have been here tonight. You have helped each of us in our faith."

It was an incredible testimony to the evening's theme, and strong reinforcement that Our Lady was coming to bring all of her children to God.

Sipping a second cup of coffee following a hearty breakfast the next morning, we began sharing Medjugorje stories. I told Victor about my sons and their reluctance to listen or change, especially Steve. "Your family is so beautiful and strong in their faith. Maybe you can tell me your secret so I can use it on my sons."

"You think all has always been well with my family? Have I got a story for you! Let me tell you about my mother—the atheist!"

Your mother is an atheist?" How, I wondered could someone with so much faith have a parent who didn't believe?

"No. She was an atheist. When we traveled to Medjugorje and heard the message—you know, prayer, fasting, and penance—I knew what I had to do for my mother. We decided to pray and fast for her twice a week until she changed and became a Christian. She was in her eighties and I knew her time on earth was short.

Victor laughed. "I told my mother what we were going to do, and she told us in no uncertain terms to mind our own business! Of course we didn't. Instead, we did everything we could to show her we loved her and continued to offer our prayers along with fasting for her conversion." Victor lowered his voice. "You know, within six months my mother joined the church!"

"Isn't that something?" I responded after a few moments. "I spend all of my time telling people about the messages of Our Lady, and it takes hearing your story to know how to convert my own sons!"

The next two days flew by. I managed to get in a couple of runs in the beautiful parks. I was impressed with Singapore and its people. This was quite a city republic. There was no litter or graffiti anywhere, no drug problems, no unemployment and seemingly none of the social ills that plague every society. That is, until I discovered in talking to Victor and Vivienne, that abortion was easily accessible and encouraged to maintain population control. It was available for as little as five Singapore dollars at any hospital or clinic.

"That is how we got Vincent," he stated. "At first, his

mother was going to have an abortion. I talked her out of it, telling her we could find a home for her baby. As it turned out, we became that home, thank God!" Little Vincent was definitely a godsend for the Wee family. Contrary to what many would perceive as a burdensome cross, he was a special gift that brought them even closer together.

Everything went smoothly until the day I was to leave for Perth, my first stop in Australia. On checking in by telephone we were informed that all flights into Australia were cancelled for a day due to a domestic airline strike. The dark forces were at it again. Now my first talk there would also have to be postponed a day. After telephoning my Australian sponsor of the delay, Victor shrugged, "No need to worry. We'll just have to extend our Singapore courtesy by treating you to the best Chinese food in the East!"

Two days later as we said our good-byes at the airport, Victor beamed with happiness. It had been a tremendous four days. In addition, arrangements had been made for Victor's center to print and distribute my book. "We'll have it out in less than a month, and please remember, all of the people who came to the talks have vowed to pray all fifteen decades of the rosary daily during your tour of Australia."

How much I had learned from Victor and Vivienne about applying the power of prayer directly to needs. And also from the unplanned stop in Los Angeles, and the visit to Larry. Sons Michael and Steve didn't know it but they were about to become primary targets of focused prayer and fasting.

12
"Have them persevere"

"Thank the people in my name for the prayers, the sacrifices, and the acts of penance. Have them persevere in prayer, fasting and conversion . . ."

"It looks as though we've a small problem Wayne. Your bag was not on the flight." Alister McLean, my Australian host, gave me the news as he returned from the baggage office of the Perth airport, adding, "but it should be delivered sometime tomorrow—no need to worry."

The annoyances were continuing. Problems had begun with the necessity of having to take an international flight out of Singapore, which included stops as far away as Kuala Lampour. No telling where my bag was! The numerous stops had made it an all-day flight and now I was due in less than an hour at a welcoming party at Alister's home.

"Well," I smiled weakly, "I'll have to make do with what I'm wearing, but I do need to clean up a bit."

"Don't worry about that," Vince Warrener, another member of the organizing committee, said. "We are about the same height and weight. I'm certain I have something you can wear until your baggage arrives, and you can freshen up at the house."

I was grateful to Vince for the clothes and toiletries. But I couldn't believe it when the wardrobe offered consisted entirely of items that were brown—my least favorite color! I grimly donned them, muttering to myself that I wasn't going to let it bother me, even though it did.

Alister's home was beautiful and spacious. Having retired from an extremely successful business career, he was actively involved in a strong, spiritual life. The simple but profound messages of Medjugorje had begun to bring peace to his life. Like so many of us, family turmoil and tragedy had caused separation from God in the past. But this ongoing miracle of daily apparitions was bringing fulfillment of faith he had never imagined.

Fortunately for the Medjugorje movement, there were many Alister McLeans who had been touched by the messages. Without their involvement and resources, Medjugorje might have taken years to develop into the global phenomena it had become in so short a time. As we sat quietly in a corner of his living room reviewing details of the ten days I would tour Western Australia, he expressed the sentiments I had heard frequently from middle and upper income people who had become involved: "I am so grateful to Our Lady for my conversion, and for the opportunity to help."

He suddenly stood and motioned toward a woman across the room. "Let me introduce you to Yolanda Nardizzi and her husband, Joe. You will be staying with them during your days in Perth."

Yolanda Nardizzi was a striking Italian woman whom I soon learned headed up a spiritual organization called the Marian Movement of Priests (MMP). She was also the English translator in Australia, for its founder, Father Stephano Gobbi. Her husband Joe was the owner of a successful real estate business, another example of people blessed with material abundance active in spreading

Medjugorje's messages. Both were involved in the planning of my Australian tour.

By mid-morning the next day, I felt very much part of the Nardizzi family which included four children ranging in age from three to fifteen. After the bustle of getting the kids to school and Joe to his office, Yolanda and I sat down for a long conversation concerning Medjugorje's apparitions and related events. "The messages given to Don Gobbi by the Madonna are along the same lines as those given to the visionaries in Medjugorje," Yolanda explained.

She told me how this very unlikely priest was chosen by Our Lady to receive special interlocutionary messages that would form and lead a special gathering of priests from around the world devoted to her in these, the end times. Without formal planning, an organizational structure had formed to develop special prayer cenacles for priests held in countries around the world. In 15 years, the MMP had burgeoned into a membership of over 70,000 priests including approximately 300 bishops and cardinals; millions of lay people were also enrolled as associate members. The messages given by the Virgin Mary at the prayer cenacles were annually collected into a book that had grown to over 700 pages with a circulation in the millions.

"It's amazing, and Don Gobbi, like many visionaries, is a most unlikely person to receive these messages and to be leading such a huge organization, but that is what makes it so unique, that and the power of its messages." Yolanda paused briefly to refill our coffee cups. "The thing is," she continued, "there is urgency in the messages of both movements and believe me, Australia needs to hear the messages of both. That is what makes your coming at this time so important."

"Thank you, Yolanda, but I still wonder at times how God could use someone like me."

"Listen, my dear American friend, God uses all kinds!

Are you familiar with the apparition of Tre Fontana and the visionary there, Bruno Cornicchiola?"

I thought a moment. "I remember reading a little about it. Isn't that the guy who was going to kill the Pope?"

Yolanda smiled. "That's him. It took place more than forty years ago in Rome, at a small park named Tre Fontana. Legend has it that it was the spot where St. Paul was beheaded."

She began telling how Bruno Cornicchiola, although confirmed a Catholic, grew to hate the Church. He had become deeply involved in politics and the Seventh Day Adventist movement. Though he coerced his wife into joining also, she secretly remained a devout Catholic.

Bruno, raised in a godless home filled with abuse from an alcoholic father, developed a rage against Catholicism, and a zeal for Communism. Filled with anger, he took his frustrations out on his wife by frequently beating her. In contrast, he had a strong love for his children. This man, so obsessed with hatred for the Catholic faith after constant brainwashing from a fanatical Seventh Day Adventist he had met while serving in the army, vowed to kill the Pope, going as far as purchasing a dagger to do the deed. He even carved on the blade, "Death to the Pope."

One beautiful Spring day in 1947, he took his children to Tre Fontana for a quiet afternoon in the open where he could compose a speech he would give the following day, vilifying the Blessed Virgin Mary. The park was notorious as a rendezvous spot for prostitutes to ply their trade, usually in a small grotto located in one corner of the park. Bruno had wanted to take his children to the beach, but they had missed the bus.

As Bruno relaxed in the warm sunshine working on the text of his speech, his children played in the little grotto. One of them came crying to Bruno that they had lost their ball. He and one of the children approached the little grotto and suddenly the child dropped to his knees and began saying over and over, "Beautiful lady!" Alarmed, Bruno tried to lift him but couldn't. He called to his other children and as they came, they too fell to their knees and began exclaiming, "beautiful lady!"

Alarmed to near panic, Bruno cried out, "God help me!" And with that, he was forced to his knees and suddenly was unable to see. Then, out of a brilliant light, he saw a beautiful woman dressed in a dark, rich green gown. She opened what would be a long and continuing conversation with this zealous anti-Catholic, by saying to him, "Bruno, my son, why do you persecute the faith?"

From that supernatural event, Bruno would became a champion of the faith and especially of Our Lady. On returning home, he knelt in front of his wife, asking her for forgiveness and from that moment he began a service of humility and obedience.

Our Lady appeared to Bruno several more times and word quickly spread of the apparitions and change in this man who so hated the Church. Several months later, he was able to keep his appointment at the Vatican, dropping to his knees in front of the Holy Father, and presenting him with the dagger he had planned to use to kill him. He told his story and of seeing the Virgin Mary; life for the Cornicchiola family dramatically changed to one of holiness and mission.

"So you see," Yolanda smiled, "our Lord uses all kinds of people." It was a touching story and one with which I could easily associate. The message that had been given to me at Trinidad actually answered every doubt that may have existed about my own mission and why I was the one given this responsibility. But in our humanity, we always question.

"There is another reason I'm telling you about Bruno," Yolanda added. "I feel Tre Fontana is directly tied to the efforts of our regional MMP group to bring spiritual conversion to West Australia. There is a sister shrine here just outside of Perth. And Bruno Cornicchiola has visited Australia twice." She went on to tell me of Bullsbruck, run by a man who knew Bruno, and with the assistance of several others, built the shrine in thanksgiving for his own conversion.

"You mean Bruno is still alive?"

"He most definitely is and Vince Lombardo is the man who knows him and has seen to the building of the shrine. He's expecting you to visit the shrine during your stay here."

It was fascinating how Yolanda could put all of these supernatural events together and make it understandable. We talked on and off nearly all day and as I prepared for my first talk in Perth, I marvelled at how persistent our Blessed Mother was in her apparition messages through the ages to bring all children possible into the light of her Son's gospel message.

That evening marked the beginning of a wonderful, exciting ten days. There was even time for a fast nine holes of golf on a very short afternoon off. It was here—and only here—that I saw kangaroos. "You're like all the Americans who come to Australia," Joe Nardizzi laughed, "You think we have kangaroos on every corner!" I sheepishly had to admit that I expected to see them all over the place.

That short recreational break was the only one during the entire tour as I traveled outside of Perth, north to a little town called Geraldton, and as far south as Bumbry. In Geraldton, one man traveled twelve hours each way by bus just to hear about Medjugorje. He had read my articles and was willing to endure this marathon trip to learn more.

I spoke twice in a small assembly hall; once in mid-afternoon and again in early evening. The little annoyances also continued. As I began speaking in the afternoon session, a fly buzzed around my face throughout the talk. Just as I finished, it left. That evening it returned again as I began speaking! The "Lord of Flies" was present! More than once, Our Lady had stated in her messages that wherever she was to bring the peace of Jesus, Satan was there to take it away.

That minor distraction was nothing compared with what happened at the end of the evening session. A couple approached after nearly everyone had left, the woman beaming but the man hesitant. "I wonder if we could have a minute with you; we want to thank you for coming and for clearing something that has been bothering us."

"Sarah, I'm not sure that is what he meant—"

The woman cut her husband short. "Oh, of course it is! Mr. Weible, you say that this Medjugorje message is a message for all people of all faiths, and that we should live our faith whatever it is. Is that correct?"

I immediately sensed she had taken something I had said the wrong way. "Well, yes, but Our Lady definitely is coming to lead us to her Son—"

"Oh, of course," she interrupted. "We are Catholics, raised in the Church and married there. But our church is so stagnant, we simply became bored with it and now we have found this new church that is so much more alive!"

The woman's husband began to squirm. "I don't want to leave the Catholic Church, but my wife met some people who became friends and they were attending this other church."

After a brief description by the husband, I knew it was a New Age church. Taking the woman gently by the arm, I asked her, "If you've been raised Catholic, then you must realize the one thing you have in this church that is unique from all others is the Holy Eucharist."

"And Our Lady," the husband broke in, "this other

church doesn't have Our Lady!"

Suddenly the woman was unsure. "But I thought you said the Virgin Mary is coming for all faiths?"

I began to gently explain that yes, Our Lady's messages were for people of all faiths; that was different than saying all faiths were the same. I pointed out that it was no accident that she came to Catholic youth and was asking for a return to the sacraments of that Church. "But regardless of what faith one is practicing," I added, "conversion of the heart to God comes first."

Nodding her head silently, the woman stood there for a few seconds, then thanked me and left. I wasn't sure she understood, but I knew her husband did. I could only pray that through this encounter and her husband's resistance, she would reconsider her decision to join the other church.

A few days later, I met Vince and Lilly Lombardo. Vince was a large man, very Italian, with an aggressive personality. He was completely devoted to the Bullsbrook shrine. "I'm glad we have the opportunity to take you there," he smiled as we began the 40-minute drive to the shrine.

"How did you meet Bruno?" I asked. "Australia is a long way from Italy."

Vince shifted the car into gear as we turned onto the main highway leading to the shrine. Driving at an agonizingly slow pace, he began. "Well now, actually my Mum is responsible, even though she didn't know it at the time. I was going to Rome with my father. Mum had heard about Tre Fontana, and as we prepared to board the airplane, she asked us to visit the shrine if we had time. It was just a last minute thought, she said.

"I completely forgot about it and really had no intention of doing so anyway. We were leaving for the airport to return home and since we had a little extra time, we decided to have the taxi driver show us some of the sights. We came to St. Paul's Church and for some reason, it re-

minded me of Mum's request. So I asked the driver to
take us to Tre Fontana. He wasn't sure where it was, so it
took a little time, but when I saw it, I was struck in a special way."

The car plodded along as Vince paused, slowly gathering his thoughts to assure inclusion of every detail of
the event. "Well, I knew I had to meet this Bruno fellow. I
convinced a priest at the shrine to telephone the monastery where he now lived and within minutes we were there.
The minute I saw Bruno, I fully believed. I embraced him
and we talked so long we almost missed our plane home."

For the remainder of the journey and on the way back,
Vince told of how the shrine came to be, and about Bruno's
two visits to Perth. It was long and involved, and while I
found it interesting, I didn't give it a lot of thought. At
least at the time.

The first leg of the Australian tour drew to a close
with a small get-together of volunteers. Approximately forty
people who had in some way or another assisted had been
invited but to the astonishment of the organizers, more
than four hundred showed up! Word had spread and the
people of Perth had come to add their own thanks. It was
a beautiful gift and before the evening was over, it had
evolved into another talk.

Again there was the problem of having to travel on
international flights as I departed Perth for a one-day stop
in Adelaide in the south. From there it was on to Sydney
for another one-night stop, before a final three days in
Melbourne, under the direction of Leon LeGrande. He,
too, was a strong convert through Medjugorje, whose story
paralleled mine in many ways.

"You might say I'm the Wayne Weible of Australia!"
he laughed. "I've been through personal family difficulties, had wonderful success in business, wrote a best-seller

book, and found conversion to God because of Our Lady's appearances in Medjugorje. Now all my work is through our Peace Center to spread the messages."

I had met Leon briefly at the end of my first pilgrimage to Medjugorje as we overnighted in Dubrovnik. He and his wife Carley had organized three meetings in different parts of Melbourne, resulting in packed capacity the first two nights.

On the morning of my last day in Australia, I sat at the kitchen table of the LeGrande home sipping coffee and enjoying my first look at a newspaper in more than a week. I planned to relax for the morning and attempt to telephone Terri around noon, since I hadn't called home in five days. Suddenly a story at the top of the third page caught my attention with the headline: HURRICANE ABOUT TO STRIKE S.C. COAST IN U.S. I nearly dropped my coffee as I read in the story that the point of land contact was estimated to hit directly at Myrtle Beach— at a time I hurriedly calculated to be just about the time I would be speaking that evening!

"Leon, quick, look at this—I've got to call home right now!"

Leon came running into the kitchen, his face half-covered with shaving cream. "What is it?"

"A hurricane is about to hit Myrtle Beach! I've got to call Terri!"

After several attempts, I finally got through, only to hear a recorded message from my wife: "Hello, just in case you call, we've moved inland and are safe." Terri's voice then changed and she added a cheery, "Once again, we're having a major hurricane, and as usual, you're not here!" That was a reference to the last time our home had been threatened by such a storm, and again, I was away.

Stunned at the news, as well as Terri's sense of humor in the face of imminent danger, I slumped onto a nearby couch. She had also included a telephone number where she and the kids were staying. I immediately began dialing the number over and over, only to be told by an operator's recorded message that all lines in the area were down due to the storm. "I can't reach her." I was near panic.

"Well, at least you know she and the children are safe inland," Leon assured me.

Carley had prepared some hot tea and as she brought it into the room she said, "Look, why don't we pray a rosary right now for protection of the whole area."

Taking the tea, I nodded in agreement; but I had difficulty focusing on the prayers. Throughout the remainder of the day, I tried to reach the number Terri had left on the recorder, but with no luck; the lines were still down.

That evening, I sat quietly in a back room of the auditorium where I would be speaking. How would I be able to speak to these people about a message of hope, when I was so concerned for the safety of my family? All at once I was filled with a sense of peace; the closeness of Jesus and His words echoed in my heart: *"Trust in Me."*

Within seconds, Leon stuck his head through the doorway of the little room. "I thought you would like to know, we just heard from Victor Wee in Singapore. All of the people there who came to your talks are praying for the protection of your family and your home. In fact, for the entire area!"

I quietly thanked Leon. It seemed as if Jesus was saying, *"You see?"*

Leon continued. "Yolanda also called; people from just about every place you've been here have called to say they will be praying for you! Now come on; the people are waiting!"

Buoyed by these events, it was an especially inspired and emotional talk that evening. And of course, it centered on trust in Jesus as the basis for ongoing conversion.

On returning to Leon and Carley's home, we immediately switched on the television to pick up the national news from the states just in time to see one of the morning news shows coming live direct from Myrtle Beach! And while damage was high, there had been no loss of life. How surreal to see the familiar downtown section of my home town from 12,000 miles away.

I again dialed the number Terri had left on the recorder and this time, I got through. Everything was fine with them and they planned to return to our home that afternoon. I fell asleep almost the minute I laid my head on the pillow, a comforting, deep sleep brought on not only by the fatigue of the day's events, but in the confirmation that through trust in Jesus, my family and all the families in the path of the hurricane were safe.

Despite the reassurances, I wished the tour was over and I was on my way there. But three days remained in the Fiji Islands, located in the Pacific Ocean some three hours by air from Australia. I arrived late on an extremely dark night, flying into the major city of Suva. From there, I had to take a late-night flight to a smaller city close to the seminary where I would be staying.

The airport at Suva was a dilapidated building that seemed to operate on an informal basis. I waited awhile at the check-in counter for domestic flights at the far end of the building. A lone woman was sitting in the waiting area, so I asked her for help. "I am the clerk," she answered without getting up or taking her eyes from the magazine she was reading. "The airplane has not yet arrived. I will tell you when to board."

Nearly an hour past departure time the airplane arrived. None of the handful of waiting passengers seemed upset that it was late. It was an antique propeller job that appeared to be held together with wire and glue, and as I boarded I began some serious prayer. The plane shook and groaned as it struggled to take off, but an hour later, landed with a sharp bump at a tiny airport somewhere in the middle of nowhere.

Father Donal McIlraith, who would be my sponsor for my stay in Fiji, was waiting. He had been to Medjugorje, and had devoted much of his priesthood to missionary work in Fiji. He drove me to the Seminary of the Pacific, his headquarters and the place where I would be staying. "I appreciate your coming and the arrangements by Yolanda," Father said to me as we had a small snack and a cold drink before retiring. "Of course, there is always a need, but especially here in these islands."

Fiji was under a strong, dictatorial government whose leader was a rigid, inflexible man with strong Catholic beliefs. "He is a bit too Catholic for many as he forces beliefs on the people and no matter the good intentions, that simply does not lead one to the faith. That is why you as a Protestant speaking about Our Lady is so important for the people of Fiji to hear."

Father McIlraith went on to say that the Fiji Islands, now under British protection, had a long history of struggle and oppression. Its resources were copper, gold and iron as well as fishing and farming. "They are a simple and poor people," Father added, "and once converted, they are devout Christians. I've enjoyed my forty-plus years as a missionary here."

There were approximately twelve other priests serving as teaching professors at the seminary, whom I met later in the morning after a short night's sleep. Most were cautiously interested in Medjugorje and listened intently as I told my story during breakfast. Later, I spoke to the seminarians, who were from all of the different island countries throughout the Pacific Ocean. It was time relished as I told them of Our Lady's messages. Many seminaries, including this one according to Father McIlraith, were leaving the Blessed Virgin out of contemporary theological teachings, along with other traditional teachings. There was also a movement to deemphasize adoration of the Eucharist and place more emphasis on an intellectual and social approach to theology.

By the number of questions and positive comments from the students, I knew this was a special time for them; it also filled Father McIlraith with joy. So much of what he experienced at Medjugorje was lost on his fellow priests. I felt this opportunity to share with these priests of the future was probably the reason for this out-of-the-way stop on the itinerary.

As though to confirm my feelings, I had an interesting conversation with the head professor on the morning of my departure. The previous evening's crowd had been the largest as people came from all over Fiji, many coming from tribes deep in the jungle area of the island. I told of the visionaries being shown or taken to heaven and hell, and talked at length on the subject.

"I must tell you," the professor began, "I have agreed with everything you have said in your talks concerning the apparitions—until last night. Do you really believe that a God of love and mercy would allow there to be a hell, much less send anyone there?"

It was a question I had been asked many times before, but usually by atheists, agnostics, or those who deemed themselves intellectuals. My usual answer was to simply say that I was only reporting what the visionaries had said. But this time I responded without forethought, "Father, I am not a theologian but if there is no hell, does that mean there is no judgment? And if so, why would Jesus be coming a second time?"

My professor-priest looked at me for a moment, then burst out laughing. "Well, I've never looked at it quite that way. Good point!"

Father McIlraith had decided to drive me back to Suva rather than take a chance on the short flight. "They don't always follow their schedule," he chuckled. "You'll enjoy the scenery along the way and this will give us an opportunity to stop and visit a fellow priest who works in the jungle with the people there. He is an American and knowing you were coming, asked to meet you if possible."

It was a three-hour drive through steaming, thick jungle. But the stop to see an American missionary priest made the trip worth the penance. Father Don Hughes was from the Northeast, he related as we sipped kuva, a strange tasting non-alcoholic drink that made the tongue and lips numb. "What did you say this stuff was made from?" I shook my head, setting the coconut shell cup down. One sip was enough.

"It's made from the root of a pepper plant and is a traditional social drink." Father Don smiled. "Haven't found too many people outside of the islands that like it."

At least we were out of the furnace heat of the interior of the car and listening to Father Don's stories about his thirty years here as a missionary was intriguing. "Listen," he suddenly asked, "did you say you were from Myrtle Beach?"

"Yes, are you familiar with it?"

"Well, I'm familiar with a hometown boyhood friend who was mayor there a short while back. His name is Bob Hirsch. Do you know him?"

I was surprised. I knew Bob Hirsch well and after a few more stories about the two of them, I suggested he write a short note that I would hand deliver to his boyhood friend. "What a small world!" I said to Father McIlraith as we began the last leg of the journey to Suva for my flight home.

After a 30-hour day of flying, I stood in my front yard with Terri, surveying the damage of the hurricane that had hit Myrtle Beach direct. Large trees were downed and many of my neighbor's roofs were severely damaged by falling trees and branches. But our home was untouched by damage save for a few missing shingles and a small tree down in the front yard.

There was no doubt of the protecting grace that came from the thousands of people from Singapore and Australia, who had offered prayers for the protection of my family and property. It was dramatic proof once again of the power of trust in Jesus.

It was the same old story: home a few days, then off again. This time to Medjugorje for the third trip there this year. But there was a new twist; it would be by way of Ireland, joining an Irish group at the request of its organizer, Heather Parsons.

Terri was concerned. "You're cramming too much into too short a time. Pretty soon, you'll be of no use to anyone. I don't think that's what the Blessed Virgin had in mind for you in this mission!"

"Well, at least I have all of December off. This woman has given up her career to establish a Medjugorje Center. She needs a little help getting started and that's why she asked me to come on this tour."

"I understand that but you better start thinking about your health. You can't keep going at this rate."

I promised her I'd slow down the next year, even though I probably wouldn't. But Heather Parsons's efforts were important. She too, had been a journalist and a very good one. And she was also an Anglican. Conversion had come through covering a story for the television publication of which she was editor. Like myself, she felt a call.

Going back to Medjugorje was no longer necessary for me in the sense of having to renew what I had received. But each pilgrimage was unique, and added to the mission. It was hard to believe that this would mark the sixth such journey since the first.

As always, there was little time to spare on arrival in Ireland. I had just enough time to check into a hotel, clean up and rush to a planned evening Medjugorje conference in Dublin featuring several speakers.

The marvels of Medjugorje's influence continued as I listened to a young Irishman who had been a fanatical activist in the Irish Republic Army (IRA). He had ended up in prison and it was there through the efforts of a priest that he found out about Medjugorje. On release, he took a pilgrimage and the rest was history. Now, no longer a member of the IRA, he devoted the majority of his time to work with youth, turning them to God.

Listening to this witness touched a memory. I had made one short visit to Northern Ireland on my first tour, but not to Belfast. Suddenly, I felt a call to go there. Turning to the man who had brought a small group from Belfast to join Heather's tour, I asked him if it were possible to arrange at this eleventh hour for me to give at least one talk in Belfast on our return from Medjugorje. It would be three days after our return to Ireland before my flight home, three days planned for rest.

Having already asked for a commitment to come to Northern Ireland at some point of time, the man was ecstatic. "You wait right here," he said as he rushed out of the auditorium. Fifteen minutes later he return smiling broadly. "It's all arranged. Part of our Medjugorje prayer group will take care of spreading the word and the priest at our church is delighted!"

I was glad Terri wasn't there. She wouldn't have been happy with the additional stop, especially in Northern Ireland.

Coming to Medjugorje is the only rest needed, I rationalized, as the Irish tour arrived early in the morning. And it was, at least for the moment. Marija was there and glad to see me, especially since she needed an escort to and from St. James Church each evening for the apparition and Mass. It was a task of pure spiritual pleasure.

Despite bitterly cold weather caused by a severe Siberian cold front that had arrived the day before, it was a restful week. And I was delighted especially in speaking and sharing with a group of Irish youth. After my talk, several of the young people began witnessing. One young girl of sixteen had come only because her mother had begged her. After two days of "nothing but church, rosaries, and climbing mountains," she was ready to return home. In a word, she was bored. By the time their particular tour was to leave, she begged her mother to let her stay on a couple more weeks.

Another young man from Dublin was convinced to take a job with one of the tour agencies bringing pilgrimages to the little village. "I didn't have an interest in what was reportedly happening here," he related. "To be perfectly honest, I was to work the three months of summer and I thought it would be a fine opportunity to get a suntan!" Now, in the bitter cold of this November, he was still here.

There were other talks and visits, but I also found time to climb the hill and mountain; and to spend a lot of prayer and meditation time in my favorite spot: the little cemetery in the fields behind the church.

I would crouch at the base of a large tomb that directly faced the sun, warming myself from the cold winds and thinking about the day Terri and I would finally be able to become members of the Catholic Church. It had already been three years; how much longer, I wondered?

How envious I was a couple of evenings later when a young man from England was confirmed into the Church during the Croatian Mass. Marija and Ivan were his sponsors. "I'm happy for that young man," I told Marija that evening as we walked along the darkened pathway through the fields on our way to her home, "but, I am also very jealous!"

Marija stopped on the pathway. "Oh, you should not be jealous," she said. "This is a wonderful conversion for him!"

"No, no, I'm happy for him," I explained. "It's just that I wish it were me." Suddenly I blurted out, "Marija, will you be a sponsor when I am able to join?"

"Of course!" she said, pulling me along the path, as if it had been decided before I asked.

That was enough to sustain me. On the flight back to Ireland, I began daydreaming of that day. I would come to Medjugorje and there would be great crowds of pilgrims there. Father Svetozar would celebrate the Mass and confirmation, while Marija and Ivan would be my sponsors. It would be so glorious!

The flight to Ireland was less than three hours, arriving in the early morning. Immediately we boarded the waiting bus for another three-hour ride to Belfast for my one speaking engagement.

Arriving near noon, we grabbed a quick meal and then toured the streets of Belfast. "Over there a British soldier was blown up in his vehicle," my Belfast friend pointed out a spot on the road now marked only by what appeared to be a washed out area. "And over there on that corner three IRA members were gunned down in a drive-by shooting."

The door of the church where I was speaking was pockmarked with bullet holes. I shuddered thinking about the senseless and never-ending killing of Catholics and Protestants, emphasizing strongly during the talk that the only solution was what Our Lady was asking at Medjugorje. "We must pray with all our hearts and souls," I practically shouted at the standing room only crowd. "It is the only answer!"

Even in Medjugorje, I related, the same hatreds were at work. "Serbs and Croats, enemies over centuries just as in Northern Ireland, are increasingly hostile in these times. While the government is now attempting to take the larger share of the economic pie of incoming tourist currency generated by pilgrimages there, senseless incidents and posturing between individuals of the two cultures has increased at an alarming rate, playing directly into Satan's hand, just as has been done here in Northern Ireland!"

The trip was well worth the effort. And there were still two days to rest before leaving Ireland. That, and the entire month of December at home with family.

But by the first week of the new year, I was ready to go again. There was still so much to do.

13
The Philippines

"Dear children, at this time I ask you particularly to conse-crate yourselves to me and to my Immaculate Heart..."

"In the name of Jesus and Mary, we welcome you to our country!" Smiling radiantly, Lydia Sison, director of the Center for Peace, Asia, laid a wreath of flowers in my arms as I cleared customs at the Manila Airport. I immediately felt at home.

There had been hesitation about coming to the Phil-ippines. An uneasy political climate hung in the air, as four weeks earlier, an attempted military coup had been quashed. It was the seventh such attempt in the last four years on the government of Corazon Aquino, a devout Catholic housewife who had been swept into the president's office in the wake of the sudden fall of despotic ruler, Ferdinand Marcos.

The near-unanimous belief among the people that these startling events had occurred with the direct inter-vention of the Blessed Virgin Mary was further proof of their total devotion to her. Corazon Aquino certainly be-lieved it. In the face of the attempted coups, she depended more on the prayers of the rosary than the protection of her military.

Having been in the air for twenty-plus hours, Lydia and her welcoming group's enthusiasm was welcome relief. With little sleep on the long flight, including a two-hour stopover in Tokyo, all I wanted now was a place to lay horizontal for about eight hours. Dropping into the seat of the awaiting car I heaved a sigh, stating that I was ready for a good rest. "Oh, but we have a full agenda for the day," Lydia quickly stated. "And right now, our Cardinal is waiting to personally welcome you to our country."

Rest was immediately forgotten. Since first reading about the "miracle" of the Philippine revolution, I found it very much related to the events of Medjugorje—even to the point that it occurred on February 25, 1986, the anniversary day of the apparitions. An audience with Cardinal Jaime Sin, who had played an influential spiritual role in the revolution was high on my list of desires in coming here. Hopefully, I would learn more about Our Lady's reported apparition during the heat of the confrontation, a fact which he had revealed at a surprised international press conference in New York City shortly after the revolution. Not surprisingly, the story was buried near the bottom of page three or four in most newspapers.

Twenty minutes later, after a tense ride through the jammed, toxic traffic of Manila, we were having coffee with the Philippines' most famous church leader. "Cardinal, I've read a great deal about the revolution and the part you played," I said after we had been talking awhile, "and especially about the appearance of Our Lady. I wondered if you could tell me more about this?"

The Cardinal laughed. "So, you have heard about that! I will be happy to tell you about 'People Power,' the power of the masses when moved by the truth of Jesus, and about how the Virgin saved her country. But my role was exaggerated!"

I sensed he was happy for an opportunity to tell the story again. Settling into his huge chair, the Cardinal began telling of the events that changed two decades of oppression under Marcos, into the beginning of true freedom for his fellow countrymen.

It began in February, 1986, as the virtual twenty-year dictatorship of Ferdinand Marcos came to an abrupt and unexpected end through a series of strange events. Corazon Aquino, the widow and reluctant political replacement of slain opposition leader Ninoy Aquino, had won the presidential election. In a stunning upset, she was elected by an overwhelming margin in the snap election, called for by Marcos himself. The Cardinal pointed out that Marcos had called for elections in order to crush the building opposition. However, through ballot box stuffing and other illegal activities, plus a total control of the media, Marcos flagrantly had himself declared the winner.

Cory, as she was affectionately called by the people, had gained enormous popularity due in part to the reputation of her late husband who had been gunned down as he descended from an airplane on his return to the island nation. He was returning to run against Marcos and hopefully restore freedom to the people. Taking his place, Cory also represented the first true opportunity for democracy.

The rigged election results were blatant and obvious to neutral observers and also to the people. Within days, millions took to the streets of Makati and Manila, spurred to action when a dissatisfied segment of the military launched an unexpected coup attempt. Unbeknown to its perpetrators, it would be this unrelated coup attempt that would allow Cory Aquino, a simple housewife, as she described herself, to assume the presidency she had rightfully won at the ballot box. Marcos responded to the rebellion and coup attempt by sending tanks down the streets of the city. He was determined to maintain his grip on the country, even if it meant massacre of the swelling crowds.

As a full convoy of tanks and other armament manned by hard-core militant soldiers came against millions of civilians, many of whom who were virtually lying down in the streets in front of the tanks, Marcos gave the order to fire on the people.

Cardinal Sin leaned forward in his chair, smiling. "What I am telling you now was told to me by many of these same soldiers who were ready to fire on the people." Reclining again, he continued. "The tanks were trying to penetrate the crowd. And the people were praying and showing their rosaries. That is when, according to these soldiers, the Marines who were riding on top of the tanks, the so-called Loyalists (to Marcos), they saw up in the clouds the form of the cross. The many sisters had tried to stop them, but they (the soldiers) told me they had already decided to obey instructions and push through. It is now just a question of ten minutes or so. You push the trigger and there you are—everybody will be dead."

Again, the Cardinal leaned forward. "Then, a beautiful lady appeared to them. I don't know if she appeared in the sky or was standing down on the ground. (Others would later tell me they thought she was a nun, dressed in blue, and that she was standing in front of the tanks.) So beautiful she was, and her eyes were sparkling. And the beautiful lady spoke to them like this: 'Dear soldiers, stop! Do not proceed! Do not harm my children! I am the queen of this land!' And when they heard that, the soldiers put down everything. They came down from the tanks and they joined the people. So, that was the end of the Loyalists."

Cardinal Sin paused, turning his hands upward. "I don't know who these soldiers are. All I know is that they came here crying to me. They did not tell me that it was the Virgin. They told me only that it was a beautiful sister. But you know," he paused, laughing heartily, "I have seen all the sisters in Manila, and there are no beautiful ones. So it must have been the Virgin!"

What a story—and what a sense of humor! Here was a powerful figure of the Philippine Catholic Church, able to add such a wonderful touch to another stunning supernatural visit by Our Lady. But being a journalist, I had to ask: "Cardinal, do you really believe it was Our Lady that the people and the soldiers saw?"

Cardinal Sin did not hesitate. "Yes. My heart was telling me, this was Mary. And since they obeyed this woman who appeared to them and did not follow orders and fire on the people, then Marcos had nobody anymore. So, he had to flee. That was the end of him."

Thus, from the Cardinal himself the story was confirmed; Our Lady did play a direct role in the freedom of the Philippine people. And no wonder. They were so consecrated to the hearts of Jesus and Mary that everywhere one looked, pictures of both were displayed. They were on office desks, on dashes of automobiles, even plastered into the brickwork of walls surrounding homes.

Adding to the incredibility of the entire story was the fact that Cardinal Sin had met with Sister Lucia, the last living visionary of Fatima, in Portugal, just before his trip to the United States and the press conference where he first told the story of the Blessed Virgin's appearance. Although living in a cloistered convent, Sister Lucia knew everything about the Philippine revolution. She had no access to newspapers, magazines, or television. Yet, she related all of the details to the Cardinal.

She then told him that Corazon Aquino was a gift to

the Philippines from God, and that if she could maintain peace and democracy there for a period of two or more years, that nation would be influential in leading China to Christianity.

This was far more information than I expected to receive. We talked for approximately half an hour more, about these things and of course about Medjugorje, which the Cardinal also fully believed was authentic.

"Now we are going to take you to the shrine which has been erected on the very sight where Our Lady appeared," Lydia said after we had left the Cardinal and were weaving our way through the congested streets. "You will be speaking there in three days at noontime. They are expecting a large crowd even though it is scheduled for the middle of the week."

Much of the drive to the shrine was spent in silence as I marveled over the time spent with the Cardinal. But that was quickly replaced by the shock of seeing firsthand the abject poverty of these people. Signs of it were everywhere.

Scores of naked infants who could not have been more than two or three years old, played in the squalor of the streets, precariously close to the road's edge, and in constant danger of the never-ending stream of vehicles rushing by. Everything seemed to be so congested and packed, including people everywhere. I felt claustrophobic and nauseous from the fumes of so many vehicles.

We crossed the Pasig River, darkened to a slimy, brown-grey by pollution of every kind, including human waste as literally hundreds of shanty homes lined the banks. They were constructed of anything that could be used for walls—cardboard, tin, and scraps of thin plywood—housing entire families in areas of less than ten square feet. The river was the only source of water and was used for all purposes including drinking, creating ongoing sickness that led to high death tolls among the young.

I shuddered, thinking of how these people had to live day in and day out. Worse, I felt revulsion at being among them, and guilt that I felt this way. It was one thing to talk about charity and love of the poor, and quite another when faced with having to actually touch those afflicted with so much suffering.

And what a stark contrast to the people sponsoring my tour. They were from middle income and well-to-do families. Yet, spurred by Medjugorje's message of penance, they were now going into some of the poorest areas to serve the most destitute. I uttered a silent prayer that I could be more like them.

We reached the shrine just as the stress of Manila traffic was about to overwhelm me. Situated at a busy intersection was a beautiful, large chapel, and on top of it, a huge, rather homely statue of the Blessed Virgin Mary, constructed out of dark grey metal. Its head was far too big for the rest of the statue. Two arms stretched out seemingly over the entire city with unusually large hands turned upwards. The women were staring at me for a reaction. "What do you think," Lydia said, "Isn't she beautiful?"

"Well—" I didn't know what to say. It was one of the ugliest statues of the Blessed Virgin I had ever seen. "It's certainly different . . ."

They all burst out laughing. "We know it is not beautiful, but it is special to us because of what happened shortly after it was completed," Lydia explained.

"You see, after the revolution, the people wanted a large statue of Our Lady to permanently mark the spot where she appeared and saved us from Marcos' soldiers. But after it was completed, much criticism came to the artist and finally, it was decided to fix the head and the hands, so as to present a more beautiful Mary to the public."

Lydia took my hand, pulling me toward the edge of the street. "Come out here so you can see it better. There, all around it," she said pointing to the statue, "they built scaffolding and everything was in place to make the corrections. All of a sudden a small tornado came out of nowhere, heading straight toward the statue! All of the workers fled to safety and as the tornado passed over, miraculously, no one was harmed and no damage was done to the shrine or any other building. Only the scaffolding around the statue was knocked down! Our Lady had spoken! The statue would remain as it is."

I looked at Lydia. "Is this true? It just doesn't sound—"

"Oh, but it's very true," interrupted Emilita Cruz, one of the ladies. "I know people who witnessed it themselves. And, so that you can see it was Our Lady behind this, you must know we do not have tornados in the Philippines!" I was entranced and could only shake my head in wonderment. This definitely was a land consecrated to the mother of Jesus.

Midway through the tour of the shrine, I began to feel tinges of exhaustion from the long trip and full morning. "We're leaving for the Roces home right now. That is where you will be staying," Lydia answered.

Again, there was the ordeal of driving through Manila traffic, and again, seeing the horrible poverty of the masses of people. At last, we pulled into the driveway of a high-walled home belonging to Marquitos and Marietta Roces. After enjoying a light meal, I asked if I could be shown to my room. "I'm sorry, but I've got to lay down before I collapse."

"Certainly," Marietta answered. "You have a couple of hours before the press conference."

"Press conference?"

"Yes," Lydia beamed. "We have arranged for all of the media to come to the Center at four o'clock today so that it can all be done at once."

I couldn't believe it! My sponsors seemed oblivious

that I had just spent more than thirty hours traveling. There were only a couple of hours to clean up and rest. "Okay, I sighed, but I hope I'll be able to wake up once I lay down— I'm dead!"

"Oh, you'll be fine," piped up one of the ladies. "The Blessed Mother will give you the strength to make it!"

How many times had I heard that, I thought as at last I was able to stretch out on a bed.

Not feeling a whole lot better after the brief respite, we entered a large conference room at the Center for Peace Headquarters to a wave of blinding flashbulbs. The place was jammed with reporters and equipment. Medjugorje and a Protestant devoted to the Blessed Virgin Mary was big news in the Philippines. For the next two and a half hours, there were nonstop interviews for television, radio and newspapers.

Afterward, we stopped briefly at a small restaurant for a quick meal before attending Mass and my first scheduled talk. Sitting quietly awaiting the start of Mass was my first opportunity since arriving for private prayer. Taking my rosary in hand, I prayed for the strength to get through the evening's events, knowing this would be the only opportunity to pray the rosary, something I had committed to do daily since January, 1986.

Feeling numb and physically sick, I got up and walked around outside after the Mass as preparations were made for the talk. The only way I could speak and make any sense would be for the Holy Spirit to take over completely; that is the only plausible answer to the standing ovation as the talk was completed. I hardly knew what had been said. "I'm glad that's over," I said to Lydia as we left the church. "There's nothing left in the tank. I'm empty!"

The moment she placed her hand on my shoulder, I knew there was more. "I am sorry we are working you so hard, but these people are so in need of hearing this message, and who knows if you will have a chance to return in the future?" Patting my shoulder, she continued: "If you can just bear up a bit longer, we have one last stop. The people of the Philippine movie industry, the actors, producers and directors, are waiting for us."

Dismayed, my voice was barely audible. "There's another talk?"

"Just a short one."

The "short one" lasted a little more than two hours. By then, I was running on remote control. It was the same sensation experienced the first time I ran in a marathon. Every part of the physical being aches with fatigue but mentally you suddenly feel acutely aware of everything surrounding you in a surreal way.

The reception by this particular group of people also helped. More than two hundred were on hand, as they had brought family and friends even at this hour, to learn more about Our Lady's appearances in Yugoslavia.

Finally, a little before midnight, the day was brought to a merciful close—at least for four hours. We had an early flight to Bacolod, a city on the southern island of Negros, for an ecumenical breakfast. It was important that the Protestants in the Philippines also know of Our Lady's call, Lydia explained before I could protest.

"There are sixteen million Catholics, 800,000 Moslems, and a half-million Protestants in the Philippines," Rogie Cruz, another member of the Center who was accompanying me on the short flight, explained when I queried him on the religious makeup of the nation. "We wanted to take advantage of every opportunity to spread the message and when this Protestant group heard of your visit, they asked if you would come to their monthly meeting as guest speaker."

I was a little surprised that I was traveling outside of Manila. "I don't mind speaking anywhere, but why in this particular place?"

"Because this is right in the heart of Communist country, where some of the heaviest fighting has taken place between rebels and the armed forces. We thought with the election of Cory Aquino it would stop, but unfortunately it continues. But don't worry," Rogie assured me, "you'll be safe."

I didn't really worry about it, but it remained in the back of my mind. However, the questions following the talk erased all other concerns. They were pointed and challenging, asking for scriptural reference to apparitions and the Blessed Virgin Mary. But it wasn't anything I hadn't heard, and learned from, at previous ecumenical gatherings. I was prepared and able to answer without offending by using other scriptural references to back the messages. "You see," I answered one of the questioners, "there is nothing new being revealed through these apparitions at Medjugorje. Our Lady has stated that everything we need to know for our conversion to God is in Holy Scripture. But we as humans are weak, and we do need signs to help us. And God, who is infinite in His mercy, allows the mother of His Son to come as a messenger to confirm for us that He is real and that He loves us."

"That was excellent," Rogie beamed as we enjoyed a quiet moment over coffee following the meeting. "Have you studied theology long?"

I had to laugh. "Listen, Rogie, I can't tell you the number of times I have been embarrassed at sessions like this one, simply because I wasn't prepared. I am not a theologian and have never taken a formal study course on religion. But I've been through the theological school of hard knocks!"

I went on to tell him of a similar event on a Christian radio show, in Tucson, Arizona. "I thought since it was a Christian radio talk show, they would accept the apparitions and see how God was at work—but they didn't. Instead," I explained, "they ate me alive with hostile call-in questions and accusations; the apparitions were Satan disguised as an angel of light; apparitions were not in the Bible; and, I shouldn't 'worship' Mary and try to take people away from the truth of the Bible. At the conclusion of the show, I was totally embarrassed and downright angry. I couldn't get out of that radio station fast enough. At my request, we went straight to a church to pray and as I dropped to my knees, I asked, 'Blessed Mother, how could you hang me out to dry like that? Where were you when I needed you?'

"Instantly, I received her answer in my heart: *'If you would spend more time reading Scripture, and less on television and other distractions, you would have known the answers.'* And then as if in confirmation, I was filled with discernment and knew the answers to the questions that had so embarrassed me!"

As we left the restaurant, I told Rogie, "I learned from that experience that although I was not a theologian, at least to be prepared by reading Scripture as often as possible, and learning to apply it in daily living."

That evening, following Mass and an early talk, I asked Rogie to come to my hotel room and pray the rosary with me. "If you don't, I'll never stay awake long enough to complete it." It was only a little after 7 o'clock when we began the rosary, and I dozed off several times. But we completed it and immediately after, I collapsed on the bed and was out for more than twelve hours. With the grace of God, I had survived two of the longest and hardest days I would ever experience in the mission.

Things didn't get easier as the Center had scheduled several talks each day, but my stamina returned to a level where it could be accomplished. By far the most difficult and stressful part of each day was driving through the city's traffic and seeing so much poverty.

But there were so many graces. I was scheduled for a noon talk at a large bank of all places, expecting only a handful of listeners since they had to come on their lunch hour. I wondered why the Center had chosen a bank as a speaking site. To my utter shock and delight, more than fifteen hundred people filled a special assembly hall in Manila's largest bank, including most of the top executive officers, who didn't seem to mind when the scheduled time overran by a full hour. Throughout the bank's offices, there were pictures of Jesus and Mary on almost every desk, something unheard of in the States. It was just one more sign that the Philippine people were deeply consecrated to Our Lady.

In hindsight, the Center had done a excellent job of reaching all segments of the population. One morning I spoke to a huge assembly of officers and enlisted men in the Philippine military. Again, I was amazed when the second-highest officer of the Armed Forces pulled out a rosary and said he carried it in place of a gun. What better example of the message of peace through prayer rather than guns?

Another morning, I was at a university located in the heart of the poorest section of the city. Rickety and in desperate need of paint and repair, this Catholic-run school which served the poorest of the poor was somehow squeezed in between the clutter of shops and offices. The students were dressed in thin, tattered clothing, but they were neat and clean, and eager to learn. A priest told me that the majority of them came from the barrios along the banks of the river.

And then came a surprise. Since my arrival, Lydia had attempted to arrange an appointment with Corazon Aquino, so I could present her with a copy of my book. It looked as though no time was available when suddenly the call came from the president's office: a fifteen-minute meeting with President Corazon Aquino had been arranged for that morning. I was elated! It was literally as well as symbolically another of the "grand castles" referred to by Our Lady in the Trinidad prophecy.

We arrived at Malacanyang Palace and were escorted to a reception room on the second floor. Within minutes President Aquino arrived, followed by a phalanx of media, and a barrage of flashbulbs as we were introduced and I presented her with a copy of my book.

"I have followed Medjugorje closely," President Aquino told me a few minutes later in a private reception room as we enjoyed hot tea. "And I want to go there for a pilgrimage when my term is over." I asked her if she planned to run for a second term. "No, eight years is enough. I think I have accomplished all that I can and I look forward to peace and privacy as a private citizen!"

The fifteen minutes stretched into more than thirty as we shared stories of Medjugorje and her ordeals as president. She was convinced that each coup attempt was aimed at not only removing her from office but killing her. "But I just keep praying my rosary and doing the best I can," she smiled.

We left after several impromptu interviews with the press on the palace grounds. A final questioner wanted to know in general what I thought of the president. I didn't hesitate in answering, remembering what Cardinal Sin had told me concerning his meeting with Sister Lucia of Fatima: "Corazon Aquino is indeed a special gift to the Philippine people during these times."

As I prepared for the final day, I thanked God for bringing me to the Philippines, but also that I was finally leaving. I couldn't remember being so stressed out during any other tour. And the reason why was there in front of me each day. It was the endless signs of acute poverty, and the sharp contrast with those who were not poor. There was little in between.

"This morning is very special," Lydia said as we left the Roches home. "Your final talk is to the rebel officers and men who were involved in the coup attempt last month." She related that the officer "with the rosary instead of a gun" had been impressed with the talk to his men and had arranged for me to speak to the prisoners at this last minute.

"That's great, and I have to admit I'm glad it's the last stop. I'm more than ready to return home and take a break."

Lydia sighed. "I understand. We are doing all possible to correct twenty years of oppression, but it will take a very long time and a lot of prayers and work."

The talk at the military base turned out to be extra special. The prisoners responded openly even though they were definitely a "captive" audience. Afterward I went though their ranks shaking hands with many of them and handing out medals from Medjugorje. Leaving the base I raised my arms to the sky. "Finished—at last!"

Just as I prepared to enter the car, one of the ladies of the Center took me by the arm. "I wonder if I could ask a small favor of you; would you be willing to make one more stop?"

I slumped into the seat, asking in a small voice, "What is it?"

"Just a block away, there is a small barrio of little homes that were struck by bombs during the coup attempt, and the mother and father of one family had to be taken to the hospital with injuries."

"You want me to go visit them at the hospital?"

"No, not the parents but their children. I was hoping you would come to their home to pray with them. They are waiting for you and are so excited that an American would come to spend time with them."

My heart leaped with fear—and anger over this woman's assumption that I would do this with no advance notice. But the overriding feeling was excruciating waves of guilt; *I did not want to go into that barrio!* "Oh, Blessed Mother Mary," I prayed silently and quickly, "please don't make me go into that place!"

But I knew I had to. This was the strongest challenge to date to truly live the messages of Medjugorje. I felt so much sorrow and helplessness for these poor people; yet, now with an opportunity to actually be with them in their daily environment, and to give something of myself in this tiny, insignificant way, I was actually trying to get out of having to do it! The woman was waiting for an answer. "Okay, if it doesn't take too much time . . ."

We walked quickly around the corner and there sprawled along the base of the high walls as far as I could see, were clusters of homes of cardboard and wood. I began to tremble. The stench was suffocating as we entered into the dark, narrow hallway leading to the home of these children. I thought I was going to be physically sick. Only then did I sense Our Lady's presence, filling my heart with her comforting words: *"These are my children also, and I am here with you."*

At once, I felt calm. Chickens and small pigs were running to and fro, but the dirt floor was swept smooth and clean. Peering into the tiny rooms along the way, I saw pictures of Jesus and Mary on the walls. We came to a small, open area and there were the children, waiting timidly for my arrival, surrounded by a crowd of adults who had also come to see this American. Each child was neatly dressed, with hair combed and eyes shining brightly with curiosity. There was hardly room to move.

The lady who had asked me to come to the barrio was smiling broadly as she called out their names in introductions. "And this is the American who has come to tell us about Our Lady and to pray with you for your mother and father!"

I could barely speak. I said a few words about Medjugorje, looking directly at the children as I spoke. Afterwards, we formed a little circle holding hands and began praying the Our Father. It was too much; tears streamed down my cheeks and I could not finish the prayer. Now I was grateful for having the opportunity to be here among these people. The words of Scripture, "Whatever ye do to the least of mine, ye do to me," echoed through my heart.

I hugged each child as I would my own. There was no longer revulsion. And then to delighted squeals of happiness, I gave each child a medal from Medjugorje blessed by Our Lady. We stayed far longer than planned, and I was reluctant to leave when Lydia reminded us that we had to go.

Five hours later I was at last on my way home. I would never forget the Philippines. The truth was, I couldn't. It had been twelve hectic days, filled with the stress of traffic, the unbelievable poverty, and the constant threat of danger.

But of far greater importance, it had been twelve days of living with and learning from a people truly consecrated to the heart of the mother of Jesus.

14

"God alone cures."

"I cannot cure. God alone cures. Pray! I will pray with you. Believe firmly . . ."

"Twelve different cities in 12 days?" I stared in disbelief at my English host.

Tony Hickey shrugged his shoulders and nervously cleared his throat, a little flustered at my reaction. "I'm afraid you've only yourself to blame. After your last tour and now that the United Kingdom finally knows about Medjugorje, you're wanted everywhere. We've a tremendous response for all twelve venues!"

Tony proved to be right. From the first event, the crowds were enormous, due in no small part to the excellent pre-tour publicity generated by his Manchester Medjugorje center and its volunteers throughout the country. Normally quiet and low-key, Tony operated the center with fervor, even though he held a full-time teaching position as religious instructor at a local Catholic high school. He had returned from his initial pilgrimage to Medjugorje filled with a sense of mission just as I had.

The Manchester Center organized pilgrimages to

Medjugorje, helped set up prayer groups and distributed materials including a monthly newsletter. One Saturday a month a full day of prayer was held, usually with a guest speaker and a special peace Mass. After several venues in nearby cities and towns, we gathered in Manchester for that special day of prayer.

From there it was on to Scotland for a weekend youth retreat at a place called Craig Lodge, nestled high in the beautiful hill country. After a pilgrimage to the little village, the owners of the lodge, Callum and Mary Anne MacFarlane-Barrow, had converted their once-lucrative business of a popular hunting lodge into a retreat house of prayer. Youth groups came once a month and more than seventy were present for the two-day session.

They came from all over the country, and from all levels of spirituality. As always they were blunt in their questions. Following a morning Mass, I talked of family, using my own as an example of what happens when the family unit is destroyed. "Even now, although my whole life is devoted to speaking about the messages, I have a son who still does not listen or believe. That comes directly from the breakup of our family, and the only thing I can do now is pray for him and hope he'll find conversion."

I concluded by saying I would be happy to answer any questions. A young man raised his hand. "Why did you go through divorce, and why aren't you Catholic, if you love this church so much?"

Taken aback, I hesitated a moment before attempting an answer. Immediately, an Irish girl near the front added: "And how can you become Catholic if you're divorced?"

Taking a deep breath, I stated that the divorce was the result of two major factors: immaturity and a lukewarm faith. "I came from a home where my father and mother were divorced, and I promised myself at a very early age that I would never do to my kids what they had done to me and my brother and sister. But I did."

I paused, wanting to make sure they understood clearly what I was about to say. "The thing is, divorce usually can't be undone. I've remarried and have two more children. But because of Medjugorje, I found Jesus—a real, live, and forgiving Jesus. And I finally found true peace. Because of Medjugorje, especially the Holy Mass and the Eucharist, I felt a strong desire to enter the Catholic faith. Now, I have to go through a process under the authority of the Church."

I briefly explained how the tribunal process of nullifying a marriage worked, comparing it to a regular trial with the "court" studying the evidence and then coming to a decision. "What about your children from your first marriage? What does this do to them?" The Irish girl, coming from a country that does not allow divorce, persisted.

"Annulment does not change the fact that they are still my children. It simply allows an opportunity to fully submit to God's will through obedience to the laws of the Church. You see," I added, "that is what conversion is all about—being obedient to God's will. Of course, as in any trial, it does not guarantee a positive result and automatic entry into the Church," I concluded, hoping this would end the personal questioning. Thankfully it did.

It was more than ironic that this question should be asked following the morning Mass. Just before coming to England, I had broken down under the emotion of it all during a daily mass in Myrtle Beach. It had been the fall of 1986 when I first filed, and still, there was no ruling on my annulment. Completely broken, I had prayed, "Lord, Your will be done. If I'm never able to enter this church, then, I accept that." In a sudden rush of inner peace, I realized I had to give Him everything.

A week later while touring Texas, Maureen Thompson, who had been on my first pilgrimage to Medjugorje in May, 1986, was at the airport as I arrived in Weslaco, a small town on the United States–Mexico border. They had flown her in as a special surprise to share the program with me since she had spent a year after our pilgrimage working as a registered nurse in a birthing clinic in Weslaco.

Maureen and I had become good friends on that first pilgrimage. She was fascinated that a Protestant would go to Medjugorje, and as she explained and taught me about the Catholic Church during the days there, she became my "Catholic Connection." Shortly after returning from Medjugorje, Maureen and her fiancée, Fred Lomady, stayed a night with us on the drive from her home to Weslaco. In the past couple of years, she and her family had assisted in arranging speaking engagements for me in the Philadelphia area. "What a surprise!" I exclaimed as I hugged her.

"Well, when they called and asked me to come, I felt it would be a good opportunity to see you and all of my friends here. Besides, I wanted to see Brother David again."

I vaguely remembered her telling me about him.

At lunch, Maureen refreshed my memory of Brother David Lopez, a Third Order Franciscan lay brother, who ran a small retreat house near the border. Its mission was to assist illegal aliens with food and shelter. The amazing thing was David suffered from severe cerebral palsy, causing him great difficulty in walking, talking, and generally caring for himself, much less in taking on the responsibility of taking care of others. Even more amazing, he had made four pilgrimages to Medjugorje.

Brother David claimed to have received locution messages from Jesus and the Virgin Mary since early youth. "I truly believe him after spending so much time with him while I was here," Maureen continued. "On his last trip, he says he received a special message about the future times."

This last bit of information intrigued me. In fact, contrary to my usual reaction to such claims of visions and locutions, I felt something special concerning this Franciscan layman. I had learned through the first years of the mission to listen carefully but to keep other apparition claims at arm's length, not wanting anything to interfere or distract from what I had received through Medjugorje.

Following the talks, Maureen introduced me to Brother David. "I wonder if I might be able to talk to you privately," I asked spontaneously, feeling a need to share with him my dilemma concerning coming into the Catholic Church.

Brother David smiled and with difficulty responded, "Of course, let's go where it will be quiet." He began to slowly make his way to a corner of the auditorium.

Settling into our chairs, he asked how he could help me. I hesitated a moment and then answered, "I don't know. I just know I'm supposed to talk to you."

I looked at Brother David for a long time as he sat in silence. He truly exuded holiness and though only 33 years old, he appeared older. But as he gazed at me through calm, brown eyes that reminded me of the eyes of Jesus, I felt tears welling in my own eyes. The emotion, pain, and frustration of the last three years in waiting to hear about the annulment poured forth. "I know I have to be patient, and I have accepted the fact that I might never be able to enter the Church but at times, it's so difficult."

"Our Lady says it will be two more years."

He said it with difficulty but so slowly, that it took a few seconds to register. I felt the impact of the last three words—two more years. But there was also great relief that at the end of that time I would become a true Roman Catholic.

Now, even in the face of such blunt questions from these young people, I was at peace.

From Scotland, I journeyed into Wales for the first time, having missed this part of the United Kingdom on the previous tour. I was met at the train station by Rose and John Walsch. They had been to Medjugorje through Tony Hickey's center and were now deeply involved in helping him. "We're very happy to have you in Wales this trip. There's a very large following of Medjugorje here, many through reading your articles. We were disappointed you couldn't include this area on your first tour."

So was I—especially now that I was here. Wales was beautiful rolling countryside, and the people were open and friendly.

Rose prepared an excellent meal before the evening's events. As we prepared to enjoy delicious homemade pie and hot coffee, she asked, "I wonder if you might do us a special favor this evening?"

"Of course, what is it?"

She paused after cutting several slices of pie. "Well, I'm sure this happens everywhere you go, but there is a family here who is in desperate need of special prayer." She went on to tell me of the Loftus family, a devout family that was suddenly confronted with the tragic medical diagnosis of terminal cancer of their ten-year-old daughter, Geraldine. "To make matters worse, they adopted a little two-year-old boy who is mentally handicapped. They purposely adopted him knowing of his condition, fully prepared to take care of him. And now this shocking news. If you could please just take the time to pray with the mother, who will be at the talk this evening."

I never got used to hearing such stories, especially involving children. "I'll be glad to. Will her little girl also be at the talk?"

"Oh, no, she's far too ill and her father is staying home to care for her and the little boy, but her mother Pat strongly feels your prayers can help."

Praying for people was part of what had been given to me through the prophecy message at Trinidad. As I thought about that I suddenly asked: "Listen, is Geraldine's home along the way to the site of the talk?"

Rose stopped preparing the coffee and came over to my chair. "It's not on the route but then it's not too far away. Why do you ask?"

I could feel an urging from within. "Rose, could we stop by on the way? I'd like to pray over Geraldine and her adopted brother."

Her eyes lit up. "Would you do that?" Before I could answer she dashed for the telephone and called the Loftus home. Flushed and beaming with happiness, she quickly hung up the receiver. "They would be absolutely thrilled if you came—but we must leave now!" And with that, Rose grabbed her coat and dashed out the door yelling for us to hurry along.

We entered the Loftus home, greeted by a grateful father. "Just last night, we watched a video in which you spoke about Medjugorje, and now you're here!" That was another amazing part of what was happening. The video and information from Rose and her husband was the first knowledge the Loftus family had of Medjugorje.

Terry Loftus led me into his living room. "This is Geraldine."

Geraldine got up from where she was sitting on the floor watching television and extended a thin little hand. She was pale, emaciated, and very white, and wore a red cap to cover her baldness caused by chemotherapy. But her eyes shone with a special brightness. Although she was shy, we were immediately friends.

In the short twenty minutes we were there, I fell in love with this little girl. Wrapping my arms around her, I asked with all my soul for God to grant a healing, asking primarily that her family have the peace to accept whatever her fate. As I prayed, I knew Geraldine needed to go to Medjugorje.

At the gentle urging of Rose reminding us of the time, we prepared to leave. I wanted to stay with this child, to spend more time with her, but I could only promise her that I would see her again. I knew in my heart that she would be healed; it was initiated by my prayers, but would have to be completed at Medjugorje. I did not know why, only that she had to go.

As we drove in silence, I remembered Our Lady's special message about healing: *"I cannot heal–only God heals."* But I also recalled her saying more than once that she needs our prayers and our efforts. To a desperate family, prayer may seem a generic answer by sympathizers. But as is pointed out so often in her messages, it serves as the vehicle for the Holy Spirit to do His work.

After the talk, a surprised mother could hardly believe that we had stopped to see her daughter. Through tears of happiness and desperation, Pat Loftus told of Geraldine having had two operations for this cruel disease, first diagnosed when she was four. "We knew she was seriously ill, but never thought of it as cancer, or something fatal. She has such a good and loving heart for one so young. We couldn't believe this could happen. Even now Geraldine is helping to raise money for a special project to help other children; that is how she keeps her mind off her own sickness."

I promised Pat that somehow, I would arrange for Geraldine and at least one parent to visit Medjugorje as soon as possible.

"Oh, in the rush of things, you missed your dessert and coffee," Rose exclaimed as she surveyed her kitchen on our return. "Would you like some now?"

Filled with the emotion of the evening, I shook my head. "No thanks, I'll catch it the next time through." I just wanted to go to bed and absorb the wonder of the evening.

The following morning before leaving Wales, I telephoned Tony to make arrangements to get Geraldine to Medjugorje. "I'm going with a group of kids from our local school in April, so possibly we could get her there at that time. I'd like it to be when I'm there."

"Don't worry, we'll arrange it." Tony could sense the importance and the urgency of getting this little girl to Our Lady's special place.

From Wales I traveled again by train to Walsingham, a very special place as I would soon discover. Picked up at the station by two Anglican nuns, I was amazed to learn that Walsingham was the site of one of Our Lady's earliest-recorded apparitions. Now, thanks to Medjugorje's influence, it was the focus of newfound pilgrimages in the UK.

"This is a shrine for both Anglican and Catholic," one of the nuns explained. "Because of the interest in Medjugorje, many are now coming here to Walsingham, and it's been a place where both Catholic and Anglican can find the Blessed Mother leading them to Jesus."

As we drove to the rectory where I would be staying, they gave me the background of Walsingham. It owed its original fame to a woman named Richeldis de Faverches, who was the lady of the manor.

In 1061, Lady Richeldis was in prayer one morning when suddenly she had a vision of the Virgin Mary. She claimed she was taken to Nazareth in the Holy Land, and shown the simple home where Mary and Joseph had raised Jesus. The vision was repeated on two subsequent occasions and the noblewoman became convinced that she was being asked to build a replica of the home at Nazareth on her land.

Lady Richeldis erected a wooden replica of the house

revealed to her in her dream, and this became the heart of the medieval pilgrimage. It is said that the site on which the house was built was indicated by a spring of water which suddenly appeared. It became a holy well and later, a statue of the Virgin Mary was placed in the house, and she became "Our Lady of Walsingham."

The eleventh century was a time of great crusading zeal as Christian Europe sought to recapture the Holy Land. Walsingham was to become a focus of devotion for those who could not afford the time or money to make the hazardous journey to Israel. The little village became known as "England's Nazareth," and pilgrimages began in ever-growing numbers.

Naturally, the talk that evening centered on the unity of the two major faiths of the UK. I pointed out that the statue of Our Lady in Walsingham was significant in that Mary's left arm encompasses the baby Jesus, while her right arm cradles a scepter as she points to her Son. "Look at this statue and see how it signifies Our Lady's role throughout the centuries," I told them. "Regardless of whether it is Walsingham or Medjugorje, whether we are Catholic or Protestant, whether we are British or American, she is the magnet that draws pilgrims to Him."

There were two remaining days of talks, at London, and the campus of Cambridge University. How Tony had arranged for me to speak to the students of Cambridge, I did not know, but I was impressed, especially with the fact that I would be speaking in an old assembly hall last used for such an occasion by Saint John Fisher, a martyr of the Church who was beheaded for maintaining obedience to the Pope. He had refused to accept King Henry VIII as head of the English Church after the king declared himself its head in defiance of Rome's refusal to grant him a divorce. The irony was not lost on me.

The turnout was excellent. I had learned that college

crowds were usually modest in size, often skeptical and sometimes rude. Earlier in the tour, I had spoken at Glasgow College in Scotland, to a much smaller crowd. There had been a strange incident, as a young girl walked out in the middle of the talk, staring with hatred at me and silently mouthing "liar!" repeatedly as she left the room. The look on her face was frightening; but I had continued without interruption, praying for extra strength from the Holy Spirit.

The Cambridge students, along with a solid turnout of people from surrounding areas, asked many questions and seemed genuinely interested. I had concentrated on the many tests of authentication by authorities of science, medicine, and theology; but I also wanted to make clear that such supernatural events had to be tested by faith alone to truly create ongoing conversion to God. Again, nothing was planned in advance, but what was given was perfectly honed for this particularly scholarly gathering.

The last stop in London was a fitting close to a difficult but rewarding tour. I had been from one end of the country to the other and felt blessed especially with the opportunity to take the message to Cambridge and Walsingham. But the highlight was Wales and praying over Geraldine.

And in a country wracked with division, Medjugorje's message was desperately needed. The divisions are not outward or wracked with violence such as in Northern Ireland, but they are there. In a land where less than twenty per cent of the population attends church of any kind, where the "center of the world" for abortion is located, according to an earlier message from Our Lady, Medjugorje was slowly but surely bringing the cure. Centers had been organized, prayer groups developed in many different parishes, and people were turning to God.

Tony Hickey wasted little time in arranging a trip to

Medjugorje for Geraldine—and her entire family. And it would coincide with my planned trip there with a group of teenagers from the local Catholic school. "That's absolutely great, Tony! How did you manage to include the rest of the family?"

True to form, Tony was reluctant to take credit. "We have some very generous followers and they were more than pleased to help."

There was a slight, but pleasant complication in the scheduling. Yolanda Nardizzi had telephoned from Australia a few days before. "Listen, Wayne, do you remember us talking about possibly arranging a tour to Rome? Well, it's been done and it's scheduled for April. We'll be in and around Rome for six days, and then go on to Medjugorje for another week, and we'd love to have you and Terri join us."

Her tour group would arrive in Rome a day before our pilgrimage to Medjugorje was due to return home. "Yolanda, I'd love to do that and bring Terri but I'm going to be in Medjugorje when you arrive in Rome and–"

"Before you say no," she interrupted, "let me add that we will be spending a great deal of time in Rome with Father Don Stephano Gobbi. He will celebrate Mass with us and we'll be able to spend some informal time with him. Also, we'll be visiting with Bruno Cornicchiola."

That changed things. I was anxious to meet and listen to Father Gobbi, having read much of the book of messages given to him by Our Lady. As for Bruno Cornicchiola, there was faint interest but it came second to being with this priest who headed up the Marian Movement of Priests. I told Yolanda I would get back to her with an answer as soon as possible.

Remarkably, it worked out if I cut one day off my Medjugorje tour, and one from the scheduled time in Rome; Terri, thrilled at the opportunity to tour Rome and

Assisi, would meet me there and we'd spend five of the six scheduled days with the Australian group before returning home.

Assisi would be special. It was the home of Saint Francis, a favorite saint for both of us. The trip there would be the only one outside of the Rome area. Our itinerary included the Vatican and a general audience with Pope John Paul II, one of my modern-day heroes whom I admired long before becoming involved with Medjugorje.

I called Yolanda to confirm that we would join the tour, happy that Terri would be able to meet these people who had been so kind to me on my recent tour through Australia. "We look forward to meeting her also," Yolanda replied, "and you'll love Father Gobbi!"

For some reason, Assisi seemed the most important part of the entire journey. I would soon understand why. . . .

15
Clothed in Obedience

"Dear children, from day to day I wish to clothe you in holiness, goodness, obedience, and God's love . . ."

It was hard to believe, but I would be making my fourteenth trip to Medjugorje. Each was unique in itself; this one because others from Myrtle Beach would be on the pilgrimage, including for the second year, teenagers from the local St. Andrew Catholic school.

The schoolkids were winners of a special contest we sponsored, where they were asked to write an essay on what their faith meant to them and why they would like to go to Medjugorje. Two students from each grade, fifth through eighth grade, were selected as winners. It was a good way to give something back to Medjugorje in thanksgiving for what it had given me. The Virgin Mary strongly encouraged getting youth involved; what better way than to take a group from the school?

This year, the priest, Father Garry Dilley would be the first clergyman of any church in our community to go. That was especially pleasing as I had asked many from various faiths to accompany me on past trips.

"Maybe at some future date," my Lutheran pastor Bill Wingard had answered when I pressed him, hoping he might also come. Theological reservations along with health concerns were given as reasons for declining. But by his answer there was hope that someday he would accept the invitation.

We arrived the first week in June to moderate weather and large crowds. Medjugorje was now a thriving community heavily dependent on the steady influx of pilgrims. In fact, too heavily dependent.

The number of Medjugorje families no longer attending daily Mass was growing. They had become preoccupied taking care of visitors. Fasting was forgotten in many of the pilgrim homes, with meat and a full menu served on Wednesdays and Fridays where only months before, breads and salads were the fare. Along with ever-increasing numbers of tiny souvenir shops set up along even the paths through the fields, there were shops selling merchandise totally unrelated to the setting and its supernatural event. On top of this many of the guides were nonbelievers.

"Boy, is this place changing," I remarked to our guide as the bus made its way toward the home where the group would be staying.

"Yes, many people come from Sarajevo and Dubrovnik to work here, and also from other cities to make money. There is much unemployment in Bosnia. Even taxi drivers come from these places to make more money." The guide was also from Split, but quickly added, "I have relatives here." The problem with the majority of guides, taxi drivers, and tour operators from outside Medjugorje, she continued, was that most were without faith. Again she swiftly assured me, "I am a Christian."

The stories of late night partying and some female guides actually having had abortions while continuing to lead pilgrimages in Medjugorje, were well chronicled. "It is a terrible situation," she sighed, "but with so many pilgrims coming now, and more than 75,000 expected for the ninth anniversary of the apparitions later this month, there is nothing that can be done at the moment."

"Well, we can only hope they find the truth of Jesus by working here. It's happened before."

The guide smiled. "Oh, yes, like Anka Blazevic."

I nodded. No matter how distressing the present situation was, it was countered by the tremendous spiritual conversion of this guide who now worked as translator and assistant for Father Jozo Zovko. Large groups of pilgrims regularly traveled the 25 miles from Medjugorje to Tihaljina, his present parish, to see and hear him. This charismatic priest had played a prominent part in Anka's conversion and often asked her to give her testimony. That is how I met her and first learned her story.

Anka Blazovic grew up in Northern Croatia in a predominantly Orthodox region. She told of her atheistic education and the contempt for the Catholic Church that had been inculcated in her by the Communist Party in which she had been active since early youth. Early in her childhood, her family had been broken by divorce and an alcoholic mother.

After a year in Mexico preparing for her degree thesis, Anka went to a meditation center in Italy. There she learned to concentrate, be silent and to find her inner self. But it was done without knowing or seeking God. Immediately she decided not to return to the world, but to go to a monastery in Holland where there was a meditation center for women.

Here her story took a special Medjugorje twist. Anka woke up one morning with a discernment that she was not to go to the monastery. Instead, she was to go to

Dubrovnik to use her fluent, multi-language skills as a tour guide. Why, she did not know. She was frightened by the intensity of the inner urge, and of the thought of returning to this beautiful but decadent city where she had led such an impure life.

Anka's first assignment as a guide was to lead a group of pilgrims to Medjugorje. To prepare for her duties, she went there alone and for the first time in her life, entered a Catholic Church where an Italian-language Mass was in progress with Holy Communion being distributed. She knew nothing about the Eucharist or about Jesus and Mary.

Suddenly, Anka experienced something special and mystical; as the recipients of the Eucharist returned to their pews, they were literally filled with a brilliant illumination that seemed to flood the church and stream toward her. Anka knew immediately in her heart that she had been favored by God with the special grace of witnessing the mystic transformation of bread and wine into the actual body and blood of Jesus. And she knew she was being called to this Jesus whom she did not know.

The pilgrims Anka led to Medjugorje did not realize that their guide was not a Christian; she climbed the hill and the mountain, visited the visionaries—and met Father Jozo, who knew immediately of her transformation without her having said anything to him. He prayed over her, gave her a special cross, and later asked her to work with him in Tihaljina. This guide now was a full child of the Virgin Mary, who would continue to lead her to Jesus.

"It is a story of hope for all of us who work here," the guide said.

"Yes, it is." I thought of the beautiful Scripture story of Jesus leaving the flock of 100 to rescue the one lost sheep. And with the rescue of one, comes a crescendo of hosannas from heaven. As long as we remembered this, nothing would stop the grace flowing from Medjugorje.

"Ah, Wayne, you are here just in time for dinner!"

I was greeted by Paolo Lunetti, a young Italian pilgrim whom I had met here in the spring of 1987. It was
good to see him again and to know that he would also be
staying at Marija's home.

Marija hurried back to the kitchen after a quick greet-
ing, to help Kathleen Martin, who was still living with
Marija and her family. I hadn't seen her since their trip to
Birmingham, Alabama, when she accompanied Marija and
her brother Andrija for the kidney transplant operation.
As with so many thousands, she too had a special conversion story, having come to Medjugorje in early 1986 and
remaining except for short excursions in Europe and the
states.

Marija beamed as she prepared the table for dinner,
happy to share conversation and food with friends. "Also
Terry from Birmingham, is coming for dinner tonight,"
she added placing another setting on the table. "He is here
with a group."

It was good to be with Marija and these friends again,
and to see her able to relax and enjoy the normal plea-
sures of daily living that had become premium since being chosen as a visionary by Our Lady. Conversation during
dinner centered on the bishop of Mostar's recent attempt
to put an end to the apparitions. He continued attacking
the visionaries personally and accusing the Franciscan
priests of staging the apparitions in order to earn money
for their communities. His latest attack came by way of a
pamphlet he had written and distributed at the Vatican
on a recent visit there.

"Yes, but it has backfired," Paulo said. "He had been
told by the Vatican not to comment personally on the apparitions and the distributing of this pamphlet has upset
many of the Vatican officials because it interferes with the
work of the commission that is investigating Medjugorje."

"It's just one more distraction from the messages," I sighed, remembering the conversation with the tour guide earlier in the afternoon.

"We must pray for the bishop," Marija interjected. "That is what Gospa is asking of us."

Of course, she was right. I quickly changed the subject, asking Paolo how he was doing in school. "Fine, so far," he answered. But I surmised he was not sure this was the right direction for his life.

Paolo was seriously considering the priesthood. He had graduated from one of the finest universities in Italy with excellent grades and eventually took a position as an economist in a large bank in Milan. But after a pilgrimage to Medjugorje, and especially after meeting Marija, his career interests changed dramatically. Quitting his job, Paolo had since made several return trips to Medjugorje and like myself, had become close friends with Marija.

But there was a difference in their friendship. It was evident when around Marija and Paolo that they had more than casual interest in each other. Deeply respectful of Marija and knowing of her stated desire to one day enter the convent, Paolo was concerned. He did not want to interfere with Gospa's plans and because of his own conversion, felt that he too, might be experiencing a call to the priesthood.

We talked for hours one evening during my last visit to Medjugorje, slowly walking around the outer perimeter of the village twice. I knew what was bothering him and was flattered when he asked my advice about becoming a priest. It was the cementing of a friendship that went beyond our Medjugorje ties. Shortly after, he had entered a university in Rome to begin preliminary studies in theology.

We continued talking after dinner, and when I told him that I would be going on to Rome to join my Australian friends, he suggested that we drive there together since he was leaving the same day. "We will stop at my home in Milan to pick up my mother, and then drive to Rome the next morning, as my classes resume the following day."

"Sounds good to me." I looked forward to the opportunity of seeing the northern area of Croatia and Italy, but more so to spending extended time with Paolo.

Later, the four of us settled into a small room to watch an old black and white television that had been given to Marija. She loved old movies and had significantly increased her use of English from viewing them. We talked and watched simultaneously, munching on popcorn and generally enjoying a quiet evening.

Suddenly, the quiet was broken by a disturbance on the street in front of Marija's home. Shouts could be heard followed by the sounds of scuffling. Peering out the window, Marija turned and headed for the door. "It is Croatians and Serbians fighting," she said over her shoulder as she quickly bounced down the stairs and into the small courtyard of her home.

We watched from the window as she talked calmly with all of the men involved. Even in the dimness of the evening it was clear they were young and had been drinking heavily. About ten Croatians had one Serbian surrounded and were pushing and shoving him around because he had been shouting Serbian nationalistic slogans.

Within minutes they began to disperse and Marija returned to the room. Her cheeks flushed and eyes dancing, she shook her head slowly. "They drink and then the fighting begins. One day soon it will turn into real war. That is why Gospa asks us so many times to pray for peace."

Such open hostility by Croatians against Serbs would not have occurred just a little more than a year ago. But hope among the Croatians was high that an independent Croatia, and Bosnia-Hercegovina was close at hand.

In early 1989, with Communism falling everywhere, the federal government became a victim of its own paranoia. A national referendum was ordered, with the Communists sure this would solidify the individual governments of the six republics that made up Yugoslavia. The last thing expected was the overwhelming defeat of Communism in the first totally free election in the Federation since 1918.

Emboldened by this dramatic change, Croatians began a purge of Serbs who had for so many years been their persecutors. Now, Slovenia and Croatia were negotiating for complete withdrawal from the Federation; the intent was to become free nations, no longer subjugated to the harsh dictates of Serbia and its dream of continued domination as Greater Serbia. Only the Serbs and Montenegrans voted to keep Communism, simply changing the party name to Socialist.

"This is why so much has changed here," Marija said. "With the good of freedom comes the bad of wanting too much, too quickly."

I began to comprehend the changes I witnessed coming into the village earlier in the day. Even little Medjugorje was getting "drunk" with the new freedom. Pilgrims were pouring in. Building was taking place everywhere, including around the church grounds. A beautiful stone plaza now surrounded the church; the road leading in to the church had been widened and many new shops and pilgrim homes constructed on both sides. A huge outdoor altar had been erected in the rear of the church and on warm summer days was jammed on all sides with pilgrims.

The conversation for the remainder of the evening focused on what many Croatians in and around Medjugorje felt was inevitable: There would eventually be war between Croatia and Serbia. Little skirmishes such as the one in front of Marija's home were happening all too frequently.

"We can only pray and fast," Marija said quietly as we

ended the discussion and the evening.

It was good to attend the morning English Mass and see the students and others from Myrtle Beach, especially to see Father Dilley on the altar. He had taken time to listen to my story and understood that I had been called to a special mission. But following Mass, he was upset.

"Listen, I'm not going to Tihaljina to see this Father Jozo! I saw him early this morning giving our guide one of the worst beratings I've ever witnessed. He was screaming at her! How can he be so holy with that kind of temper?"

I immediately knew why our guide had received such a reprimand. "Father, this is the way these people live. The Church is the center of their lives and the priests are the real leaders."

"But what excuse does he have for acting that way? What did she do that was so horrible?"

"She was organizing a group of pilgrims to take one day of their pilgrimage and travel to Dubrovnik for sightseeing and shopping. Father Jozo and the other Franciscans stress to the tour companies and guides that the pilgrims come for a spiritual week and it should not be interrupted by things of the world. Look around here at all of the distractions. That doesn't excuse the excess of his actions but maybe you'll understand his concern."

"I understand," Father Dilley responded, "but he shouldn't have done it in front of us."

"Well, he may be holy, but he's still human. Listen, Father Jozo knows these guides. He knows which ones are here for the right reasons and those who are not. He doesn't want them to be lost anymore than he would a visiting pilgrim."

Father Dilley did go to Tihaljina with the rest of our pilgrimage, and was relieved to see Father Jozo hugging our guide after his talk. "You're right about his gift of preaching," Father Dilley said as we watched the pilgrims mass around Father Jozo. "He's a powerful speaker, and after hearing Anka's story, I can see why he got so upset with our guide."

The remainder of the pilgrimage went well. I was sorry to have to leave a day early but anxious to get to Rome where Terri and the Australian group would be waiting. The drive from Medjugorje took more than ten hours because of a steady drizzle of rain that began as we entered Italy. My only regret at driving with Paolo was the terrific speed at which he drove, and the weaving in and out along the mountains. But he was a superb driver and I had my opportunity to drive a few hours at rates of speed impossible in the States. It was exhilarating!

We spent the night, arriving late in Monza, and enjoying an outstanding dinner prepared by his mother, Millie. Six hours after leaving Milan the following morning, we arrived in Rome which literally took my breath away.

"Can you believe we're actually in Rome, I mean actually here with Yolanda and Joe, and the others from Australia?" I was bubbling over to Terri after Paolo had dropped me off at the hotel where the group was staying.

She was just as excited. "It's great and we have a super itinerary including going to Assisi." I knew that part would be special for her as Saint Francis was also on her favorite saints list.

"And don't forget about the time we're spending with Father Gobbi," Yolanda added. She and Joe had already met Terri and spent several hours in conversation while awaiting my arrival.

Vince Lombardo, also with the group chimed in, "He's going to meet with us here at the hotel for a private question and answer session, something he's never done with lay people before." Vince reached over and squeezed my arm. "And you'll have the grace of meeting Bruno Cornicchiola at the monastery where he lives."

"I don't think that will be possible for us, Vince," I said as I looked over the written itinerary. "The group is due to see him on the last day. We have to leave for home on that day." Vince was disappointed at this news, but for some inexplicable reason, I was not disturbed at missing meeting Bruno.

The next few days were everything we could possibly have hoped for. How happy I was to be with these special friends from Australia. It was a whirlwind tour, including a general audience with Pope John Paul II. Paolo's mother went with us to see the Pope, and Paolo was able to join us for Mass with Father Gobbi as celebrant.

Paolo was able to spend additional time with us between studying and his classes, taking us one evening to a remote Franciscan monastery high on a hill overlooking Rome. We entered into a small chapel. Suddenly he called us over to a plaque embedded in the tile floor. "Do you know what this spot is?" He said excitedly as he read the inscription. "According to this, it is the exact spot where Saint Peter was martyred!"

This discovery and a myriad of special little graces filled the days. But an unexpected stop at a monastery about an hour outside of Rome would bring a grace far greater than all of the others combined.

We had just attended our second Mass with Father Gobbi, after which he joined us for lunch at a nearby restaurant. As we made our way through the narrow country roads on our way back to the hotel, Yolanda suddenly stood up and asked the driver to stop the bus. Grabbing me by the arm she dragged me to the front of the bus along with Joe and Vince. "Listen, this is the monastery where Bruno Cornicchiola lives. You've got to go and see him now!"

"Yolanda, I don't really need to see him. He may not be here. Besides, I believe his story." I did not want to get off the bus.

"That's not it, I just know you have to go and see him—now!" With that she pushed me out the door where Joe and Vince Lombardo were waiting. "You need Vince to introduce you and to interpret. Joe can help."

Exasperated, I looked at Terri who gave a helpless look and wave as the bus pulled away. "But how are we supposed to get back to the hotel?"

Yolanda stuck her head out of the window. "You'll find a way. Our Lady will help you. I just know you have to see him!" And with that the bus disappeared down the road leaving us standing there not quite sure what to do next.

"Well, I guess we better go and see if he's here," Vince grinned. He rang the bell at the entrance gate of the monastery which was enclosed in a tall, ancient iron fence. After a brief conversation over the speaker, the gate clicked open. "The brothers are in the chapel for afternoon prayers and we're asked to join them," Vince stated, striding swiftly toward the building.

We entered a small chapel to hushed chanting of the rosary by a group of about fifteen monks. I knelt in a pew near the front, hoping Bruno wasn't there. Why, I wondered, was I so reluctant to meet him? Suddenly from the back of the chapel came a high-pitched, strained voice leading the decades of the rosary. Vince leaned over and whispered, "That's Bruno."

I relaxed momentarily in the peace of the prayers, resigned that I would have to meet Bruno Cornicchiola. Later, Joe and I waited in the pews as Vince went into a back room where Bruno had immediately disappeared on completion of the prayers to see if he would meet with us. "What's wrong with Bruno's voice?" I asked Joe, noting during the prayers the effort it took for him to lead us.

"According to Vince, Bruno is physically attacked directly by Satan himself many times during the night. He chokes him and then drags him outside the gate of the monastery. The monks have confirmed that they have had to let him in often in the early morning hours, since the gate remains locked during the night."

I looked at Joe and was about to question the story when Vince returned. "He'll see you, but only for a few minutes. We're lucky to get that with no advance notice."

"You mean we're stuck here in the middle of nowhere just so we can spend a couple of minutes with this man?"

Vince moved closer and lowered his voice. "Cardinals and bishops come from all over the world to see him and hardly receive more than ten to fifteen minutes. We're blessed to spend time with Bruno, even if for only a few minutes."

Vince led us into the room where I was introduced to a small, frail man with snow white hair and beard. He had to be at least in his eighties, but his eyes were alive and blazing and as we looked at each other, I suddenly knew this meeting was important.

Speaking rapidly, Vince interpreted as I told Bruno my story, keeping it as brief as possible in consideration of the time. But I related everything, including the divorce and the long seven-year absence from all churches.

As I finished, Bruno stared hard at me and began speaking. "He says he has difficulty with Medjugorje because the people are not obeying the bishop who is in charge there, and he cautions you to proceed slowly until there is a clear directive from the Church," Vince explained.

"Tell him there is a commission consisting of all the bishops in Yugoslavia investigating the apparitions, and that this bishop himself has not followed the Vatican's directives concerning the investigation."

"He says it does not matter. The bishop is still head of the Church in that area, and he is to be obeyed."

My doubts about the meeting with this man returned. Just as I was about to stand up and politely end the meeting, Bruno smiled. "But he is pleased that you want to enter the Church, and as a former Protestant himself he would like to help you. He asks how long you will be in Rome?"

I relaxed again, wondering how he could possibly help. "We've got three more days."

Vince smiled broadly, shaking his head affirmatively after a long exchange with Bruno. "He says if you return here Monday, he will help arrange for you to come into the Church right away!"

My heart leaped; but the reality of the situation overrode the emotions. "That is very kind of him but tell him I'm married again and we are presently awaiting a ruling on an annulment."

Another long exchange. Vince, now feeling the embarrassment of having to interpret such personal exchanges, paused before translating. "This is difficult for me, but Bruno states—and he does so with compassion and not in judgment—that if you are living together as man and wife, you are living in sin in the eyes of the Church."

I felt a terrible discomfort. I now knew why I did not want to see this man. "But we were married by a minister and I've asked for forgiveness."

"Yes, but he stresses again that in the eyes of the Church you are not married until you receive an official ruling," Vince said softly. "He says in order to fully submit to the will of God, that you and your present wife should give the gift of celibacy, and live as brother and sister until the situation is resolved."

I gulped hard. A numbness left me seemingly paralyzed for what seemed a long time. There was no question in my heart that this was coming directly from heaven; and no question about my own willingness to comply. The problem was, how to tell Terri? And how would she react?

Bruno was smiling broadly as tears filled my eyes. He reached over and patted my shoulder. "He will pray for you and knows you are in the hands of the Blessed Mother," Vince smiled. I shook Bruno's hand, only able to utter a weak thank you for taking the time to see us.

Vince let out a loud whistle as he glanced at his watch. "Do you realize we've been with him for an hour and a half?"

It seemed only minutes. We were ushered into a small kitchen where hot tea had been prepared. And the preparer, a policeman from Rome who was a lay member of the monastery's order, insisted on driving us back to our hotel.

Arriving at the hotel just in time for dinner, the look of relief on Terri's face said it all. Yolanda, sitting across from her began apologizing. "Don't bother," I answered, "it was an incredible experience!"

"Here, sit down, all of you and tell us about it!" Yolanda was brimming with anticipation of the story.

Joe looked at me and then his wife. "I'll tell you about it later. Right now, I'm starved!"

As we returned to our room, Terri again asked about the meeting. I told her something very important had happened and to please give me a little time to pray about it and then I would explain. We were going to Assisi the next morning and I knew that was the place where I needed to talk to her. Surely, since St. Francis was so special to her, she would understand.

But she didn't.

We stood on the stairs leading to St. Francis' tomb at Assisi. I don't know why but I had chosen that place and moment to begin telling Terri what Bruno had said about our marriage. Terri was furious, her eyes flashed with anger as she struggled with her emotions. Members of our group were all around us as we prepared for Holy Mass in the little chapel that served as tomb for St. Francis and several of his closest followers.

"I can't believe you would tell me this here after I've waited so long to come to Assisi," she hissed as we moved to the very rear of the chapel and pulled our chairs back into the corner.

I was shocked and didn't know what to say. The Mass, so special in this holy place, was filled with tension. I kept asking myself what had gone wrong. As our group began filing out, we remained and I haltingly related the rest of what Bruno had said. She began to cry. And now I was even more flustered. Terri rarely shed tears. "What you're saying is that our children are illegitimate, and that our marriage is not valid and–"

"No, no, not in that sense. I just know that this is something we have to consider." I didn't know how to explain it and Terri had no desire at the moment to hear any explanations.

How could it have turned out this way? Completely frustrated, I quickly left the chapel area leaving Terri sitting there. For the next two and half hours, the bulk of the time we had left in Assisi, I walked through the streets trying to sort things out.

Returning to the chapel, I found my wife, now calm, quietly walking through the building. We looked at each other briefly but said nothing. It was time to leave, and we had seen little of Assisi. I didn't care, grateful that the storm was over and the emotions were quiet. After boarding the bus, Terri took my hand in hers, again without saying anything. Words at this point were unnecessary.

At the hotel we sat in the cool of the evening in a far corner of an outside patio, and finally talked. "Well?" I looked inquiringly at Terri, still unsure of what was going on in her mind. She just looked at me until I burst out with, "Look, I know this is difficult. But, we don't have to accept—"

"Yes we do," she said, startling me.

I started to object again but she held up her hand. "What changed your mind?" I asked.

Terri smiled and took her time before answering. "You know, after you left I sat there in front of St. Francis' tomb for a long time and a lot of thoughts drifted in and out of my mind. But the strongest thought was that St. Francis was asked by God to restore obedience and faith to Church doctrine. And I guess the longer I sat there, the more I knew that God was now asking us to do the same. That's why we applied for the annulments in the first place."

I started to say something. "Just a minute, I'm not finished. The thing for both of us to understand is that a commitment to live as brother and sister in obedience until the annulment process is completed has nothing to do with that process! It needs to be a freely given gift or sacrifice that is intended to draw us closer to Jesus."

I sat there dumbfounded. There was nothing more to say. Once again, in a way far beyond normal understanding, another important piece of the mosaic of the mission was put in place.

16
Courtney

".... Especially, dear children, pray that you may be able to accept sickness and suffering with love the way Jesus accepted them."

We returned home united in that we would do what Bruno Cornicchiola had advised. After further discussion, we went to our church and quietly kneeling in front of the tabernacle, promised to attempt to live in celibacy until a positive ruling on our annulments was officially received.

There was a peace felt by both of us, as though we had passed a difficult test. But it was short-lived, interrupted by return to the reality of daily living and all its nagging little problems. The latest was one that occurred frequently: my son Steve had lost his job—again. And again, he needed financial help.

I was mad. "Why can't you do something with your life? Why are you always having confrontations with people?" Out of chronic frustration with this problem, I could only yell at my son over the telephone as he told me of his latest dilemma, reversing the charges as usual.

"But it wasn't my fault, Dad!" Steve started to explain what had happened.

"It's never your fault," I answered in anger, cutting off his explanation which I had heard a hundred times before. The conversation ended as it had so many times: in total anger and frustration that a twenty-five-year-old couldn't get his life straight.

Sitting at my desk in the study trying to cool off, I wondered why my fasting and prayers seemed to work for others, but not my son. Especially since I had really concentrated on him after hearing the story of Victor Wee's mother in Singapore. I felt a sudden urge to pray for Steve and sunk to my knees. "Blessed Mother, please help me help my son!" It was a plea from parents I had heard often in the course of the mission. Immediately my heart was filled with an unexpected message: *"Send him to school."*

My head jerked up. Had I heard right?

"Put him in school!" There was no mistaking the second time. I immediately went to the living room where Terri was reading, telling her what had transpired.

"He barely graduated from high school," she began. "He's never indicated an interest in going to college, so what makes you think he can even get in? I think it's a waste of money, and you need to pray more on this one!"

I did. The result was the same. I left for Columbia the next day for another father-to-son chat with my son.

Throughout the two and a half hour drive, I thought about Steve, how he had always been my "thorn." He was always in mucky little trouble, unable to conform to society; and, he had had the strongest negative reaction at the time of my divorce. To make matters worse, I was forced to go to court shortly after Terri and I were married to accommodate his plea to come and live with us. He was twelve at the time, and I knew he would be in constant trouble if I didn't take control. That wasn't easy for Terri, and tension between them was always present.

We won the court battle but it was costly for my son.

His mother became bitter and an estrangement developed to the point she never came to visit him or arranged for him to come to her home in Columbia. And even now with the changes taking place in the other children, Steve remained the same. It was him against the world—including members of his family.

After the usual lecture in which I expressed for the thousandth time how he had disappointed me in just about everything, I sat Steve down and told him to listen carefully, because this was his last chance. "Steve, you know of my involvement in Medjugorje, and what I'm about to do comes straight from the Blessed Mother. It's the only reason I'm doing it because frankly . . ."

Steve looked at me quizzically. "What are you talking about?"

I took a deep breath. "Do you still want to go to school?"

"You mean college?"

"Yes, college. The University of South Carolina."

My son blinked, not believing what he was hearing.

"I'm willing to put you in school, to pay for your tuition and books, but you've got to get a job and pay for your room and board. And I'm not doing any of the legwork for enrollment. You've got to do that. If you don't get a job to take care of living expenses, and if you fail to take care of the enrollment requirements, then you won't go. That's it."

There was complete surprise and shock on his face. "One last thing," I continued, "if you make below a C grade or flunk out, the deal's over!"

Steve stood up, and hugged me. "Dad, I love you! I can't believe you're doing this for me!"

As I hugged my son back I thought to myself, "Neither can I!"

Changes were noticeable immediately. In the next few weeks, Steve obtained a job that would allow him to attend school and work nearly full-time. He also took care of all the enrollment details and was set to enter summer school by the first of June.

Even Terri was surprised. It was a proud day when I drove my oldest son to the university for his enrollment. "What does your mother think of all of this?" I asked.

Steve's eyes lit up and he turned in the seat. "Oh, I haven't told you what happened on Mother's Day. I went to see Mom and she started in again about the divorce and my leaving to come live with you. And you know what that leads to; I usually just get up and leave to avoid further arguing."

I knew that scene all too well. "What did you do?"

"I don't know why but for some reason I didn't get mad. I told Mom that this had been going on for ten years and it was about time it stopped and that we needed to talk. Well, she didn't want any part of that, but Lisa who was with me told her to listen for once." Steve then related that they talked for more than two hours, amidst accusations and tears. Finally, they hugged and promised to try and start anew.

As Steve finished the story, I fought back tears and silently thanked Our Lady. I was convinced this was the start of my son's conversion.

I was thankful for the beginning of summer. Physically and mentally drained from twenty-two individual trips taken in the first five months of the year, Terri insisted there would no added venues during the next three months. "You are officially on vacation," she stated with spousal authority upon my return from the last scheduled trip in May.

It was nice to have a normal life again. Days were spent attending Kennedy's Little League baseball games, and Rebecca's dance recitals. In between, there was golf and a few evenings dining out with my wife.

The only work being done was preliminary planning for the manuscript of a second book, a sequel to the first one. There was no rush as the deadline was early Spring of 1991, with publication slated for June. Thus, I was able to work at a leisurely pace and enjoy the everyday activities of family life.

A favorite chore assigned to me by Terri was to pick up Rebecca and two classmates after school and take them to dance class. Courtney, one of the little girls, was always the last one to the car. "Courtney," I would fuss with mock-sternness, "why are you always late?"

Smiling, she would climb in the front seat and hug me and answer in a sweet, little-girl voice, "I don't know, I just am!" Of course I melted. Courtney soon came to be like one of my own children.

Thus, it was with shock we received news on the first Sunday morning in June: Courtney had collapsed at home and had been rushed to the emergency room of the local hospital. Just a few days before, she had attended Rebecca's sixth birthday party and was noticeably not her usual spirited self. She was tired and did not want to participate in the array of games Terri had scheduled.

"The diagnosis at the emergency room is that she has a tumor at the base of her brain," Terri said solemnly as she hung up the telephone after talking to a mutual friend of Courtney's family. "They're flying her by helicopter to Duke University in Durham, North Carolina."

I was devastated. Prayer for Courtney, and for her parents, began immediately. Early that afternoon, Courtney's mother, Kathian telephoned Terri just before departing for Durham. "Please ask Wayne to pray for Courtney," she pleaded. "We have to drive to Durham and we're leaving in a few minutes."

"He's already started," Terri reassured her.

We really didn't know Joe and Kathian very well; only through school functions and the dancing activities in which our daughters were involved. They had only recently moved to Myrtle Beach from California, and didn't know too many people. But Kathian had attended one of my talks locally concerning Medjugorje and had read the articles. After the call we sat in silence. Finally, Terri asked, "What are we going to do?"

"We need to go to Durham, to the hospital, so I can pray over Courtney."

Terri nodded in silence. There was no need to discuss it; we both were convinced that is what I was supposed to do. She telephoned Kathian at the hospital the following morning telling her what I wanted to do and asking if it was okay for us to come.

"Oh, thank you, thank you! Of course it's all right!" Kathian was extremely grateful—and desperate. Courtney was still in a coma and had not responded to treatment. The tumor was inoperable; two of the top tumor specialists were doing all that was medically possible.

"They have told us that there is nothing more they can do," Kathian said tearfully. "We can only hope and pray, so please come!" Within the hour we arranged for friends to take our children overnight and were on our way.

During the long, four-hour drive, little was said. We were both praying constantly. I prayed with intensity. And doubt. It was not doubt in the power of prayer but in the fact that I was the one being asked to do this. And, it was the enormity of the disease that created the lack of confidence and trust, and brought back the often-asked question: why me? Would I ever just accept the fact that God chooses and we are to respond? That healing prayer was one of the gifts given with this mission?

Despite the doubts and questions, I had to do it. Courtney, for reasons not fully understood at the time, was very precious personally, and somehow important to the mission. For this reason, I found myself bargaining with the Blessed Mother. Since I had committed my life to the mission, maybe she would work a little harder on this request for healing to her Son, Jesus.

It was late night when we arrived and checked into a motel, leaving immediately afterwards for the hospital. The elevator door opened to the children's intensive care unit and there alone in the large waiting area were Courtney's parents.

"I can't thank you both enough for coming," Kathian said, hugging us. "I've already arranged with the nurses for you to see Courtney, so if you're ready, I'll take you to her now."

Still filled with some uncertainty, I motioned for Kathian to lead the way. She quickly ushered me into the ward and my heart leaped with the sight before me. There was Courtney, tubes attached seemingly everywhere to her little body, and monitoring machines beeping steady signals of vital signs. She was still in a deep coma. Trembling, I took a rosary from my pocket that had been blessed during the time of an apparition at Medjugorje. "Kathian, I know you're Protestant, but this rosary came from Medjugorje and—"

Oh, thank you, thank you!" Kathian said as she took the rosary and wrapped it around Courtney's wrist. "I was raised Catholic and I'm familiar with the rosary."

That surprised me, as part of my hesitation was knowing they were Protestants. They might not comprehend the importance of Medjugorje's message of prayer and fasting so necessary in cases of healing. I hoped they would understand beyond a desperate reaching for anything that might help their little girl. Joe had only recently begun attending church and I was pleased he had agreed to our coming.

I pressed on. "I also have this holy oil and I'd like to anoint Courtney if it's okay with you."

"Yes, yes, please!" Kathian urged. "Anything you want!"

For the next three hours I prayed over Courtney. Every now and then her eyes would flicker; but that was the only sign of life as she lay motionless. Each time doubt seeped into my thoughts, the fervor of prayer was increased.

Finally, it was time to leave. Joe had come in to give Kathian a break and was bowed in prayer with me, gently gripping his daughter's still hand. But there was one more prayer I wanted to say. Silently, I pleaded, "Saint Therese, little flower of Jesus, please, please, give a sign of flowers—anything. Just let us know that Courtney is going to pull through this."

As I walked out of the ward with Joe, there in front of us on the glass windows across from the elevator doors, was a huge display of posters with all kinds of flowers drawn in crayon by children. I laughed in relief, wondering why I hadn't seen them when we arrived. I knew it was the answer to my prayer to Saint Therese!

Stopping, I grabbed Joe by the arm. "Joe, she's going to make it through this! I know it!" I then told Joe about my prayer to Saint Therese. "You may think this is a little strange, but it never fails!"

But immediately after telling Joe, doubt crept in again. What if she doesn't recover? Neither Joe nor Kathian thought it was strange. They were ready to believe anything.

Joe and I returned to the motel to grab a few hours of sleep. I would be driving home later and he hadn't slept since arriving. Terri stayed on the remainder of the early morning hours talking with Kathian and praying for Courtney. When we left, Courtney's condition had not changed.

That evening, I asked Terri to call Kathian at the hospital. The line stayed busy for over an hour. Finally she got through. "She's awake! She's awake!" Kathian was practically screaming, overwhelmed with excitement. "She awoke and began crying and asking for her daddy!"

When Terri relayed the information, we all let out a shout of joy. I prayed a thank-you prayer to the Blessed Virgin—and to Saint Therese for her beautiful sign. But then we received an even more beautiful sign.

"Terri, I was getting ready to call you," Kathian began once we had settled down. "I have to tell you and Wayne what happened just before Courtney came out of the coma." Kathian paused to control her emotions. "My best friend in California called and told me about a strange dream she had last night. She is a Lutheran and doesn't know anything about Medjugorje, or Wayne, or what he does. And she doesn't know a whole lot about the Virgin Mary."

Again Kathian paused. "She told me that in her dream, the Blessed Virgin Mary was holding Courtney in her arms. And there was a man she did not know standing next to the Virgin Mary with his hand on Courtney—praying!"

When Terri related the story to me, I had to leave the room. As I sat in numb joy in the quiet of my office, I was too overwhelmed to even cry.

17
All My Children

". . . You are all my children. Certainly, all religions are not equal before God, as St. Paul says. It does not suffice to belong to the Catholic Church to be saved, but it is necessary to respect the commandments of God in following one's conscience."

Courtney was home in a few weeks. She was not healed of the brain tumor and would require ongoing medical treatment, but she had survived an all but impossible medical crisis. And the prophetic dream of Kathian's friend in California confirmed what I already knew in my heart: Courtney now belonged totally to Our Lady.

Thankfully, some normalcy was returning to her young life, although parents and friends knew Courtney would never be the same. As much as I hoped and prayed, there was no great expectation, or disappointment, that my daughter's little friend wasn't completely healed of the tumor. Rather, I felt an instinctive sense she was living on borrowed time.

My prayers now were for peace and acceptance by Courtney's family of her condition. Throughout the mission I had learned in similar life-threatening or terminal crises to first pray for the grace to accept whatever cross is given as a prerequisite to asking for actual physical healing. That, in essence, is why Our Lady stressed penance so frequently in her messages. It simply meant that we are to take up our daily crosses without complaint.

On a less dramatic scale, there was a mini-miracle: Steve made an A in his first course taken in the early summer session at the University. He seemed determined to make the best of his opportunity. But there was no noticeable change spiritually. I had asked him to make an effort to attend church services on campus, any church, so long as he attended regularly. That had not happened. "I will," he said to me repeatedly. "Just let me get settled.

Trusting what Gospa had said about his attending school as the starting point of conversion, I could only wait patiently for signs of its beginning. Even at this stage of his anticipated conversion, I had to accept that he too, was now a child of Our Lady.

The remaining months of summer weren't nearly as dramatic as May and June. But they were packed with events and trips. July kicked off with a visit from Paolo, who arrived the first week, having accepted our invitation to visit in order to sort things out. He had dropped out of the university at Rome after only six months, putting to rest thoughts of the priesthood. "It just wasn't meant to be," he related as we caught up with each others lives the evening of his arrival.

From this and recent conversations, it was evident that Paolo was frustrated. Unemployed and living at home, he could easily have returned to his profession as an economist, but decided against it. "How can I return to that life of the world after Medjugorje?" he said, adding, "But, at the same time, I must find work."

He did not want to be dependent on his parents but a renewed spiritual commitment sparked by pilgrimages to Medjugorje, came first. Just any job would not do. It was enough to make my Italian friend unsure of just what God was asking of him, and his only peace seemed to be the extended times spent in Medjugorje with Marija.

That kindled another concern, a huge one: He and Marija had fallen in love.

It didn't just happen. Kathleen and other friends had sensed it from the time the two of them first met. But with Marija's well publicized intention to become a nun, and Paolo attending school in preparation to possibly enter the priesthood, no one, including Paolo and Marija, expected this. The last thing Paolo wanted to do was interfere with what the mother of God was doing through her visionaries at Medjugorje.

Through time spent with them, I had long-suspected they were more than Medjugorje acquaintances, but only after Terri returned from a recent trip to Medjugorje was it confirmed. "They're in love," she stated rather matter-of-factly when I had asked about the two of them.

"You're wrong on that one!" I had laughed. "They're both going to pursue a religious life."

"Maybe they are, but I'm telling you, they are in love!"

Uncertain, I asked, "How do you know?"

Terri gave me her patented side-glance with a slight smile. "Because I'm a woman and women sense these things."

And when Paolo arrived, he validated my wife's intuition, talking openly of the possibility of marriage and about their future. "But first," Paolo said taking a deep breath, "I must find a good job."

I suddenly had an idea. Paolo was extremely fluent in English and had read my book; would he consider translating it into Italian and help find a publisher in his country? "You could serve as my agent and it might help spread the message there," I added.

Paolo shrugged after a few moments. "Well, we can look at that possibility since at the time I have so much free time."

It didn't really matter whether the book was published in Italy. My sole intent in offering this was to give Paolo something to occupy his time while looking for the right job. Anything above that would be a bonus.

Several days later, Paolo accepted my proposal and I immediately began gathering everything he would need to do the translation. Time flew by. Soon, we were saying good-bye to him and I was on my way to another speaking engagement.

I flew to Los Angeles the first week of August, accompanied by Father Svet, to speak at a Medjugorje conference organized by the prayer group that had sponsored my two previous tours in California. It was the first such conference in the state, and had originated after my last visit as we gathered at the Starbuck's home for a light meal the night before my departure. After praying the rosary, Elaine Starbuck said rather offhandedly, "I wonder what we can do next to keep the spreading of the Medjugorje message going?"

"Well, you could organize a Medjugorje conference like the ones that are springing up all over the country." I answered just off the top of my head, but without hesitation. Kay Sentovich saw that as a sign and soon the group was in deep discussion on whether they could put together such an event. Within weeks formal plans for a three-day conference had been completed and scheduled for early August the following year.

Asked by the group if I would personally invite Father Svetozar to be the main speaker and representative of Medjugorje, I took advantage of the opportunity by persuading him to come to Myrtle Beach a few days in advance. Terri was pleased when he accepted. This priest, so very special to her, had been a spiritual guide to the visionaries and had authored two insightful books on the apparitions. His latest, titled *Pilgrimage,* was her favorite which she often gave as a gift to family and friends.

Father Svet was a powerful example of what Gospa was asking of each of us through the messages of Medjugorje. Prayer, fasting, and penance was not something new to this Franciscan priest who grew up within a few miles of Medjugorje. "Even before Medjugorje's apparitions, this was a strong part of our every day living," he told us with an unassuming shrug as we talked on the evening of his arrival.

The next morning, Father Svet concelebrated Holy Mass with Father Dilley, who asked him to give the homily. Terri and I felt as though we were back in St. James Church in Medjugorje, as we sat listening to his mesmerizing words that reached directly to the heart. Judging by the reaction of those around us, it struck everyone the same way.

It was a time of relaxation and joy for the entire family as well as our guest. The only problem was it passed far too quickly.

The conference was excellent and a personal reunion of sorts for me. Foremost was seeing Kevin and Mary Starbuck—and their newborn baby girl! As predicted, little Mary Margaret had easily become the "apple of their eye," and the catalyst for transforming them into a family of renewed faith. Mary was ecstatic. "She is the most precious gift and all of the other kids love her. I just can't believe that everything you said about us having another child has come true!"

In addition, Michael O'Brien had been invited as one of the speakers. "But he'll only sing," Elaine told me. "We wanted him to give a testimony but he said he hasn't reached the point where he can do that yet."

Knowing where Michael had come from spiritually, I understood. It was as though he had one foot in Medjugorje, and the other still in the world of rock music.

Full transformation to an active child of Mary would take time for him, just as it would for my son, Steve. "I'll talk to him," I responded.

Cornering Michael at the first opportunity, I lectured him like a Dutch uncle; his story needed to be told in order to help other young people. Our Lady had chosen him to be an instrument for them. And I told him about Steve. "Look, Michael," I said after telling him how I received the message from Our Lady to put Steve in school, "I know deep inside that Steve isn't going to change overnight. And neither are you. But this is the next step. I really believe you are ready for it!"

But he resisted. "I hear what you're saying and I know that one day . . . but I just can't do it in front of these people," he confessed after nearly two hours of discussion. "I mean, they're different. It's not like a rock concert crowd!"

I put my hands on his shoulders. "You never thought you could sing religious songs either, but you did. You need to do this because Our Lady is asking you to do it, just like she did in the beginning when you received that note from Vicka. Just think about that and then who knows what might happen!" I left it at that, hoping through some small miracle it might register.

And it did.

Michael insisted I introduce him. I accepted, hoping it would encourage him to give witness. I related to the audience how we had first met, about the note, and how he had finally answered by recording the religious songs. After doing so, I moved to a side corner of the stage.

Ending his first song, Michael glanced over at me with a look that can only be described as one of pure terror. But suddenly, he began speaking about his pilgrimage to Medjugorje and of receiving the note from Vicka. Mixed in were bits of self-deprecating humor. The audience of more than five thousand loved it; and the young people flocked to the side area of the stage as he sang his last song, wanting an autograph or simply to be near him or shake his hand. The words of the message Gospa had given to Michael through Vicka echoed in my mind: *"You will bring young people to God with your talent. . . ."*

The prayer group had done a superb job in their schedule of speakers. It was well balanced and representative of different segments of Christian faith. I was particularly touched on Sunday morning as I knelt in quiet prayer in a room on the second floor close to the auditorium. I had already spoken and now had time to just sit in peace in this little room set aside as an adoration chapel with the Blessed Sacrament exposed. Here was Jesus present in the small host encased in a golden monstrance.

I was filled with a mixture of longing and awe. How I wanted to be able to receive Jesus in full communion with the Church! Suddenly the words of the speaker on stage below could be clearly heard. He was speaking about the Eucharist and his longing to one day receive Jesus through this incomprehensible gift of grace.

Curiosity got the best of me; I arose from my kneeling position and went to the door to see who was speaking. It was a Protestant minister. He had been invited to give ecumenical balance to the conference and underline again that all people of all faiths were Gospa's children. As I listened, he ended by saying, "And there is no doubt in my mind that I will one day soon convert to Catholicism . . . because I truly believe that Jesus is present as flesh and blood in the Holy Eucharist!"

I returned to the little adoration room, kneeling there in silent gratitude, thankful for this and other conferences that were bringing the children of all faiths together under the guidance of Our Blessed Mother.

18

"Speak about the events"

"Preach my messages. Speak about the events at Medjugorje. Continue to increase your prayers."

The California conference marked the beginning of busy travel time again. I was glad; I enjoyed being home, but after a month of not giving talks I began to get "antsy." It was not out of need for attention or glory, but a desire to carry out the mission. There was still so much to do and so many places to go. But admittedly, the daily involvement kept me constantly immersed in the messages. That was a grace I never wanted to lose.

"Just be sure you always do it for the right reasons," Terri cautioned as I packed for yet another pilgrimage to Medjugorje.

"Terri, I promise you, when the day comes I feel Our Lady telling me the mission is completed, I'll gladly come home and live in quiet and peace with you and the children." Pausing from my packing, I reached over and touched her arm. "But this trip is special."

"You always say that!" she laughed.

But it really was. Somewhere during this period, I felt

an urging by Our Lady to bring clergy to the little village, a reminder that they are as much in need of conversion or renewal as the laity. That point had been underlined in the last few months as I encountered both resistance and embracement of Medjugorje from Catholic and Protestant clergy alike.

In late October, I would be taking three priests, three seminarians, and three Lutheran ministers among an entourage of 75 pilgrims from across the country. Recruitment began with a priest I met in March during a stop in Memphis, Tennessee. His was a story as dramatic as that of Father Stephan Gobbi of the Marian Movement of Priests—and as flamboyant as Father Ken Roberts' playboy-to-priest saga.

Joe Tagg had known since high school that he wanted to become a priest. But like so many candidates for service to God, he struggled with the decision. Prior to first entering the seminary fourteen years ago, Joe earned his law degree and was an outstanding attorney with a lucrative practice. He had given all that up to enter the seminary.

Suddenly, days before his ordination, Joe was filled with self-doubt. After long hours of prayer, he decided to call it off. This, of course, created distress for his bishop and embarrassment for his family whose many friends had already sent ordination gifts. A week later, the young lawyer returned to his practice and began to amass the material benefits of a carefree, single young man.

"I was enjoying life," Father Joe recalled as he told me of his arduous route to the priesthood. "I never missed the Sugar Bowl, always had tickets to the final four basketball tourney, and belonged to all the right clubs. I went to Super Bowls and championship fights in Las Vegas. I'd be less than honest if I didn't tell you that I went through a strong grieving process at losing the good life when I finally made up my mind to really be ordained."

I asked him what prompted the second call to the priesthood. "I was in New Orleans for the '87 Sugar Bowl and for some reason, I suddenly got to thinking about my vocation again. I went into the cathedral and walked up to the statue of the Sacred Heart of Jesus and asked Him to please help me out of this indecision. I asked for some sign to seek ordination, or be set free."

Joe walked away from the cathedral that day, determined to spend the next year in prayer and soul-searching, hoping for signs along the way. It didn't take long. "That is where Medjugorje—and you—fit in," Father Joe smiled. "It was a couple of months later that I received a copy of your articles on Medjugorje. I was impressed that a Protestant, a Lutheran, would be involved in this. I didn't know where Medjugorje was, or anything about it before that."

Four days later Joe received a telephone call from the bishop's office. They needed his help in obtaining the personal goods of a priest who had died of a heart attack in Memphis, after the airplane on which he was a passenger had been diverted to Memphis in a last-ditch effort to save his life. The young attorney had done legal work for the bishop's office before and was glad to help.

"I'll never forget what happened at the police station," Father Joe continued. "As they were emptying out the late priest's personal goods from a large envelope, a Sacred Heart badge rolled out of the envelope and over to where I was on the other side of the desk, coming to a stop right in front of me! I was shaken as I recalled my prayers in the cathedral in New Orleans. Sitting in my car outside the station thinking about this and the fact the God had lost another priest, I suddenly heard an inner voice saying, *'Why don't you take his place, Joseph?'* There was little doubt what I had to do. A year later, after entering the seminary a second time, I was finally ordained."

There was little doubt what I now had to do after hearing Father Joe Tagg's story: "Father, you've got to come to
Medjugorje with me this fall!"

That was the beginning of the special pilgrimage. In
July during my trip to Saskatchewan, Canada, I found another seminarian "picked" by Our Lady. Maurice Frolleau
had no unusual or startling story. Very quiet in his ways,
he had wanted to be a priest as long as he could remember, was totally devoted to the Blessed Virgin, and was
only a few months away from ordination. I asked him to
join us.

In August, during a two-day tour in Fort Wayne, Indiana, I met Father Ron Reider. Jim Stoffel, a good friend in
Myrtle Beach, and orginally from Indiana, had asked me
to go to Fort Wayne for a talk. "I'll even come with you
and we'll schedule a round of golf," he stated. From that I
knew Jim had an ulterior motive. "Yes, I do," he confessed.
"This priest I've known for a long, long time needs to go
to Medjugorje. And he loves golf. So, I thought we might
set up a friendly little game and maybe during the match
you could invite him to go with you this fall."

Jim failed to tell me Father Ron was not a believer in
Medjugorje! He agreed to the golf match strictly as an
opportunity to play golf and to appease his friend. But he
was reluctant to hear about or discuss Medjugorje.

After several holes of casual conversation about my
mission and the many trips I had made there, I asked him
straight out if he would like to come with our group. "I
very much appreciate your offer but no, I don't really care
to go!"

After the match, I asked again at the urging of Jim.
"It's just not for me and to be perfectly honest with you,
I'm not too keen on apparitions of the Blessed Virgin with
all the claims of rosaries turning gold and the like . . ."

I looked at Jim and shrugged. But Jim wasn't deterred.

"At least he's coming to your talk tonight, so we'll just have to pray that he listens to the message."

The talk was to take place in a large theater directly across the street from the hotel where I was staying. As we returned to the hotel, there was a long, double-line of people waiting to get in the theater with more than an hour to go before the beginning of the evening's events. Father Ron was taken aback. After the talk, he came to me. "Is that offer to go with you to Medjugorje still open?"

I looked at him with surprise. "Yes, of course it is! What changed your mind?"

Father Ron hesitated, looking away so that I wouldn't see the emotion building within him. "Let's just say I feel a calling and leave it at that!"

That was good enough for me, and Jim was absolutely delighted. "Wow," I thought, "this is going to be some pilgrimage!" But that wasn't the end of the recruitment; it seemed as if Our Lady was working overtime!

September found me in New Mexico and in the company of a priest with severe multiple sclerosis. Father Don Kapitz was in a severe, degenerative state of this crippling disease of the muscles—but he wanted to go to Medjugorje. He could hardly speak above a whisper. Despite his handicap and present state, I sensed that Gospa wanted him there; maybe, I thought, for a physical healing.

"Father Don, it is not an easy trip and there's no way you could go up the hill or mountain. If we could have someone who could come with you and care for you . . ."

"What about the two seminarians—and myself?" Len Rabb, a nurse and one of the people who had invited me to come to New Mexico, interjected, looking at me expectantly.

I nodded, remembering two young men presently in the seminary who had come to one of the talks. They were on fire spiritually and a lot of it had to do with Medjugorje.

Within a couple of days, arrangements were made for Father Don, Len, and the two seminarians to join the October tour.

As if three priests and three seminarians weren't enough, I asked my Lutheran Paster Bill Wingard once again if he wanted to go, since he was now retired from his pastoral duties. I was determined to balance the trip with Protestant clergy as well. Again, he could not go.

But Irv Donor could. The minister of music from my Lutheran church had also read the articles. Having been involved with Taize, an interdenominational movement centered in Taize, France, he was an advocate of ecumenism and intrigued by Medjugorje's call to people of all faiths. At Bill Wingard's suggestion, I asked him to go in his place.

Irv was deeply grateful and willing to go. "But I have to check with the pastor. If he gives permission, I'd love to go!" The pastor gave his permission and Irv Donor was added to the list. I was ecstatic to actually have another Lutheran from Myrtle Beach who would now experience Medjugorje.

But I wanted a Lutheran pastor as well. As it turned out, I got two. Remembering that David Eastes, a Lutheran pastor from New Bern, North Carolina, had come to one of my talks, I decided to call him. He first heard about Medjugorje through a flyer announcing that a Lutheran would be speaking about apparitions of the Blessed Virgin Mary in Yugoslavia, at a Catholic church in a nearby location. David came to the talk and was struck like so many before him. Having always felt a closeness to the mother of Jesus, he felt he now knew why. "I haven't been the same since coming to your talk, and now, to think I might actually be able to go. I don't know how to thank you."

I pressed on. "David, do you know of any other

Lutheran or Protestant clergy that might desire to go?"

It turned out that he had shared his experience and information on Medjugorje with a fellow Lutheran pastor and good friend, Richard Mokry. Richard, a serious student of Lutheran theology, also accepted the invitation, although more as a study project than one affected by its good fruits.

There was just one hitch: we were leaving on a weekend and that particular Sunday was Reformation Sunday, when Lutherans celebrate the founding of their denomination. "It's all tentative based on whether we can obtain permission to be gone on that Sunday," David related to me by telephone a couple of days after our initial conversation. He was crestfallen, sure that this would force them to miss the pilgrimage.

But again, things miraculously fell into place; their respective congregations agreed to their making the trip and substitutions were found. Permission from church officials was also granted. It was a definite sign that it was the right mix of clergy for this pilgrimage.

The group was now complete. Soon after departure, the Lutheran contingent and several other non-Catholics on the pilgrimage had melded in with the others. They prayed the rosary and shared stories and by the time we arrived in Medjugorje, they had been "adopted" by the predominantly Catholic group.

It was good to see Marija and Kathleen again—and Paolo, who had come a few days before. By the time our pilgrimage was settled for the evening and I arrived at her home, it was after 10 o'clock; still, Marija insisted on preparing a small meal. I knew better than to resist. Besides, it afforded me the opportunity to sit around for two more hours catching up on the latest happenings in Medjugorje. Sleep could come later.

"I have just returned from a trip to Czechoslovakia and Russia," Marija said casually as we settled in her small living room for a coffee after the meal. That caught me offguard.

"You were actually able to speak to the Russian people about Our Lady's apparitions?"

"Yes, also in Czechoslovakia. The people knew about Gospa's apparitions here in Medjugorje. We would stop at a church to prepare for the apparition and one hour later, the church would be filled with people!"

I was envious. Russia was the country I most wanted to go with the mission but the opportunity had never developed. I listened in awe as Marija enthusiastically talked about her trip, resorting to Italian from time to time and asking Paolo to translate. She had been accompanied on the journey by the pastor of St. James Church in Medjugorje, Father Leonardo Oric, and Czechoslovakian bishop Paolo Hnilica, who had made the basic arrangements for the tour. This bishop, who had spent years in Communist prisons because of his uncompromising defense of his faith, was a personal confidant of Pope John Paul II. He had served as liaison for the Pope in his meeting with Soviet President Mikhail Gorbechov, earlier in the year.

"The people wanted to know everything about Our Lady and her messages," Marija said with a happy glow of remembrance reflecting in her eyes. "They were very devoted and anxious to hear about Medjugorje."

But, they almost did not make it into Russia. The entourage had traveled by automobile through Czechoslovakia, slowed by the theft of Marija's purse which contained her passport. After what she described as endless hours of waiting, filling out red-tape reports, they were finally able to secure a temporary passport and board a flight for Moscow.

Even in the heart of the city that housed the feared Communist government power that had wreaked social havoc for so long, thousands came to see and hear Marija. As she talked about the trip, I could not help but think of the millions of prayers offered for the conversion of Russia in the last seventy years. There were startling changes taking place now, as Communism was losing power, just as Our Lady had predicted during her Fatima apparitions in 1917. Possibly this seemingly insignificant tour by one of Gospa's special chosen was a sign that those prayers were finally being answered.

"But these people still need much prayer," Marija added as she ended the story of her tour. "They do not have food and clothing like we do here in Medjugorje. I was surprised at this, and happy to come home. Here we have plenty of everything!"

There was one other little detail I found intriguing about Marija's Russian journey. During the long hours of travel by automobile and airplanes, Father Oric learned far more about the apparitions and visionaries of his famous parish, than he had in his short tenure as pastor of St. James. Up to that point, he had managed the parish but remained somewhat distant from the visionaries and details of Our Lady's visits.

"Yes," Marija said as we prepared to go to our rooms for the evening, "I think he now understands more clearly why Our Lady has come to Medjugorje."

That was an interesting development, I thought as I was finally able to stretch out horizontally on a bed for the first time in thirty-plus hours. But for some strange reason, I was not ready for sleep; my mind was racing with the details of Marija's Russian tour.

How I had longed to take the mission to Russia! I knew

I was supposed to go sometime; that had been a thought deep within me since the beginning of the mission. With all the political changes that had occurred, finally freeing the multitude of republics that made up the Soviet Union from the oppression of Communism, I hoped that a tour could be arranged. Several offers had been proposed during the past year but nothing had materialized.

As I lay in the still of the night, I realized again where I was. "I guess you'll send me there when it's time, Blessed Mother," I muttered sleepily as the fatigue of the day finally won out.

Well-rested after sleeping past 10 o'clock, I hurried down the pathway through the fields toward St. James Church for the English-speaking noon Mass. It was a beautiful, bright day and I thanked Jesus for the good weather. I wanted everything to be perfect for this contingent of pilgrims—especially the Lutherans and other non-Catholics.

The church was packed as I made my way to the rear and took a place near the wall. Glancing over the throng of worshipers, I spotted my Lutherans near one of the doors.

We exchanged brief waves as the Mass began with a thunderous rendition of the hymn, "Amazing Grace." I was startled and pleased at the same time. What better start for my Lutherans than to hear this hymn universally recognized as one of the most popular of Protestant hymns!

The feeling of well-being came to a crashing halt ten minutes later when the English-speaking Franciscan priest began his homily by informing us that today marked "a day of infamy" in the Roman Catholic Church: "This is Reformation Sunday, which is celebrated annually in Protestant churches . . . the beginning of the greatest schism in Church history . . . the very foundation of Protestant-ism!" His voice rose to a roar and stayed there for the next thirty minutes, lambasting everything Protestant from the history and writings of Martin Luther, to the modern-day evangelical crusades of Billy Graham.

I was devastated. So were my Lutheran pilgrims whom I saw leaving about halfway through the homily. How could this good priest who worked so diligently for the English-speaking pilgrims, choose this particular time to launch such a broadside against Protestants? For the first time in any Catholic Mass, I was anxious for it to end so I could find Irv, David, and Richard, and hopefully repair the damage that had been done.

I found them huddled together near the rear of the church under a tree, talking. "Look, I'm sorry. I don't understand why he would do that, but please don't judge Medjugorje on one man." I didn't know what else to say.

Irv was on the verge of tears. "I just couldn't stay in there and listen to that. This is supposed to be a place of peace and unity." He was filled with hurt and anger. "To be perfectly honest, I'm ready to go home—now!" Richard and David had remained silent but it was evident they felt the same way.

"I promise you, this is an isolated incident. Just try and enjoy the rest of the day."

Calming down, they agreed. "I guess we really don't have much choice since we're stuck here for the next five days," Richard said, resignedly.

I didn't see them again until late that evening at the Croatian Mass. At least, I thought, they're here at the Mass, and Irv was smiling as he motioned for me to join them. "You know, we climbed that little hill this afternoon, the one where the Virgin Mary first appeared. And something happened that made us all feel better."

I wondered if they had witnessed some phenomena.

"What did you see?"

"Oh, no," Irv said quickly. "It was nothing we saw. A man from our group was sitting in that little cafe at the foot of the hill as we were preparing to go up. He motioned for us to come to where he was and said, 'Don't judge us by what you heard in the Mass this morning.' We talked for awhile longer and by the time it was over we felt our peace return. The climb up the hill was wonderful!"

I breathed a silent sigh of relief.

"But there is one thing; we wondered if you might be able to spend some time with us. Richard has some questions."

I knew the questions Richard had; I'd heard them dozens of times and had deliberately kept a distance from my Lutheran pilgrims so they could experience Medjugorje for themselves, and come to their own conclusions about its authenticity and purpose. Richard was primed to raise age-old theological differences. "Well, let's give it a few days more; then we'll talk . . ."

Reluctantly, they agreed.

Monday was a day of peace, a day I hoped to just be another pilgrim and absorb the grace of Medjugorje. Climbing Podbrdo early, there were several small groups of pilgrims on the hill and I was immediately recognized. After spending a few minutes with them listening to anecdotes of their pilgrimage experiences, I thanked them and began to make my way toward the other side of the hill. Suddenly one of them called out, "Hey, are you still giving a talk tomorrow after Mass?"

Several of the tour leaders had asked if I would speak to their groups and I had agreed. Arrangements had been made to use one of the large tents that had been erected several hundred yards from the rear of the church, strictly for such purposes. After assuring them that I would be speaking, I was finally able to slip off to a quiet spot to be alone and pray.

Such encounters with individuals and groups had become an ongoing responsibility of the mission now. Publication of *Medjugorje: The Message* had taken care of that, stripping away the last vestige of privacy and bringing with it recognition far greater than anticipated. More than one conversation now began with the words: "I read your book and that's why I'm here. . . ."

But that was fine as long as I kept in mind who the real author of the book was—and its purpose. It was Gospa's book; its purpose was to bring conversion to her Son. I was merely another instrument allowed to put my name on the cover. As long as that remained in the forefront, it would continue to be a powerful tool of conversion.

As I looked over the beautiful panorama of this special little valley, I marveled at what Our Lady had accomplished with the book. In the two years since publication, more than 150,000 copies had been sold in the United States alone. It had been translated into Spanish and several other languages and was spreading in other English-speaking countries. In short, it was doing exactly what it was intended to do and that was simply to bring people to God.

After a late breakfast, Paolo and I reviewed his progress in translating the book into Italian. He had made moderate progress but assured me it would be done soon as his father, Dino Lunetti, was now assisting him. "My father is convinced that it will do well in Italy, and wants to complete the project as soon as possible," he said as we completed the review.

I began to get excited about the possibility of the book being published in Italy. "Paolo, do you really think it has a chance of being published in Italy?"

Paolo looked at me with surprise. "Of course, or I

would not be taking the time to do the translation."

We spent the remainder of the day on an assortment of little chores and later drove to Mostar to shop for food. And, as usual, we arrived back in Medjugorje with barely enough time to take Marija to the church for the evening apparition. After escorting her to the door of the tower, we took a seat away from the crowds to pray the rosary and attend the Mass.

It was a perfect ending to a perfect day; a day that for the most part, I was able to be just another pilgrim at Medjugorje.

I squeezed into the front side door of St. James Church the following morning, pleased to see so many English-speaking pilgrims at Medjugorje; and pleased to see Father Don Kapitz in his wheel chair on the altar, surrounded by the other priests from our group.

Father Don had made the long trip in good fashion, thanks to the aid and comfort of his fellow priests and the seminarians. The priests had spent hours listening to confessions, a major part of bringing the reality of Medjugorje's holiness to priests. That was especially true for Father Ron Rieder, who told me, "I've never heard confessions like these—anywhere!"

As Mass began, I noted that the music sounded a bit more professional than usual. Glancing toward the front left corner of the church where the organ was located, I was shocked. Irv Doner was playing the opening hymn, surrounded by several members of our group that were serving as a choir! And the same Franciscan priest who had given the homily on Sunday, was the main celebrant!

"Can you believe this?" David Eastes whispered as he sidled up next to me.

"What—how?"

David laughed softly. "It's a long story!"

Regardless of what had brought it about, I was thrilled. "David, let me borrow your camera. I've got to get a picture of this for Irv!" Taking his camera, I made my way toward the corner and clicked off a couple of pictures. Raising the camera to take one last shot, I suddenly felt a sharp pain as a man next to me shoved his elbow into my side. He glared at me and I immediately knew it was done deliberately. Anger welled up inside of me and I wanted to punch him back—hard!

Remembering where I was and knowing people were watching, I fought for control. "Excuse me if I got in your way—"

"Excuse me, indeed!" He virtually hissed in a distinct British accent. "This is not a tourist spot! This is a church!"

There was no explaining about the importance of the picture. I turned and made my way back to David and Richard.

"What was his problem?" David asked, having witnessed the act.

Still shaking, I waved my hand. "It was nothing important. It's okay."

Personal anger from the incident all but took the joy and beauty of the Mass away, and the special grace of a Lutheran playing the organ at a Mass in Medjugorje. Until the time came for the sign of peace to be given and shared. I sought out the man that had accosted me and looking him directly in the eyes, I smiled, took his hand and said, "God's peace be with you."

He was too startled to answer.

Irv beamed when I was finally able to corner him away from the crowds moving toward the tent. I only had a few minutes before the talk but I wanted to know how he had ended up playing the organ. "I decided to go and see that priest," Irv began. "I told him I was a Lutheran minister of music, and that there were two other Lutheran pastors here as well as some other Protestants. I expressed my disappointment at his attack, pointing out that I came here because I was led to understand it was a place of unity and peace."

"And what was his answer?"

"Well, he said, 'This is the way it is.' But I wouldn't accept that, and I told him he had been away from the States too long. There was great dialogue among the faiths and we had to learn to live with each other despite our theological differences. Suddenly, he asked me if I would play the organ for the English Mass. We talked a while longer and I knew his asking me to play was his way of saying he was sorry. When I returned to the house, several members of our group said they would serve as a choir because the hymns he had selected were difficult."

I was pleased things had worked out so well. It was a powerful lesson and proof that Medjugorje was indeed a place of peace and unity. "Hey listen," Irv said as I started to leave. "If it weren't for these wonderful Catholics in our group who prayed for us after the Mass Sunday, it probably wouldn't have worked out so well." And then as an aside, he added in a lower voice, "And the thing is, they're charismatics and they pray in tongues. That's something I've always been uncomfortable with, but I must admit I felt a strong sense of peace before meeting with the priest."

Hurrying to the tent for my talk, I noticed the man who had poked his elbow in my side was sitting near the front. His eyes widened as I was introduced, and it struck me that he only now knew who I was. We exchanged embarrassed, sheepish smiles; but we knew that everything was now okay between us.

And everything was okay with the clergy—including

the Lutherans. It was pure pilgrimage. My task had been simply to get them to Medjugorje. As always, Gospa did the rest.

19
Father Jozo

"Dear children, I want you to comprehend that God has chosen each one of you, in order to use you in His great plan for the salvation of mankind . . ."

Unable to put it off any longer, I met with Irv, Richard, and David that evening just before dinner. Richard had a pad filled with questions. They were the usual ones concerning infallibility, worship of Mary, why Protestants could not receive Communion with Catholics.

David was a little nervous. Other than the incident on Sunday morning, he was enthralled with the village. "We just wanted to ask you a few questions," he said, turning to Richard, who promptly began rattling off differences between Catholics and Protestants. As I listened, I thought how difficult it was for theologians of any faith to understand, much less embrace, the childlike simplicity of God's love. By constantly dissecting each line of Scripture or doctrine and having to have definite fact or thought for every particle, they missed the pure joy of acceptance on faith.

After fifteen minutes of give and take, I held up my hand. "Wait a minute guys. I can answer your questions or refer you to one of the priests in our group, or we can continue to debate, but that's not what this place is about. Here you simply have to put your theology in your back pocket and let your heart lead you. Medjugorje isn't meant to bring us together ecumenically in a formal sense. Our Lady comes to unite us through our love and desire to serve God."

I continued, telling them about the messages Gospa had given relating to the different faiths. "She always comes to lead us to her Son. And, she comes for the people of all faiths, asking each of us to turn to Jesus and follow His way of love. That doesn't mean all faiths are equal," I concluded, "What's important is the sincerity of heart in truly seeking God. Beyond that, we'll have to let Him sort out the rest."

Turning to Richard, I asked, "Does that answer your questions?" Thankfully, that brought the discussion to an end. And while it probably didn't answer all of Richard's questions, it seemed to give him and the others momentary peace of mind.

Our bus rumbled through Ljbuski, early the next morning on its way to Tihaljina, a small parish twenty-five miles from Medjugorje where former St. James' pastor Father Jozo Zovko was now assigned. Going to see and hear him had become an integral part of every Medjugorje pilgrimage, orginating ironically, with Paolo's father Dino. A couple of years earlier, he had taken a group of Italian pilgrims to see this charismatic priest, who at the time was forbidden by the bishop of Mostar to even set foot in Medjugorje.

Moving to the rear of the bus, I took a seat next to Irv and the two Lutheran pastors. "You're in for a real treat listening to Father Jozo; I think he'll put into perspective what we talked about last night."

Irv nodded and then asked, "Is he charismatic?"

"Yes, but probably not in the way you're thinking. Why do you ask?"

"Well, many of the people at our house are charismatics and they prayed over us again last night. Now mind you, I have nothing against it, but I've never really cared for that way of worshipping. The funny thing was, I felt a deep sense of peace and warmth when they prayed over me for my family."

I laughed. "Frankly, I think all of us are charismatics who truly believe in the Holy Spirit. But Father Jozo has a beautiful gift of preaching and praying over people; and many of them are slain in the spirit."

"What does that mean?" Richard asked.

"When he prays over a person they are filled with the Holy Spirit and they simply faint in a semi-conscious state of great peace."

By the look on their faces, I could see they were unsure of what to expect. "Hey, don't worry about it. Just open your heart and see what happens. Everything's worked out so far, right?"

"But why doesn't Father Jozo come to Medjugorje now?" David asked. "I understand he is no longer forbidden to come there."

"He does sometimes, but it's easier now for the pilgrims to come to Tihaljina. Besides, the trip is worth it just to see one of the most beautiful statues of Our Lady ever created. It has unofficially become the signature statue representing Medjugorje."

"Why is the bishop so against the apparitions?" Richard inquired. "Doesn't that raise questions from church authorities, not to mention other denominations, as to the authenticity of the apparitions?"

"You have to know the background," I began, explaining that the bishop had accused Father Jozo and the other

Franciscans of manipulating the visionaries and perpetuating the "hoax" of apparitions at Medjugorje in order to make money. After his release from eighteen months in prison, the bishop assigned him to Tihaljina as one more futile attempt to stop the apparitions. And of course, it failed.

Banning Father Jozo from Medjugorje was sadly one more lost battle in a war against the apparitions conducted by the bishop. Ironically, in the beginning he had been a strong advocate, visiting the parish almost daily and praising the young visionaries for their open honesty.

Many felt the change came when the bishop was threatened with jail by the local authorities, just as they threatened Father Jozo. He suddenly transformed from the apparition's champion to its strongest foe, using a local squabble between secular and Franciscan priests as the impetus to now challenge its authenticity. And when his priest was sentenced to jail for refusing to shut down his church and stop the apparitions, the bishop offered weak resistance verbally, but did nothing further.

Later, the bishop was mortified when the Vatican threw out his commission's study on the apparitions because of its outright prejudice, and forbid him from making any public statements concerning the investigation—an order which he constantly ignored. Now, the responsibility of investigating the apparitions was under the authority of the collective bishops of Yugoslavia.

"And that is without precedent. Never in the history of the Church has a local bishop been removed from such an investigation," I concluded as we pulled into the parking lot of Father Jozo's church.

"In case anyone's interested, today is Halloween," a woman yelled as we descended the steps of the bus and made our way toward the church. I thought nothing of it until we had settled in the church and Father Jozo began the opening prayers.

For the next twenty minutes we prayed fervently in an almost impossible stillness and quiet. Suddenly it was shattered by a piercing scream as a middle-aged Italian woman in the rear of the church fell writhing to the floor.

Pausing only momentarily, Father Jozo continued the prayers, as Anka told us not to be alarmed but to continue to pray with him. But the more he prayed the louder the woman's screams became. Several people who were trying to help her were violently pushed away as the woman seemed to suddenly have exordinary strength. Then she began vomiting and growling gutteral words. It was a scene straight out of the worst horror show.

"My God, what is happening?" David asked.

"She is possessed with demons," a woman from our group responded. "We need to pray for her as hard as we can!"

People began to leave the church from the rear entrance, wanting to get as far from the woman as possible. Father Jozo now made his way off the altar and went directly to the woman and began to pray over her. "Please do not be afraid and do not leave," Anka said reassuringly. "Father Jozo will help her and you can help him by praying for her healing."

And for the next three hours, we did. In the course of our prayers, others fell into similar fits and Father Jozo would move from one to the other. Finally things returned to normal. Time seemed compressed; we had been inside the church for more than four hours and yet it seemed like only minutes. And incredibly, the same woman who had undergone such a fit in the beginning was now singing hymns with us in total peace, a serene smile on her face.

There was no time left for Father Jozo's talk. After more prayers, he anointed the priests from the groups who were up on the altar with him, and began moving through the crowd, praying over individuals. The priests followed and were frightened and then amazed as people began to be slain in the spirit by them as well as Father Jozo. And in large numbers. Catchers were assigned to go behind each person as the priests and Father Jozo placed hands on their heads. They were kept extremely busy.

"I don't know about this," Richard said as Father Jozo made his way toward us.

"Just relax and let the Holy Spirit take over." I wondered if he would go down. He did. And so did Irv; but David Estes did not.

Ten minutes later, as David helped them to their feet, Richard and Irv were smiling dazedly and telling him how peaceful they felt. And I couldn't believe my ears when Richard added, "It was one of the most wonderful and incredible experiences in my life!"

Moving away from the crowds, I found a little time to pray quietly in front of the beautiful statue of Our Lady of Grace, as she was named. My eyes filled with tears as always. I felt that Gospa was right there with me every time I came to Tihaljina and prayed in front of this statue.

Later, I thanked Anka and Father Jozo, wishing I had more time to spend with them. But the look in Father Jozo's eyes was enough; he hugged me and said something to Anka who laughed. "He says your heart is like chocolate, and encourages you to continue on your mission."

It was a simple confirmation, but a precious gift from this holy priest.

"What an experience! I never thought of Halloween as being a day of demons before, but after this . . ." Irv could only shake his head.

"The same thing was happening to people in Medjugorje this morning before we left," someone piped up from the rear of the bus, as we left the outskirts of Tihaljina.

David had remained quiet since boarding the bus. After awhile, he turned to me. "Why did Richard and Irv experience the slaying in the spirit—and I didn"t?"

I shrugged. "David, I've never experienced it myself, so don't think that because you didn't, something is wrong."

"But I wanted to feel that peace! I wanted it in the worst way but it just didn't happen!"

"That should serve as confirmation that it is truly the Holy Spirit at work. Richard didn't want it and he got it!" I looked at Richard, who grinned sheepishly and nodded.

David leaned closer and in a near whisper asked, "Wayne, would you pray over me when we get back to Medjugorje? I'd really like to experience that peace."

What could I say? I had never had anyone slain in the spirit when praying over them. "I don't know if it will happen, David. I've never done that before."

But David pressed on. "Would you try?"

I agreed, telling him we would do it on our way to Dubrovnik when we stopped in Slano, a small village about halfway between Medjugorje and Dubrovnik.

Early the next morning, our group gathered at the foot of Krizevic. This was the last day of the pilgrimage and the final event was climbing the mountain and praying the Stations of the Cross. It turned out to be far more than that.

To the amazement of everyone, the priests, seminarians, and Lutheran clergy, along with a few other men from the group, carried Father Don Kapitz in his wheel chair to the top of Krizevic! Father Joe Tagg led the way and insisted on carrying him the entire distance, while the others rotated between stations. It was an incredible act of love and bonding for all the clergy.

At the top we prayed, sang a couple of hymns of

thankgiving, and then made our way to quiet little cor-
ners to be alone. Coming over a small ridge, I came upon
Father Ron Rieder kneeling on the hard stones, weeping.
I backed up quietly, not wanting to disturb my
once-reluctant pilgrim priest in his moment with Jesus and
His mother.

We slowly pulled out of the little village on our way to
Dubrovnik to await a next-morning flight home. It had
been a tremendous pilgrimage; the nice thing was, it wasn't
over yet.

Stopping in Slano, a beautiful little fishing village on
the Adriatic, we gathered for a last Mass together, and
afterward, individuals came forward to give witness of what
the pilgrimage had meant to them.

The Catholic witnesses were grateful for the opportunity to have met and shared with Protestants; to know that
there really were very few differences between the faiths.
And the Lutherans, Irv, Richard, and David came forward
to witness as a threesome. It was a fitting end.

"But there's one more thing before we go," David said
to me as people began moving out the door toward our
waiting bus. "Remember, you promised that you would
pray over me."

I took a deep breath. "If that's what you want but I
can't promise you anything."

"I understand but I would very much appreciate it."

Most of the little group of Charismatics that had been
so open and helpful to the Lutheran clergy, along with
Richard and Irv, hastily gathered around David. I began
praying over him. Soon there was a beautiful, musical
rhythm of praying in tongues coming from the group. I
made the final sign of the cross on David's head and in
what seemed like slow motion, he sank to the ground, aided
by those around him.

As David lay in peace, Irv was laughing and crying at

the same time. "I can't believe what just happened: I was actually singing in tongues!"

We were the last to board the bus and the happiest pilgrim of all had to be David, who at last felt the peace of the Holy Spirit pass through him. "How do we take this back to our churches?" he asked as he sank into his seat.

"David, you'll find it to be a lot easier than you think. Just tell it the way it happened. Gospa will do the rest."

Two weeks after our return home, I received a letter from Father Ron Rieder that began: "Dear Wayne, I wish words could express thoughts and feelings adequately; I am so grateful for having gone to Medjugorje. I will never be the same. It was the greatest week in my life. . . ."

It was indeed, a very special pilgrimage.

20
Abandonment

"If you would abandon yourselves to me, you will not even feel the passage from this life to the next life. You will begin to live the life of Heaven on earth."

January, 1991: the beginning of another year of heavy travel. I had already completed two tours and was home long enough to pack clean clothes before heading out again.

"I guess this is as good a place and time as any to give you this." Terri handed me a letter from the Diocesan Tribunal as I sat in quiet meditation on the soft carpeting of our bedroom.

I looked at her face but she was revealing nothing. "Is it . . . ?" I was afraid to finish the sentence.

"Just read it," she replied, sitting down beside me.

I tore open the envelope. Surely it wasn't a negative ruling by the Tribunal on my nullity of marriage; she would have told me immediately. But was it granted already?

Unfolding the letter I began reading: Dear Mr. Weible, We have received a decision from our Appeal Court which upholds the decision in your favor. . . .

I jumped to my feet. "It's been granted! I can't believe it!"

Terri tugged at my leg. "Keep reading."

I looked at her quizzically but sat back down and continued reading. Yes, the nullity was granted, but on condition that I go to counselling for an "indefinite period of time. . ."

"I don't understand. How can they do this to me?"

"What they're saying is you have to go to a psychologist to prove you are of sound mental health, which they don't think you are. I think it's a tactic to keep you out of the Church. Besides, didn't Our Lady say it would be two years?"

"Yes, but I thought maybe I was being given a special grace since I was working so hard to spread the messages." I knew immediately how selfish and immature that reasoning was, but I was crushed—and livid. There was no thought of prayer now. All reason had vanished.

Frustration increased as I realized that in two months, the entire family was due to go to Medjugorje for the Easter holidays. It was the ideal time for us to enter into the Church! Since receiving the message from Gospa that it would be two more years, I had sustained myself with my dream of entering the Church at Medjugorje. Marija and Ivan would be my sponsors, and Fathers Jozo and Svetozar would perform the rites. The church would be full and it would be a great and joyous occasion. I daydreamed about it so often, it seemed real.

I waited a couple of days to cool off and then called the Tribunal offices. Telling them of our plans to go to Medjugorje and my hopes of entering the Church there. I asked—begged in fact—that they waive the condition of counseling. Sorry, was the response, the condition stands. I felt totally abandoned.

Terri let me vent the entire range of emotions for several days before sitting me down for a talk. "Now, if you're through with all that, maybe you'll listen. Regardless of the motive behind this, you have to understand it is simply the method being used by heaven to allow you time to grow spiritually. You need to remember the special power of your mission as a Protestant speaking about the Blessed Virgin Mary. She said it would be two years and you should know by now that's what she meant. So, you need to pray about it, accept it, and get on with life."

I nodded weakly. It made sense. Terri's annulment had been granted in June, on the 25th, the anniversary of the apparitions. We accepted that as a sign that our vow to remain celibate was bringing the desired grace. Still, I was angry that the Tribunal saw me as "rigid and inflexible" when they had nothing to base such judgment on other than a psychological test I had taken as part of the case preparation; and then to make the prohibition indefinite.

Terri seemed to discern the purpose. "It's probably because of your involvement in Medjugorje. You know how cautious they are about alleged apparitions. And the fact that you are a layman—and a Protestant one at that!"

Resigned and feeling totally abandoned by the Church I loved so much, I agreed to begin counseling in February. Later, Terri also participated at the urging of our counselor. He felt her participation could only help. Thus, at our own expense, we entered into weekly sessions that would continue for nearly nine months.

The sessions became part of a growing list of struggles that had developed in the months after my return from Medjugorje in November. The most pressing, and heartbreaking, was the state of Lisa and David's marriage.

David, a reserve in the National Guard, had attended five months of officer training school in Texas, beginning in January. It was the first extended separation in their five-year marriage; but it became the catalyst for a permanent one. Shortly after his return home, David informed

Lisa that he no longer wanted to be married. After attempts at counseling failed, they began a trial separation
that by late November become permanent.

It was a shock to Lisa, but not to me. The tribulation
of the abortion had never been resolved between them.
There had been no prolonged arguments; no previous
troubles, nothing that would lead to this. But the shadow
of that one dark moment of their past lingered.

David showed no desire for any type of spiritual commitment. When Lisa returned from Medjugorje and started
attending the Baptist church of her upbringing, and later
daily Catholic Mass, David balked. There was no pressure
put on him to join her, but talk about Medjugorje and
religion bothered him to the point where it showed in his
demeanor. By October, the marriage was over. Official
proceedings for legal separation and eventual divorce commenced.

I could only comfort my daughter and encourage her
to continue trying to live the messages of Medjugorje. "I
will," she said tearfully over the telephone, "but I feel so
abandoned and alone. I just pray that one day Our Lady
will send me a good Catholic boy."

"Hey, I'll put that at the top of my prayer list!" I said
trying to cheer her up. "In the meantime, I've got a little
surprise for you. How would you like to go with me to the
New Orleans Medjugorje Peace Conference?"

Lisa was speechless, which for her, was a small miracle
in itself. "Daddy, that would be great. That's my birthday
weekend. I'd love to go!"

Her birthday was the reason I asked her to go, but
there was an ulterior motive as well. Since returning from
Medjugorje, Lisa, like myself, became entranced with the
Catholic Church. However, she had made no commitment
to convert, something I hoped would happen. Possibly the
three days of exposure to the faith at the conference would

encourage her in that direction.

It turned out to be the perfect antidote for my daughter. She spent time with Father Svet and Father Ken Roberts, both of whom were on the speaker's program. It was a time of counseling and assistance by the right priests at the right time. Medjugorje visionary Ivan was also there and Lisa was especially taken by his talk which focused on youth and the family. This young man had matured into an excellent speaker, being far more than just a superficial attraction to the conference. He had been traveling throughout the country for the past month giving such talks, learning from each stop, and creating tremendous interest in the messages.

The final push came from Mimi Kelly, director of the conference. Knowing my motive for bringing Lisa, she went out of her way to be helpful since she had a daughter about Lisa's age, and like me, had been through divorce. As a result, her daughter Christina had been through some rough teen times and Medjugorje had been her spiritual turning point. Christina's influence and sharing was more of the right medicine for Lisa's situation. And when Mimi arranged for us to be present for Ivan's evening apparition with Gospa on December 2, Lisa's birthday, it was the *coup de grâce*. Tears of sorrow were turned to tears of joy as she said to me, "Daddy, I'm going to begin instruction into the Catholic Church as soon as possible!"

I sat wearily at my desk two evenings after returning from New Orleans, rummaging through a growing pile of letters from people who had read my book. Mixed among the letters were scraps of paper with notes outlining a new book, the initial attempts of what was to be the sequel to *Medjugorje: The Message.* But I was having difficulty getting it into a working manuscript outline so that I could begin actual writing. A tentative publication date had been set for June, 1992, more than a year and a half away but close enough to where I was beginning to feel the pressure.

"I'll never get this started," I thought as I sorted mail from book notes. I was leaving in the morning for three days of talks in St. Louis, at the request of Rich and Connie Bampton. Finally, in exasperation, I opened my brief case and shoved the pile of notes and letters inside, promising myself that I would catch up on both during the tour.

Late into the evening after the first night's talk, I read the letters, sorting out those that required an answer. It was late, and there was a two-hour drive to the next speaking site in the morning, but I was determined to get them answered so that I would have time to work on the new manuscript.

The letters were filled with stories of struggle and conversion from those who had read my book and became part of the Medjugorje story; they were sad, tragic, enthralling and uplifting, all at the same time. While I had always received a steady load of mail, it had increased markedly since the book's publication. I was always overwhelmed during marathon sessions of reading them.

"You just make yourself comfortable back there and do your work," Rich said as we headed out on the interstate from St. Louis. "You've got plenty of time and it's a good road."

"Thanks, Rich, I'm going to answer a few letters and work on the outline of the new book." I opened my laptop computer and grabbed the first letter to review its contents. It was a poignant story of inner struggle from a woman who felt abandoned by God—until reading about Medjugorje's apparitions. The book, she stated, had changed her life. Contemplating the woman's story, I suddenly felt that warm, gentle presence of Our Lady speaking to my heart. After a few moments, I tapped Rich on the shoulder. "Excuse me, but you've got to hear this."

I read the letter out loud, leaving out the name and some personal details meant only for me to read; afterwards we sat in silence. "That is an incredible story," Connie said. "You must be very proud at what the book is doing."

"Well, it isn't because of the writing, and to be honest, I'm humbled that Our Lady let me put my name on it. She's the reason it's touching people."

Returning to my computer, I started to answer the letter. But the presence of Gospa was still there. "You know, I need to do a book about these letters. It's been on my mind for a long time, and Terri has told me numerous times I needed to do it. I thought I'd put it together after the sequel to the first book, but just now I felt Our Lady saying to me: *"Do the book on the letters first!"*

"Well then, do it!" Rich laughed.

I answered the entire stack of letters before arrival at the speaking site, exhilarated and relieved with the thought of doing the letters book. The sequel to the first could wait.

One trip remained before a long break for the holidays. Sister Margaret Catherine Sims, my spiritual director from my first trip to Medjugorje, had asked me to come to Boston for several talks. I was glad to go, happy to see her again and tell her about my new writing project. She had become my unofficial "spiritual mother" since that first pilgrimage.

"That sounds like a great book," she said as we left the airport. "When do you plan to have it out?"

"Well, I telephoned my publisher immediately with the sudden change of writing plans. They agreed without hesitation that this would be okay. I took that as a strong confirmation that it was to be done as Our Lady requested."

"Of course," Sister Margaret smiled, "did you ever doubt that?"

I just smiled back. This strongly charismatic nun with a penchant for bluntness was a tireless worker for Gospa. She headed up Medjugorje Messengers, an organization manned by volunteers whose goal was to evangelize New England. She had been to Medjugorje more than 40 times and was well acquainted with the visionaries and Franciscans. "We wanted to get Father Jozo to come and be with you for these three days, but you know him. He's just not ready yet to take on international travel."

It didn't matter. The crowds were tremendous, eager to learn more of the apparitions and their impact on individuals. Thoughts of my nullity dilemma, Lisa's impending divorce, and even the new book, were temporarily forgotten.

The second evening I was speaking at a large auditorium in Lowell, Massachusetts. I was immediately greeted by a woman from Connecticut, who knew of my desire to take the message to Russia. She had made tentative arrangements for a trip. "You will be able to reach thousands in large stadiums. It's all but arranged if you accept," she told me just before the talk on the first evening.

Pumped up by this news, I spoke with a special fire, ending the session by telling the audience about the impending trip to Russia, and asking for their prayers.

Crowds of people immediately surged to the base of the stage for autographs of the book and tapes which were on sale in the foyer of the auditorium. As the last person left, a man wearing an unusual hat hesitantly approached. He had been standing nearby, waiting patiently for the last person to leave.

Visibly shaken, he asked if he could have a few minutes of my time. "Of course, how can I help you?"

"I know this may sound strange to you, and believe

me, it's never happened before," he stammered. "But . . .
I feel that the Blessed Virgin Mary just spoke to me while
you were talking about your possible trip to Russia. She
said you need to go to Poland—and I'm supposed to help
you get there!"

I looked at him for a long time. "I'm sorry, what's your
name?"

"Stan, Stan Majewski. I'm Polish, but I was raised in
Australia, and have lived here in the States for a long time."

"Stan, if this is meant to happen, it will. We'll both
pray about it and see what happens."

He laughed nervously. "This is really strange because
I don't know anyone in Poland who is involved with
Medjugorje. I just know I'm supposed to help you."

I had received many similar offers of help throughout
the years of the mission. Most never materialized. Again,
I told Stan to pray about it and, scribbling my office telephone number on a scrap of paper, gave it to him adding,
if he still felt compelled to do it, to call me.

The following morning, Sister Margaret picked me up
to drive me to her convent for a short talk to the sisters. "I
had the strangest dream last night," she began. "It was
like a prophecy. I've been praying about it all morning. I
dreamed that there was a horrible war taking place in
Medjugorje and everything was being destroyed, with thousands of people killed. It was so realistic and terrible because many of the people killed were women and children."

She went on for a good fifteen minutes, remembering
the dream in its minute points. Then, as an afterthought
she added, "The strangest thing happened at the end of
the dream. A man wearing a funny little hat suddenly came
up to me and said, 'Wayne must go to Poland!' "

Startled, I asked, "Did you see him at the talk last
night?"

"What man at the talk? I'm talking about my dream!"

I quickly told her about Stan Majewski. "Wayne, I promise you, I didn't see anybody up front. In fact, I was in the foyer helping with the books and tapes!"

Sister Margaret was sure the trip to Poland would be arranged. "It's hard to understand sometimes the way God speaks to us, but I know from experience this is no coincidence. You'll be going to Poland!"

"That's okay with me. I can add it on to the Russian trip. But I hope the other part of your dream is only that—a dream."

"So do I," Sister Margaret replied, "but I'm not very optimistic with the rumblings presently taking place over there!"

Sister Margaret's prophetic dream seemed to be coming true all too soon—but not in Medjugorje. Tensions were high throughout December over the very real possibility of a third world war stemming from the imminent invasion of Kuwait by Iraq. Once again, the Middle East was the center of confrontation.

The Christmas celebration of the birth of the King of Peace, was tempered by Gospa's somber message given through visionary Marija on Christmas day: *"Today, I invite you in a special way to pray for peace. . . . Pray, because Satan wants to destroy my plan of peace. Be reconciled with one another, and by means of your lives, work that peace may reign in the whole earth."*

The threat of war and its side-product, terrorism, brought pilgrimages to Medjugorje to a halt. The village suddenly returned to the way it was in the days before the apparitions, much to the chagrin of the people in the process of adding more rooms to homes, more souvenir shops, and more restaurants. Our planned family trip to the little village for April now seemed in jeopardy.

January's schedule took me from Detroit, Michigan, to the Grand Caymens in the Caribbean; back to Minneapolis, Minnesota, and then to Mississippi. In the middle of all this was the news concerning my annulment.

By the time I arrived in Greenville, Mississippi at the end of the month, I was as sick as I had been in years. It was a combination of exhaustion, traveling from hot to cold climates—and mental depression. I would stay in bed all day, arising only to prepare for the evening's talk. Book store autographing sessions and other daytime functions were cancelled. Strangely, while hardly able to even kneel for the rosary before each evening talk, I would suddenly feel fine, give the talk and within half an hour, be sick again.

But on the last day of the tour, I had had it. I was ready to cancel and head home. One of the ladies who had arranged the Mississippi schedule was a nurse and had been taking excellent care of me, but as good as it was, I was still sick. "We understand if you have to cancel tonight's talk, but it's a real shame because you were to speak in the largest Baptist church in Greenville. It's the only place big enough to hold the crowd."

That did it. "I can't pass that up. We've stuck it out this long; just give me something to get me though the day!"

It was the perfect place to again stress that the mother of Jesus came to Medjugorje for all of us. Using the Persian Gulf struggle as an example, I pointed out that she wanted us to seek peace as well, so that we might come together as one family led by Jesus. "Just this week, the Virgin Mary gave this message to Marija," I told them in concluding a short but fervent talk. Pulling the message from my pocket, I began to read: *"Dear children, today, like never before, I invite you to prayer. Your prayer should be a prayer for peace. Satan is strong and wishes not only to destroy human life but also nature and the planet on which you live. . . ."*

As we prepared to leave, I thanked the Baptist minister for opening his church to the message of Medjugorje. The look on his face indicated he wasn't quite sure about what had transpired in his church, but shaking his head he said, "This, of course is all new to me, but I certainly am impressed with your sincerity, and the response of the people, especially those of our congregation. And, we must pray for peace and hope this situation in the Middle East doesn't lead to Armageddon!"

For awhile, it looked as if it might. Iraq's quick invasion of Kuwait led to an even quicker buildup of forces from nations around the world. In the next forty days, the world prepared for the worst in the predicted high-casualty land battle for the freedom of oil-rich Kuwait. The largest oil spill in history was deliberately released into the Persian Gulf in a horrendous act of ecological terrorism; putrid, black smoke created by nearly 600 oil wells maliciously set ablaze engulfed the entire region. The words of Our Lady's January message were coming true: ". . . Satan is strong and wishes not only to destroy human life but also nature and the planet on which you live. . . ."

But then words she had given in the early days of the apparitions also leaped to mind: *"With prayer, you can stop wars and change the laws of nature."*

As suddenly as the land war began, it came to an abrupt halt. Kuwait was liberated and the world breathed a collective sigh of relief as global holocaust was averted. I was convinced that it was the direct result of worldwide prayer by people of all faiths, though the threatened loss of oil supplies also played a major role.

Shortly before we were due to leave for Medjugorje, I received a telephone call from Stan Majewski. He was in Puerto Rico, leaving momentarily for Myrtle Beach to meet with me, and due to arrive in a few hours. I was not happy with his coming to my home town unannounced, knowing little about him other than the brief meeting in Lowell. But it was too late to change his plans. Accommodations were booked for him in a nearby motel with a meeting scheduled for the first thing in the morning.

"I'm sorry to come without notice but I wanted to tell you in person about my trip to Medjugorje and Poland, and the arrangements I've made for your tour," he began as we sipped coffee at the motel restaurant.

"Stan, I'm not even sure I can go to Poland this year. Why didn't you call me as we discussed before making the trip?"

Stan gave a nervous little laugh. "This whole thing is so strange, I just felt a need to go to Medjugorje first for confirmation, and then on to Poland if the confirmation came. It did, and I simply wanted to see you in person to tell you about it."

I leaned back in the chair and smiled. "Okay, tell me your story." I sensed this was Our Lady's work and I needed to listen. If she wanted me in Poland, I would go.

Stan's face lit up as he moved his chair closer. "By the way, my Polish name is Stas, and if you're going there, you'll need to get used to a few Polish words." He laughed nervously again and continued. "I have to tell you that after you left Lowell, I kept hearing in my mind, 'The doorway to Russia is Poland.' That's when I decided to leave as soon as I could. I wanted to go to Medjugorje first and see Father Jozo for confirmation."

Stas told me about arriving in Dubrovnik, with no way of getting to Medjugorje. He didn't have much money and knew he had to be frugal. Finally, he was able to hitch a ride to the village with a group of pilgrims from Puerto Rico. "They were wonderful people and that's why I was there before coming here, just to see them and tell them about my trip to Poland."

He had seen Father Jozo only briefly, telling him the story of Our Lady's message to him about bringing me to Poland, leaving convinced that he had the confirmation as Father Jozo said he would pray for its success. Eight weeks later, after traveling across Poland several times, he contacted a prayer group that had formed as a result of Medjugorje. "Up to that point, bishops and priests would have nothing to do with a tour to promote the apparitions, especially by a Protestant. They told me to go to the Lutheran Church." Now, he continued, with the aid of this prayer group and two priests, a nominal tour was being arranged. "If you can go, that is," Stas concluded.

Amazing, I thought. Here is a man in his middle 40s, who has also suffered the pain of divorce, has a small landscaping business and only recently became interested in Medjugorje. And now, Our Lady has him arranging this trip. We talked awhile longer, filling in details and tentatively set the tour for sometime in October. Putting him on the plane for Boston, I made him promise to telephone our office when plans were firm so we could schedule the dates.

We decided to go through with plans to go to Medjugorje for Easter, despite warnings from friends and family that terrorism was still a threat to international travel. But the trip was peaceful and a delight since Marija and Milka were both at home. Marija spoke of the rumblings of imminent trouble throughout Yugoslavia, as Slovenia and Croatia made plans to withdraw from the federation. Remembering Sister Margaret's dream, I asked her when she thought it might occur. "I don't know. Maybe this summer."

That surprised and alarmed me; I knew Serbia wouldn't sit idly by and watch their economic suppliers simply disappear around the bend.

Conversation turned to other things, and I told Marija about plans to go to Poland. "I'll probably stop in Italy to see Paolo and his father about the book on the way home," I added.

"That is good, and maybe I will be there also!" Terri and I smiled, knowing that Marija was spending a lot of time now with Paolo's family. There were no formal plans of marriage yet, but it was accepted that it would occur at some future date. We left early the next morning with Milka driving us to Dubrovnik.

During the flight home, I thought of the things that had happened in the last few months. My counseling had started and I knew that once completed, there should be nothing to deny entrance into the Catholic Church. Lisa, while still despondent over the breakup of her marriage, had pulled herself together through pastoral counseling and was taking instructions to become Catholic. And, I could now look forward to going to Poland and Russia.

Of far more importance though, the world had averted what could easily have developed into another global holocaust. And in my heart, I knew the prayers, fasting and penance from those touched by Medjugorje, had played a major role. The words from one of Our Lady's messages at Medjugorje echoed in my mind: *"If you would abandon yourselves to me."* And then her words confirmed by the endless examples of grace when we listen: *"I will never abandon you!"*

21
Children of the Sewers

"Pray, and do it with fervor. Include the whole world in your prayer. Pray, because prayer makes one live."

Lillian Gorman was brimming with joy. "I am so happy you are finally coming to my country to speak about Medjugorje!"

"It's an honor. I've wanted to come to South America for a long time now. I appreciate your efforts to organize the tour, and since Our Lady has given us this unexpected little sign by seating us together," I added with a smile, "I'd say it's going to be a powerful trip!"

Lillian giggled shyly. "I was afraid maybe you had decided not to come."

I had deliberately waited until the last possible moment to rendezvous with Lillian, giving cause for her alarm. Having earlier secured a seating assignment, I had been on the telephone for nearly an hour with David Manuel. The second book was completed and I had spent several days with him wrapping up the editing. But there were parts that troubled David—and he was pushing hard for changes.

Already fatigued from travel and working furiously to complete the book, I was in no mood for last-minute changes with which I did not agree. In undisguised anger, I ended the marathon telephone conversation by telling him to publish it as it was, and then walked around Miami International Airport trying to regain composure.

Seeing Lillian at the gate just before boarding, we discovered we had randomly been seated together. I had looked forward to being alone, but realized immediately Our Lady's hand in this, and was now glad for Lillian's company. Not really knowing her other than our meeting at the New Orleans conference in December last year, I listened intently to her story of why and how she wanted me to bring Medjugorje to Colombia. She told me about a man named Jaime Jaramillo, who had founded a foundation to aid the thousands of abandoned street children in Bogota.

Jaime's involvement with the "children of the sewers" as they were called, began at the early age of nineteen. A young street girl who had been doused with gasoline and cruelly set afire by police was left to die on the street. She was a victim of a heartless new police policy of making examples of children caught stealing from the merchants. Even more cruel, people ignored her, walking over or around her. But Jaime, deeply touched and shaken by the cruelty and apathy of the people, took her to a hospital emergency room for treatment.

Days later, he paid the hospital bill, picked her up and asked where she lived. The child led him to an affluent street, then to a manhole in the street and pointing to it said, "This is where I live—down there!" It was then that Jaime Jaramillo took it upon himself to begin a one-man outreach program to care for these children.

Jaime came from an affluent family and a cultured background. At first, he was mocked and laughed at, and then rejected by friends and family members. He was viewed by the general public as an eccentric. But like other eccentrics, such as St. Francis of the past, and Mother Teresa of the present, he continued his mission.

Now thirty-two years old and extremely successful as a petroleum engineer, Jaime is a legend throughout Colombia. Married to a beautiful young woman who helps him by overseeing the operations of the foundation, and the father of their two little children, he somehow is able to balance a homelife with the arduous task of taking care of the street children.

"I came to the New Orleans conference from my home in Memphis, Tennessee," Lillian added, "so I could bring material on Jaime, hoping to get others involved. That is when I decided to ask you if you would come to Bogota to meet Jaime, and speak about Medjugorje. But I did not realize how difficult it would be."

She explained that Colombia was a very traditional and conservative Catholic country, and Marian apparitions without approval of the Church were definitely not a part of their devotions. Knowledge about Medjugorje was virtually non-existent. But Lillian had a niece now living there who had lived in Memphis for a long time. This young woman named Leila, had gone to Medjugorje with Lillian, and was thus the only source of help in arranging the tour. She began working on it and eventually a small prayer group of dedicated volunteers was formed. Now, a full schedule of talks had been arranged in Bogota, Medellin, and Cali, the three largest cities in Colombia.

"Leila has done a good job and a young man from Memphis, whom she has been dating is there now as well, so you won't be the only American," Lillian concluded.

"Has Jaime Jaramillo been to Medjugorje?" I asked.

"No, but I hope we can arrange for the two of you to meet sometime during your stay in Bogota."

With three cities in only eight days, I didn't hold much hope for a meeting with Jaime. "Maybe he'll come to one of the talks and we'll have a few minutes."

We were met at the Bogota airport by a sizeable delegation of tour volunteers. Leila was an engaging young woman filled with excitement now that the tour was starting. "There is a reception at my home, with some good Colombian food, and you can meet the other volunteers. Then we'll take you to your hotel for a good night's rest," she added after introducing me to Roy Peters, her American boyfriend from Memphis.

"I certainly hope you have time to meet Jaime Jaramillo," Roy said in a quiet voice as we walked to the cars, "maybe even visit one of his safe houses he has established to help these kids."

I told Roy it was dependent on the timing of the talks. On the car ride to Leila's home, he told me about Jaime coming to Memphis. "From the time I met him, I knew he was special. I wanted to help so we convinced him to come to Memphis for some talks to help raise funds. He told me this week that upon his return home, he received many phone calls from Memphis parents, thanking him for what he said about family and values. He also said that during his time in Memphis and since, no child had died in the sewers, and no one was hurt. That is highly unusual."

The more I heard, the more I wanted to meet this man. I began to sense Our Lady had something special planned for me concerning him.

"We hope people come to the talks, especially the first one in the morning," Leila said. "I've been worried because it is at a very large church on a military base. The talk is at 10 A.M., and it is on a work and school day."

Those concerns became secondary on arrival at Leila's home. One of the volunteers informed her that a call had come from the archbishop's office in effect canceling all of the talks, saying they could not be held in the churches. "But who was calling?" Leila asked plaintively. The volunteer did not know. There was suddenly mass confusion.

I looked around the large living room at the somber faces. "Wait a minute here, let's not panic!" But inside, I was dying. Had I traveled thousands of miles here just to have everything canceled? "Our Lady's message at Medjugorje is to pray, fast, and do penance," I plowed on. "I suggest we begin this tour by praying the rosary. The rest will be up to Our Lady's intercession!"

And with that everyone dropped to their knees as I led them in an intense prayer of the rosary. I didn't eat much of the "good Colombian food." I was anxious to go to the hotel and sleep, hoping everything would work out by morning.

And it did—well beyond expectations! We left for the first site, not sure if anyone would be there or if the church would be open, hoping that news of the cancellation was a mistake. As we approached the base, there was an abnormally slow movement of automobiles on the road. "It's probably an accident," Leila said, "or maybe its a special event."

My talk was the special event! The church was open and literally hundreds of people were pouring into the streets and surrounding parking lots. Included in the crowd were many priests and nuns, and busloads of school children. "Would you look at this!" Leila squealed with delight.

I let out a long sigh of relief—and happiness. "I didn't think Our Lady would bring me this far and have no one to listen to her messages."

People were standing elbow to elbow, even in the choir loft. The entire assembly prayed the rosary with a fervor and the talk lasted more than two hours. I told them the basic story of Medjugorje and of my involvement, ending with something new added to all my talks in the last month. "I would like to close by giving you two gifts; one from me and one from Our Lady. At Medjugorje, Our Lady gives those who come there a very special blessing, using the grace given her by Jesus. I now give all of you here Our Lady's special blessing!" The crowd began to kneel *en masse.* "Secondly, I promise you that from this moment on, I will pray for each and every one of you every day for the rest of my life. Jesus knows you and your needs so I will offer every one of you to him!"

We then closed with a consecration to the Immaculate Heart of Mary, as I added, ". . . who always leads us to her Son!"

Word spread like wild fire and that evening was more of the same. Thousands crammed into a large church which, again, was open. "I have received no word of any prohibition," the priest responded upon our arrival. We had asked to assure we were not being disobedient to orders from the archbishop.

But the next morning, we found the church closed, the priest not sure about allowing the talk. With another turnout of thousands, a makeshift stage was hastily put together in the parking lot. The prayer group had preplanned in the event of a lockout and before it was over, thousands more had come from nearby apartment buildings. Again, a fervent praying of the rosary and consecration to Our Lady. Afterwards, it became a huge block party with people filling the streets, singing, dancing, and clapping their hands.

As we dined in a small restaurant, one of the volunteers entered and informed Leila that the afternoon session had been cancelled, "But tonight is okay."

In light of what had already occurred, we felt fortunate it was the only cancellation. "One good thing is we can spend more time with Jaime," Roy said, referring to a short meeting of approximately an hour which had been arranged at Jaime's nearest safehouse. "It will give you the time to see his facilities and speak to the kids."

Studying the pamphlets Roy had given me on Jaime's foundation, I learned that it was called Los Ninos de Andes—The Children of the Andes. Bogota is a city built in a valley 8,600 feet above sea level and a drizzle of rain is almost constant. Because of this, an underground drainage system for neighboring hills meshes with the city's crude sewer system. Thus, the roof over the abandoned children's heads consists of streets and building foundations, with manhole covers and large drain pipes serving as doorways.

The street children had taken to their underground world because it became too dangerous to sleep outside at night. Army and police forces had militarized the city as a result of car bombings and shootings, direct byproducts of the multi-billion dollar cocaine trade that had become the major export and worldwide symbol of Colombia.

The children were attacked, doused with gasoline and ignited by paramilitary personnel; to eat they rob, and when they become involved in a life of crime, they eventually get into drugs and other criminal activities. Merchants, fearing the loss of revenue and angered at the thievery and peskiness of the children, hired criminal hit men to rid the sewers of them as though they were an epidemic of rats. They viewed Jaime as a cause, and thus, targeted him as well.

But his reputation grew by quantum leaps. In the last several years, Jaime had been kidnapped twice by gangs that prey on the affluent for ransoms. Each time they let him go unharmed when they discovered who he was. I shook my head as I read the last brochure. "This guy is something!"

"Yes he is," Roy said. "Last year he was nominated for

the Nobel Peace Prize, but he never completed the papers necessary to place his name among the candidates. He said he didn't have time."

Finally, I was face-to-face with this man whom I had learned so much about in so short a time. He was a little taller and a little heavier than me, with striking features and eyes filled with kindness. "So, you are the one speaking about this place in Yugoslavia where the Blessed Mother is appearing?"

"Yes, and you are the one living her messages by assisting these children."

There was immediate friendship and respect between us. "Come, I will give you a tour so that you can see and meet some of my children."

As we entered the main building, a small toddler came down the hallway toward us, followed by a small teenage girl who quickly scooped him up in her arms. Jaime told me the child had been born in the sewers, the mother being sixteen years old; she also had a six-month-old baby, both children fathered by an eighteen-year-old she had met in the sewers. "They have been together for three years and only last month was I able to convince them to come here. Would you like to see the baby?"

I followed Jaime into one of the small side rooms to find the little baby asleep on a lower bunkbed, the father napping on the upper bunk. On completion of the tour, I turned to Jaime. "Can I see you outside alone for a moment?"

He followed me into the front area of his complex. I had felt the inner urging of Our Lady again. She was asking me to go into the sewers, to see for myself this horror of abandoned children. My initial reaction was the same feeling I had in the Philippines when I was asked to go into a barrio to pray with little children. But this time, even though reluctant and apprehensive of the danger of such a move, I asked, "Jaime, would you take me into the sewers to see these children?"

Jaime was only mildly surprised—and pleased that I wanted to go. "But it is dangerous. Many of these children have become hardened criminals and drug addicts. They have killed."

"I understand, but I need to go. I think the Blessed Mother wants me to go there with you."

"You could become very ill." He told me how members of the CBS television crew of the *20/20* program had become so sick that many of them were hospitalized.

"Jaime, I've got to go down there with you!"

It was settled. We arranged to meet at my hotel after the talk around 11 P.M. Throughout the evening, I was edgy, wondering what was in store. It was amazing knowing that even though Our Lady was doing the asking, I still had doubts and fears.

I waited at the hotel, dressed in jeans, dress shirt and one of my favorite sweaters Terri insisted I bring. Now I was glad I did as it was drizzling rain with temperatures in the low fifties. There was one minor complication; a couple who had come to the talk and heard I was going with Jaime, had come along, hoping he would take them also.

We waited until midnight. The couple gave up and left. Still, I sat in the lobby until 1 A.M.; still no Jaime. That surprised me as he had a car phone and always kept in touch with family and others during his excursions into the sewers. At last, and with great relief, I went to bed; it wasn't meant to be. Maybe I hadn't really heard Our Lady asking me to go . . .

I was awakened at 5:15 A.M. by the shrill ring of the telephone. It was Jaime. "Hello, Wayne, I am sorry that I was unable to come last night." His voice was heavy with fatigue and emotion.

"That's okay, I understand your schedule–"

"No, it wasn't that. A terrible thing happened; I was trapped in the sewers all night with two little children and couldn't get out to call you."

Jaime had gone into the sewers to prepare the children for my coming. He told how a large drainage pipe blocked with refuse had suddenly ruptured and filled the pipe line he and the children were in with rampaging water. "I went down early to clear the way for you to come so that you would not be harmed, and found these two little ones. The water caught us and swept the little boy from my grip, but I was able to hang onto the little girl. We were trapped until just a few minutes ago."

I didn't know what to say, numbed by the events he had just described. After a long silence, Jaime asked, "Do you still want to go with me?"

"Yes, I'll be ready in a few minutes." It wasn't bravery, or foolishness—or sense of adventure. I had to go now!

Hastily dressing, I met Jaime in front of the hotel a few minutes later. We set out at breakneck speed through the steady rain, routinely running red lights along the still-quiet streets. "Aren't you afraid the police will stop us?" I queried, hoping he would take the hint and slow down.

"My friend, you do not stop on the streets if possible," he answered with a slight smile. "It is too dangerous, especially in this area!" Suddenly wheeling around a corner, Jaime came to a stop on a narrow side street. "We will stop here for food to take to the children. Please bring the bags."

I grabbed the large sacks lying on the car floor and hurried after Jaime into a small combination cafe and grocery store. It was immediately discernible that the people knew him. Taking the bags from me, Jaime began pointing out items to the clerks who raced to fill the order, while the cafe customers stared in mild curiosity.

Thoroughly soaked and shivering, a man in ragged

pants and shirt was standing just outside the wide opening of the store, hungrily watching the loading of the food
sacks. Jaime motioned for him to come into the store and
instructed the clerk to give him anything he wanted to eat.
The man rushed to the counter, thanking Jaime profusely
as the clerk and customers stared at him with disdain. A
boy of about 10, seeing what had transpired rushed up to
Jaime, speaking rapidly in Spanish. Jaime tousled his long,
wet hair and told the clerk to take care of him as well.

"The two of them live on the streets. I try to help them
also," he explained as the beggars gulped down sandwiches
and hot coffee.

As we prepared to leave with the sacks of food, a man
in a stylish long leather coat suddenly stopped Jaime, handing him a small card. He thanked the stranger and we
headed for his car with the two street people insisting on
helping. "That man," Jaime said, motioning to the man in
the leather coat leaving the cafe, "he is a famous football
star here in Colombia. He has promised to help me with a
donation."

"Do you receive much help locally?"

Jaime shrugged. "Yes, we have many problems in our
country with the drug cartels, but there are also some good
people. The government also helps some because it is good
for their public image. But you see these two," he said
motioning toward the two beggars busily loading the food
bags into the rear of the car, "there are thousands like
them that receive no aid."

Just before leaving, I gave each of them a Medjugorje
medal, and as we drove away, they screamed thank-yous
and made the sign of the cross.

Ten minutes later, I was carefully following Jaime across
a small lot in the now-increased rain, clutching a bag of
food and trying to keep from slipping. This was it. The
entrance into the sewers was a large drain pipe with a pu-

trid, torrent of cloudy water roaring along the bottom. Within seconds, my white running shoes were covered with mud as I struggled to keep from falling into the water. The stench was overwhelming. Jaime, wearing waist-high boots and a slicker, trudged through the torrent toward the dim entrance.

Once inside the tunnel, he let out a series of loud shouts. Bodies suddenly began emerging out of crevices, and from the darkness of the backstretches of the sewer. The children were all ages and sizes. Glancing only briefly at me, they eagerly turned full attention to Jaime and the food bags. It was an incredible sight.

Fifteen minutes later, as we made our way out of the tunnel and back to the car, several of the children followed to get more food for others deeper inside the maze of pipes. "Will they actually take the food to the others or will they keep it for themselves for later?" I asked Jaime.

"They will give it to the ones who are sick or hiding inside the lines. There is a bond of honor between them no matter what they may have done."

I suddenly felt sick—not from the water or stench, but from the impossibility of it all. Getting into the car to escape the cold and rain, I wondered what would these children do if there was no one like Jaime to care for them? One boy, about eighteen, stood near the car, shivering in a cutoff shirt, thin pants and no shoes. I got back out of the car and took off my sweater, handing it to him in silence. He took it with a slight nod of his head.

I wanted to return to the hotel. I had seen enough. But Jaime wasn't through. "We have one more stop. There is a girl with a baby I want to see about coming to the home."

It was a solid fifteen minutes away and traffic was beginning to pick up. I glanced at my watch noting that I had approximately an hour and a half to clean up and get to the airport for my flight to Medellin. "Do not worry.

We will make it," Jaime said. Somehow, I didn't believe him.

We pulled up under a busy overpass onto a muddy field close to the culvert where the woman and the baby were supposed to be. Again, about seven or eight children appeared as Jaime approached with the last bag of food. But within minutes, a police van also arrived. After a brief discussion with Jaime, several policemen began herding the children toward it with Jaime in close pursuit, bargaining with them. The police wanted to take us all to the precinct and sort it out there. But Jaime persevered.

Once again, Jaime's reputation saved us. He convinced them to let him take the children away from the culvert. We quickly loaded all of them into his car, and with the help of several of the officers, managed to get the car out of the mud and onto the road. It was a foregone conclusion now that I would miss my flight.

Jaime drove the children to the home of one of his volunteers who would see that they got to one of the safe houses. "Don't worry about your connection. I will get you another," he said, picking up his car phone and calling his office. Within minutes, he had me booked on a later flight.

Pulling up to the entrance of the hotel, I was suddenly in no hurry to leave this man. "I'm going to help you, Jaime. I promise you, I'm going to help raise funds for your safehouses."

Jaime smiled serenely. "You have already helped just by coming with me. Say a prayer for the little ones I found in the sewers last night, and for all my children."

Hugging him, I vowed I would pray for them everyday. "I'll see you again, don't worry!" I hurried into the hotel with only twenty minutes to clean up and leave for the airport. But at the moment, I didn't care. All I could think about was those children living in the sewers.

22
As Never Before

"Today, in a special way I invite all of you to prayer and renunciation. For now as never before, Satan wants to show the world his shameful face by which he wants to seduce as many people as possible onto the way of death and sin . . ."

Medellin was a continuation of the excellent work done by Leila and her volunteers, as a huge crowd gathered on the afternoon of my arrival, only hours after leaving Jaime. The adrenaline of the early-morning forage into the sewers of Bogata was still fresh as I talked of the messages of Our Lady at Medjugorje, hitting especially hard at the illegal drug industry.

This sprawling city was home to the world's largest and most powerful drug cartel, the source for production, packaging and marketing of killer cocaine, Satan's magic powder. I compared the power of Our Lady's messages of prayer, fasting, and penance, against the power of cocaine with its message of addiction, destruction, and death. There was no hesitation to point out Medellin's role.

Halfway through the talk, held in a large open-air church, dark clouds quickly gathered; suddenly, loud claps of thunder and ominous streaks of lightning seemed to surround the church as a howling wind swept through the church. The usual annoyance of the evil one was now life-threatening. Some of the overflow crowd ran terrified from the building; others screamed in fear. With a loud pop, the microphone suddenly went dead.

I prayed as several men fiddled with the mike. Almost as quickly as the "storm" developed, it dissipated. And the public address system came back on.

But Satan was not finished. I was in one of his favorite playgrounds; he was making sure I understood that. A well-dressed woman approached as we prepared to leave. She was angry. "Excuse me, but I want to tell you that you have no right coming here and accusing Colombians of spreading drugs. You have many people in your country also who are involved in drugs."

"I'm sorry if I offended you or any of the people. But this is the center of the cocaine industry and I only point that out to make the people aware of the need to follow the messages of prayer and fasting to eradicate it."

"Yes, but many of these people are forced to work with it in order to survive. It is dangerous for you and for them to talk about it in public."

Before I could answer, others came to my defense. In seconds, it turned into a full-blown, heated argument. The woman, outnumbered, abruptly turned and walked away. "Do not worry about her," one woman said. "The people need to hear what you are saying about drugs."

The evening was more of the same. Finishing the talk and opening it to questions, a man, visibly upset, began a long monologue in rapid Spanish. My translator was embarrassed. "I don't know if you want to address this man's question. He is asking how you can be allowed to speak in this church and preach the word of God when you have been through divorce—and you are not Catholic."

"It's okay, I'll answer it."

Waiting for quiet from the crowd's reaction to the

question, I walked to the podium, picking up a Bible which had been used at the beginning of the talk by the welcoming priest. "We read in the Old Testament the stories of Moses and King David," I began, holding the Bible up. "Both of them were guilty of committing the terrible sin of murder; yet, God chose them and gave them missions. He chose Moses to lead His people to the Promised Land, and He called David, the 'apple of His eye.' I feel He is doing the same with me, although I am not a Moses or a David. I am one of you. Like many of you, my life had been changed because God chose me and asked me through His mother to spread His word. That is the only qualification I have for being here and being allowed to witness to you."

There was a loud, supportive ovation and again, many turned on the questioner in my defense.

Several days later in Cali, I felt the peace return. I was limited to giving talks in a rather small assembly hall located just off a busy street in the uptown section of the city. It was hot and stuffy because of the crowds which filled every nook and cranny, cooled only by a large doorway that led to an open air garden in the center of the building. The talks were being broadcast live over a popular radio show and for that reason, I was seated at a table, having to speak into the microphone.

It was not my usual style; I liked a podium and having to sit while speaking was difficult. But on this last day, and the last talk of my Colombian tour, there was a pleasant surprise. The audience included five elderly Franciscan priests, their brown robes a familiar sight. In concluding, I again told the listeners I wanted to leave them two gifts: "The first is from Our Lady; it is her special blessing which she gives us at Medjugorje, a blessing that is a grace from Jesus. Now, I give it to you."

With that, I raised my hands and extended them toward the audience. As I turned to my right and toward the Franciscan priests, a small bird suddenly flew through the doorway and perched momentarily on the shoulder of one of the priests before flittering away.

There was a murmur from the crowd, most of whom witnessed the scene, as I smiled and added, "That, my friends, is a very special sign of her peace. May it remain with you and with all Colombians who respond to her call!"

But I found little peace in returning home. My wife was perturbed that there were two engagements scheduled during June. "I know, I promised no engagements during the summer months," I responded weakly when confronted by her. "This will definitely be the last time, but these two are important."

Terri threw up her hands. "This conversation is a broken record played each June! They are all important—I know that. The point is you cannot keep up this pace!"

Terri admitted attending the second Notre Dame Conference was vital since my new book, *Letters From Medjugorje* would be available to the public for the first time. Following that, I would be one of many speakers at a huge pro-life rally in Washington, D.C., to be held on the steps of the U.S. Capitol later in the month. "And after that you have a full schedule of personal travel with your family. So, you see my point?"

. I nodded with a wane smile.

We would be leaving immediately after my return for a week-long family reunion in Nebraska, followed by several shorter excursions. It would be a full summer, ending with the annual trip to Medjugorje for the winners of the essay contest we sponsored for the schoolchildren from our local Catholic school.

The Notre Dame trip turned out to be a time of rest and reflection; and the sale of the new book went well. Skipping some of the scheduled events of the conference, I managed to sleep a little later and enjoy a couple of runs through the campus. There was even time to pray for extended time in front of the Blessed Sacrament. I returned home far more rested than expected.

It was a good thing. With a solid field of speakers the organizers of the Washington, D.C. pro-life rally expected thousands to fill the grounds at the base of the Capitol. Father Ken Roberts was present, as well as Father Philip Pavich, an American-born Croatian in charge of the English pilgrims at Medjugorje for several years now. I was excited to be part of such an important gathering.

The excitement was short-lived as barely three thousand people turned out on a cloudless, scorching day. We sat on a wooden platform constructed on the Capitol steps, cooking like so many pieces of bacon on a grill. The rhetoric was excellent and the few in attendance were enthusiastic, but it was one of the toughest speaking engagements of the mission, having to sit in the broiling sun for nearly four hours.

Near the end of the program, Father Ken nudged me. "Look up in the sky directly over us. Can you see it?" he asked, pointing skyward. There was a small but clearly distinct rainbow in the otherwise unbroken hue of deep blue sky; it was directly over the Capitol. "That's a sign from Our Lady, letting us know heaven is pleased with the efforts even though the turnout is small," he commented, pointing it out to others on the platform.

It was comforting to hear a priest make such a comment, especially one with Father Ken's credentials. A gifted theologian constantly in demand for weekly missions throughout the states, he was now a special mentor and good friend. We shared many hours at conferences around the country, and I depended on his guidance in preparing for entry into the Catholic Church. Most impressive was his ability to know and explain the doctrines of the Church and Holy Scripture; yet, he was able to accept in a child-like manner the little gifts of grace from heaven.

It was a good start to the summer. However, July brought devastating news; little Courtney Crocker, after battling for thirteen suffering months, died of the malignant tumor at the base of her brain.

I was brokenhearted beyond comprehension. In all of the years of the mission, no single individual had so affected me even though there had been a multitude of similar cases. I hadn't really known her very long, but there was something extraordinary about this little girl. She was the epitome of redemptive suffering. In the thirteen months since her miraculous recovery from a coma when I prayed over her, Courtney lived a life of suffering that I felt enabled many souls to receive the grace of conversion.

While growing progressively worse in the months following her recovery from the coma, Courtney managed to continue in school. At first, she was able to walk about and participate in a limited way with the other children. But soon she needed a wheelchair and by springtime, Courtney was no longer able to attend school. She became an inspiration not only to the children, but to people throughout the community. Now, she was a little angel who would always be with me in my mission.

I had prayed and fasted for this little girl. But deep inside was full knowledge that she, too, had a mission: a mission of suffering for the redemption of others.

News from Medjugorje was also grim with growing apprehension over the threat of war in former Yugoslavia. Isolated attacks were becoming frequent as age-old hatreds smouldered, fanned by the ongoing breakup of the Yugoslav Federation. Chaos reigned as factions struggled for control.

Slovenia, too far north for the Serbian aggressors to sustain control, was the first to declare outright its independence; and then on June 25, 1991, the 10-year anniversary of the apparitions, Croatia followed suit, doing so at precisely the time of the daily apparition of Our Lady. It was not a coincidence.

The predominantly Croatian population of Medjugorje celebrated along with their brothers and sisters, sure that Bosnia-Hercegovina would be the next republic to declare independence. But 24 hours later, there were tanks and jets spraying destruction and death throughout Croatia. The Franciscans, at the prodding of the U.S. Embassy in Belgrade, urged the huge crowds of pilgrims to leave Medjugorje immediately, fearing a major attack on the popular shrine village. For the second time in the last seven months, only a handful of pilgrims were left in Medjugorje.

Fears were based on the systematic destruction of Catholic churches, convents, and monasteries in growing numbers. The Catholic Church of Croatia was reeling as threats and troop movements indicated that Bosnia was next. The rebel Serbs in Croatia and Bosnia moved confidently, knowing that the Federal Army's power far outweighed the hunting guns and disorganized green troops of the republics. And of course, all pilgrimages from the United States to Medjugorje passed through Dubrovnik, already jittery in anticipation of Serb invasion.

That was the situation as I prepared to take twelve teenage girls and approximately forty other pilgrims to

Medjugorje in late August. Amazingly, no one wanted to cancel, including two Protestant girls who were part of the school group!

Meeting with the parents of the girls in the school conference room two weeks before departure, I finally asked outright: "Why would you allow me to take your children to Medjugorje knowing the dangers of being so close to a war zone?"

There was quick response: "Because they are going with you, and we know Our Lady will take care of you!" That only added to my concerns.

I telephoned Medjugorje as often as possible checking on conditions. "Everything is good," Marija stated when we talked just before the last meeting with the students and their parents. "You come—Gospa will take care of you!"

There it was again.

A week before we were due to leave, I walked to my car to drive to our last group meeting at the school. It was also the last opportunity to cancel; I was still apprehensive. Opening the car door, I noticed the setting sun which was in my line of sight; it was dancing, spinning and pulsating in full phenomenal glory! "Okay, Blessed Mother," I smiled, "I get the message!"

Loud, extended applause burst spontaneously from the students and parents alike when I informed them we were definitely going to Medjugorje, "since Our Lady has given us such a strong sign of confirmation that we're to come!"

Along with the schoolkids, a teacher and two nuns from the parish were included in the contingent from Myrtle Beach. One of them, Sister Mary Alice, who taught math and science at the school, was from the "old school" of Catholic sisters—strict and tough; after meeting her, I was determined she was going to Medjugorje.

She had given Kennedy a low grade on a science project turned in past deadline. The project was in the car the morning it was due, but running late, I shooed Kennedy from the car so he would be on time—and the project was left in the car.

"Don't worry, I'll go see her and straighten everything out," I assured my despondent son. "Surely she will change your grade when she realizes it was my fault for getting you to school late."

Terri turned from her cooking. "You've never met Sister Mary Alice, have you? She goes strictly by the rules!"

"But she's a nun. She'll understand!"

"Good luck!" Terri smiled knowingly and returned to her cooking.

The following afternoon I met with Sister Mary Alice in her classroom. "So you see, Sister, it was my fault; he had the project in his book bag, but I wanted to read it before he turned it in. I forgot to put it back in his bag. And since we were late getting to the school that morning, it was forgotten as he rushed to make class on time." I smiled my sweetest smile, sure of a positive response.

"I'm sorry, but I cannot change the grade. If I make an exception for him, I'll have to make it for others." She stood there, unsmiling, arms folded, indicating the meeting was over.

"But Sister, it was my fault; and the project was turned in by his mother a little later that same day—"

"I can't help that. It was his responsibility to get it in on time. The grade stands."

"You don't know it yet, Sister, but you're going to Medjugorje!" I muttered to myself as I left the school building. Sister Mary Alice did change the grade after considering the circumstances. And she was surprised and pleased when I asked her and Sister Pat, to join us for the pilgrimage. "You could serve as chaperons for the kids," I added as a reason for the invitation.

By the second day in Medjugorje, the kids were near

rebellion. They came to me *en masse*, with one chosen as spokesperson. "Mr. Weible, can't you get Sister Mary Alice to like, lighten up a little since we're not in school?"

"Yeah, she doesn't want us to shop or anything—just go to church," another added.

I shook my head in frustration. That morning, Sister had grabbed me after the Mass. "Listen, these kids aren't getting anything out of this! They're not coming to Mass, or paying attention. All they want to do is shop and eat pizza. You need to talk to them!"

I had promised her I would; now, it appeared both sides were frustrated. "Look," I began, " Sister simply wants to make sure you're getting something out of the experience of being here. How about if we do this: you come to the front of the church this evening at 6 P.M., when the rosary begins. Pray with me and stay until after the time of the apparition. Then, if you've already attended the morning Mass, you can do what you want; but if not, you need to stay for the Croatian Mass." I looked around at the twelve teenage girls. "That sound okay to you?"

Within seconds they had agreed.

That evening, we assembled on the front steps of the church as the rosary began. Halfway through the second decade, one of the girls suddenly let out a loud gasp. "Look at this!" She held up her rosary. Several of the silver links had changed to a gold color!

"Mine is changing, too!" another exclaimed.

And then another: "Oh, look at the sun! Its spinning just like you talked about during the meeting at school!"

Immediately, there was silence as all of them fell to their knees and began fervently praying the remainder of the rosary, their heads bent so low as to almost touch their legs. Sisters Mary Alice and Pat walked by, staring in disbelief. "What did you do to them?" Sister Mary Alice whispered.

Smiling broadly, I turned my hands upward to heaven. "I didn't do a thing—but Our Lady did!"

The fervency continued through the time of the apparition. Gospa came to Marija and Ivan who were in the tower in front of our little group. As the apparition ended, Lauren, the oldest of the girls at 17, timidly tapped my shoulder. "Mr. Weible, I saw an image of a lady in a blue mist leaving the window of the tower just now. Is that the Blessed Virgin?"

Had any of the other girls told me that, I would have questioned their emotions. But Lauren was shy, quiet, and more mature than the others. I knew what she had seen because it had occurred to other pilgrims at the time of the apparition. "Yes, Lauren, I think you have just been given a very special grace, and you need to tell the others about it."

She shook her head. "Oh, no. I don't want to do that—" But with a little more coaxing, she did. Each evening thereafter, the girls gathered on the steps for the evening prayers and apparition. Other pilgrims came by to marvel at young people so deeply involved. There were no more special signs, other than they, themselves.

We managed to include fun time as well. Remarkably, Father Ken Roberts had come to Medjugorje at the same time as our pilgrimage, also with a group of teenagers! The two groups got together to sing, listen to talks, and generally enjoy themselves. They spent time with Ivan and Marija who went out of their way to accommodate so many young people in Medjugorje at one time.

In such a setting, it was hard to imagine the threat of war as close as the beautiful snowcapped mountains surrounding the little valley. Flare-ups had upgraded to full battles throughout Croatia, and rumors of troops congregating in these hills and mountains for invasion of Bosnia, had us on edge. Worse, there was talk of clashes in and around Dubrovnik—and at the airport. I prayed that we would be able to leave in a couple of days with no problems.

There was another concern. Popularity of the book had made being anonymous impossible. I wanted to spend all my time with the young people, but other requests for talks and prayers from groups and individuals were overwhelming. Two days before we were due to leave, I left the girls after our prayers and hurried to the back of St. James Church, to the furthermost bench from the outside altar. It would be the last opportunity for personal quiet time and I wanted to sit alone in peace and enjoy the Mass.

Luckily, no one else was in the area. But that was short-lived. Four pilgrims, two men and two women, came to the front benches, about fifty yards away. One of the men seemed ill and was bent over in evident pain, coughing uncontrollably, while the others surrounded him in concern. I felt an urge to go to him to see if I could be of any help, but quickly dismissed it. I wanted to be alone.

"You should go and pray over him!" It was the familiar sense of Our Lady speaking to me.

Incredibly, I responded with: "I'll just pray for him from here." The minute I thought it, I felt a mixture of remorse and incredulity that I could say no to Gospa! Still, I closed my eyes and began praying for the sick man, rationalizing that it was the same as going to him.

Within moments, I felt a tap on the shoulder. Looking up, I recognized the woman standing next to my bench as one of the women with the man who was ill. "Excuse me for disturbing you. Are you Wayne Weible?"

"Yes I am," I answered with a weak smile.

The woman, in her twenties, rung her hands and then pointed to the man in the front benches who was still bent over. "Please excuse me for disturbing you during the prayers, but that man is very ill and we were wondering if you would come and pray over him?"

Before I could answer, she broke into tears. "He's my brother, and that's my mother with him and his friend." She hesitated momentarily and her tears intensified. "He has AIDS, and is dying. We brought him here, hoping for a healing and—" She was unable to continue.

I was devastated. How could I possibly pray over him feeling this way? "Listen, I will be happy to pray over your brother," I began in a small voice, "but would it be okay if we did it tomorrow evening? I promise you, I'll be right here at this same time if you'll bring him then."

"Oh, yes!" The young woman grabbed my hand as she continued, "We're just grateful that you would take the time."

It was a difficult evening—and night; I didn't sleep much. Why did I say no? How could I have said no, knowing it was Our Lady asking? But contrition was softened by inner assurance that even after initial reluctance, she was pleased her prayer request for this man would be answered.

I took a deep sigh as I thought of how our humanity always seems to get in the way. It wasn't the first, and probably would not be the last time I would have difficulty saying yes—even though it was the Blessed Virgin doing the asking. The scriptural parable about the father asking his two sons to do a certain task came to mind. The first son, although saying no, did what his father asked; the second son said he would do it, but then he didn't. Too many times, I was like the first son.

The condition of the young man with AIDS also dominated my thoughts. His sister had given me a little background. Her brother Paul, and his companion Ed, the other man with them, had lived together for seventeen years. They truly loved each other and were dedicated in their profession as teachers in the public education system. Ed was H.I.V. positive, had no living relatives, and was a Protestant, while Paul was Catholic.

And it was the love of a mother and sister that had brought them to the little village. They believed the mother of God was appearing here, and had brought them hoping for a miraculous healing for Paul—and a spiritual healing for both.

Sitting with the two men the next evening, I related to them my hesitation to come and pray over Paul, even though I felt the Blessed Virgin Mary was asking me. "I tell you this so that you know in your heart that both of you are also her sons. She loves you and cares for you, and that's why she asked me to pray over you." Taking a deep breath, I continued. "I must also tell you, your life-style is wrong; it is a sin, and you must realize and accept it before hoping for a physical healing. I do not say that in condemnation of you because I love you as brothers in Christ."

Paul looked up and nodded his head. "Yes, I understand that and accept it," he said quietly. Ed, not sure about Medjugorje's apparitions and its ramifications, remained silent. As a Protestant, this was new and strange to him. But at this stage he was open to anything that might save his companion's life, as well as his own if necessary.

With that I put my arms around both men and prayed fervently for them to surrender completely to Jesus and be at peace. And then I prayed Paul would be healed physically.

After a brief chat, I was convinced Paul accepted whatever God had in store for him, as I added, "Remember, Our Lady brought you here. She loves you both. As long as you know that, you can handle anything!"

I walked away, knowing that two more souls had been at least exposed to Gospa's motherly love at Medjugorje. To accomplish it, she had used two willing souls, and a reluctant one. Would I ever learn?

"Well, what are we going to do now?" Maria Cartwright, our travel agent who had accompanied us on the tour, had just returned from the Yugoslav Airlines ticket office. "Our scheduled flight is cancelled and they are saying we might have to wait several days before we can leave here."

We were huddled in a far corner of the terminal, out of earshot of the pilgrims, especially the teenagers. Having already spent four hours awaiting our flight, this was ominous news, exactly what I feared might happen. Rumblings of imminent invasion had turned this normally busy airport into a ghost town. The last thing I wanted was for our group to stay in a city threatened with bombings.

"Maria, is there no other airline scheduled to land here? Can we make arrangements on another airline?"

Frowning, Maria answered. "I don't know about another airline, but I'm not going to accept having to stay here!" With that she headed for the ticket office again.

Telling the group that our plane was still delayed and we didn't know what time it would arrive, the beginnings of panic began to show on a few faces. "Hey, wait a minute," one of the teenage girls exclaimed. "We need to pray! Let's pray the rosary and ask Our Lady to get us out of here!"

"That's a great idea, Bianca, why don't you lead us?" I was beaming with pride as they gathered together with the other pilgrims surrounding them and began the prayers of the rosary. "And thank you, Blessed Mother—again!" I uttered silently as we prayed.

Two hours later, after Maria had bargained with the Yugoslav airline officials, an aircraft was sent to transport us to Split, and then to Ljubiana, where finally we boarded a Lufthansa jet for Frankfort, Germany. We overnighted there and found enough seats the following morning to return to the States.

I didn't relax until every teenager was reunited with family. For them, the intense situation in Dubrovnik and the extra day in Germany was exciting drama that only added to an already memory-packed trip. But the lessons and memories of prayer on the steps of St. James Church each evening, would far outlast the excitement of the last day.

Lying in my bed late into the night, I thanked Gospa again for the privilege of pilgrimage to Medjugorje for the seventeenth time; little did I realize, it would be my last for a long time to come.

23
Wrapped in Her Mantle

". . . I want to wrap you all in my mantle and lead you all along the way of conversion. Dear children, I beseech you, surrender to the Lord your entire past, all the evil that has accumulated in your hearts . . ."

"You left Medjugorje just in time. The situation is bad and I cannot return home because it is not safe!"

I was talking to Marija by telephone, having called Paolo in Monza, to arrange a short visit. Paolo's father Dino had completed the translation of my book and was requesting I come to Italy to finalize plans for publication.

Now I had another reason to stop in Italy. "I'm sorry you can't return home," I consoled her, "But at least we will be able to visit in Italy after my trip to Poland."

Marija had departed Medjugorje for a visit to her brother in Munich, Germany, shortly after our pilgrimage left for Dubrovnik. Numerous skirmishes between Croatians and insurgent Serbs, supported by the heavy artillery and air power of the Federal Yugoslav army, were now flaring across Croatia, making travel dangerous.

"There are more than 17,000 troops near Medjugorje at this time," Paolo related via the extension telephone as we discussed the situation. "And according to news reports, there are 200,000 refugees coming into Italy, Bosnia and Slovenia."

Reports stated there was at least one American pilgrimage stranded in Medjugorje, with no air transportation in or out of the country. Some refugees were also in Medjugorje, and many villagers had left for safer places. The men were manning outposts around the valley, armed only with hunting rifles and little else. It was hard to imagine this place of peace under seige; and while there were no confrontations as yet, it was inevitable Bosnia would be the next target of the Serbs.

Bosnia-Hercegovina was the ripest of the plums coveted by the Serbs. Bordering Serbia to the west, it was rich in farmlands and factories, with two flourishing cities, Mostar, only seventeen miles from Medjugorje, and Sarajevo, a former host city to the Winter Olympics. Conquering this republic fit nicely into the aggressor's dream of creating a Greater Serbia.

It wasn't as if Our Lady hadn't warned the people of what could happen. For more than ten years, she had come daily to teach, direct, and implore all who would listen to pray and fast for peace. In August, her monthly message given to Marija and meant for the entire world, was ominous and blunt: *"Dear children, today also, I invite you to prayer. Now, as never before, my plan has begun to be realized. Satan is strong, and wants to sweep away plans of peace and joy and make you think that my Son is not strong in His decisions. Therefore, I call all of you to pray and fast still more firmly! I invite you to renunciation for nine days, so that with your help, everything I wanted to realize through the secrets which I began in Fatima, will be fulfilled. I call you, dear children, to grasp the importance of my coming and the seriousness of the situation. I want to save all souls and present them to God. Therefore, let us pray that everything I have begun be fully realized."*

It was one of the strongest, most direct and unusual messages given by Gospa in the history of Medjugorje's apparitions; and, it followed a pattern of urgent warnings begun in the period just before the Gulf War. She now seemed to be speaking directly to the people involved in this imminent danger. Marija said when Our Lady gave this message, she was very serious. "And now we have this horrible war. You tell everyone to pray for peace in Croatia and Bosnia!"

I was anxious to reach Italy and learn more about these events. But first, there was Poland . . .

Stas Majewski was disappointed. There were only two talks planned in the eight days I would be in Poland, one in Crakow, and one in Warsaw. Additionally, plans for Russia had fallen through. "I'm sorry you're not going to Russia, and I wish there were more stops in Poland, but maybe next time," he stated as we talked by phone, wrapping up last minute details.

But he had done a good job, espcially considering he knew no one connected with Medjugorje in Poland prior to his arrival there to arrange the tour. He had met stiff resistance from bishops reluctant to welcome a foreign Protestant layman talking about apparitions of the Blessed Virgin Mary. To me, it was high accomplishment to have secured two talks, both of which would take place in Catholic churches under the auspices of the local bishops.

But the spare time between the two stops would not be wasted. I should have known from the outset; nothing done concerning Our Lady is ever wasted. Settling into my hotel, I immediately left to explore the streets and sights of Crakow, site of the first talk.

Churches were everywhere. This quaint, historyladened city was known as a "City of Churches." It was also the former home of Pope John Paul II. How thrilling to walk the streets, visit the churches and pray in the chapels where he grew up and later served his people as a servant of God's holy priesthood!

Entering a beautiful, old church a little before 5 P.M., I was startled when many of the worshipers, deep in prayer prior to the Mass, suddenly left the pews and prostrated themselves full-length on the cold marble floor. Young and old alike. It was a dramatic, beautiful sight—and welcoming sign that I was in a land of deep faith.

The Mass was as holy and reverent as the preceding prayer service, which I later learned was the Divine Mercy Chaplet. I remembered that the chapel where this chaplet originated was located just outside of Crakow. In the early 1930's, a nun named Mary Faustina Kowalska, received profound revelations and extraordinary spiritual experiences, the revelation by Jesus Himself of the gift of Divine Mercy. In essence, she was a visionary just like Marija and the others of Medjugorje.

The ebullience of these events faded as I entered the small gift shop at the hotel. There on the counter where it could not be missed, was a full array of soft pornographic magazines, including the most popular editions from the United States. I approached the woman behind the counter and asked, "How long has this material been available in Poland?"

The woman smiled slightly. "Only in the last few months. We are trying to get more, but it will take time. There are many changes taking place in Poland now."

I couldn't help but ask the next question: "Aren't you embarrassed to sell these magazines?"

Her smile disappeared and she shrugged. "It is my job and this is what the people want." With that, she walked away from me, not wanting to continue the conversation.

How sad, I thought. Here was a predominintly Catholic country that through the enduring faith of its people, had been the catalyst in defeating Communism in Eastern Europe. Now it was being infected with the worst materialism from the Western world. The people were like children who had been locked in a dark room for a long time, suddenly let out in the sunlight. There was a sense of bewilderment. Events leading to monumental political changes had occurred so swiftly, that they didn't quite know what to do in their daily living which was suddenly free from oppression.

The majority rejoiced in their newfound freedom and thanked God. But others were focused only on developing the worldly ways of the West as fast as possible. It was a blunt reminder again that wherever the grace of God flows, Satan will be there to counteract it.

Grace returned the following morning when I met Zofia Oczkowska. Fluent in English and deeply committed to Medjugorje, she would serve as guide and translator. "Yes, I am one of the few from Poland who has taken a pilgrimage to Medjugorje, and of course, I have read your articles. I am a tour guide by profession and am available to show you our holy city!"

Zofia was also interested in translating my book into Polish. The articles had already been translated and had served as publicity for the talks. "These translations are needed since few people know about Our Lady's apparitions in Yugoslavia. I will be honored if you allow me to translate your book."

It was clear meeting Zofia was no coincidence. She had been a major key for Stas in setting up the two talks. Arrangements were made that morning over coffee to begin work on the book as soon as I could get the materials to her. We spent the remainder of the morning touring the city, and after an excellent lunch, Zofia asked, "Is

there anything else you would like to do—shopping for instance?"

"Yes, but more important, could you arrange a visit to
the Divine Mercy chapel?"

Zofia smiled. "I intended to include that in our tour.
We will go this afternoon at 3 P.M."

I was awed as I walked into the little chapel just as the
nuns, dressed exactly in the same habit as that worn by
Sister Faustina, began the special prayer chaplet given to
Sister Faustina by Jesus. I prayed in front of the famous
Divine Mercy picture of Jesus as He had appeared to her,
and I sat next to her tomb embedded in the wall of the
chapel. I had first learned of this prayer chaplet on my
second trip to Medjugorje, and had prayed it daily since.
It was a series of prayers recognizing the total abandonment of Jesus at the hour of 3 o'clock. The devotion ties
so closely with the messages given by Our Lady at
Medjugorje. Now, to be here in person . . .

The talk was more than I could have expected, with
the church overflowing, much to the surprise of the priests.
Afterward, during questions, there was hesitancy, again
reflecting the people's awe of finding themselves free to
live and worship openly a faith that had been practiced
covertly for so long. At the end it was a mob scene, with
women and men rushing forward to grasp my hands, eyes
glistening with tears of joy! It lasted more than three hours
and they didn't want to leave or stop asking questions.

After a day of leisure and a little shopping we headed
for Warsaw, with stops along the way at Auschwitz, and
Poland's most famous Marian shrine, Czestochowa. I was
accompanied by a woman named Barbra, and a driver.

What a contrasting example of good and evil in these
two places. Auschwitz, only an hour's drive from Craków,
was the infamous Nazi death camp established during
World War II primarily for the extermination of Jews, along

with other minorities and dissidents. One could feel the evil just walking the grounds where millions of innocent men, women, and children had been cruelly put to death. We had been there less than an hour, but I wanted to leave. "Barbra, I've seen enough—let's go!"

Barbra, a quiet woman of few words, gave an understanding smile. "There is just one more place I would like you to see. It is the cell of Saint Maximilian Kolbe."

Peering into a small 10-foot by 10-foot cell with only a four-foot ceiling, I was glad Barbra had brought me here. St. Maximilian, a Catholic priest thrown into Auschwitz for openly celebrating Mass and distributing church literature, had been martyred here. He had volunteered to take the place of a Jewish man who had a family, and had been sentenced to die in the cell with more than two dozen Jews.

Placed in these claustrophobic quarters with no food or drink, their torturers waited for them to die of starvation. But St. Maximilian led them in prayer and songs of praise. The captors were finally forced to put the survivors to death by lethal injection.

As we drove away in silence, I was reminded that even in the most horrible events perpetrated by man, God's grace always manages to shine through. Thinking about the events now taking place in Croatia, and threatening to spread to Bosnia-Hercegovina, and even Medjugorje itself, I hoped that would be the case there as well.

We arrived in Czestochowa, just a little before 3 P.M. "We must hurry; they show the icon precisely on the hour," Barbra said, heading for the huge church.

This shrine, so dear to the Polish people, was one of the most famous shrines in all of Eastern Europe. I could see why. It was home to the "Black Madonna," an ancient icon considered to be the most beautiful of all icons. We arrived at the exhibit area just as a blast of trumpets sounded, accompanying the raising of a large silver cover, intricately covered with holy artwork. The icon itself was breathtaking. Legend has it that the Black Madonna was painted by Saint Paul, on planks of wood from the table used by the Holy Family.

Suddenly, there was a procession of priests and we realized we would celebrate Mass before the icon. I quickly moved as close as possible, standing just outsite the iron grating separating the small enclosure in front of the icon. During Mass, I felt the Virgin gently touch my hand as though to say, *"Thank you for coming to my shrine!"*

It would be hard to top the time spent at Saint Maximilian Kolbe's cell, and in front of the Black Madonna, but the talk the following day came close. It was held in a cavernous church overflowing with people. Following the rosary at 4 P.M., I spoke for more than two hours, interrupted by Mass, then resumed with questions for another hour and a half. It was a marathon session that left me totally exhausted but pleased.

Stas Majewski didn't know it at the time, but the two talks accomplished far more than he could have imagined. Word of Medjugorje spread rapidly throughout Poland, and before my return home, bishops who had said no to him were now clamoring to have me come to their dioceses. I knew I would return to Poland.

Paolo guided his car expertly through the maze of traffic clogging the highway. "So, we have two days to do some work for the book and then we are off to the country for the weekend. Marija is having some dental work done while she is here and we will meet her and Margaret along the way."

"Sounds good to me. I'm glad Margaret's here as well."

Margaret Townsend was from Scotland, and was one of
Marija and Paolo's close friends—as well as mine. We were
on our way to Paolo's apartment for a quick lunch with his
parents before embarking on a tour of prospective publishers for the Italian translation of the book.

Paolo's mother Millie gave me a quick hug and bustled
back to her cooking. "My wife is very happy to see you
again, and finally we meet in person!" Dino Lunetti, a
gregarious, animated man had been to Medjugorje frequently. I liked him immediately as we shared stories over
Millie's delicious lunch. "I feel I know you like one of my
own sons as I have been through your book many times in
the last six months. I also know Terri, Kennedy, and
Rebecca, and your older children as well!"

"My father has done most of the work on the translation and the corrections," Paolo interjected. "Without his
contribution, it would not have been completed."

Dino waved his hand. "He exaggerates. We have shared
the work, and I think your book will do well in Italy."

As we mapped out the afternoon's schedule, I noticed
a picture of the Blessed Virgin Mary on the wall near the
table that was similar to the one on the cover of my book—
except it was clearer. "Dino, where did you get that picture?"

"Ah, you like my picture! It was given to us by a friend
who knows Pino Casagrande, a man who claims to receive
apparitions from Our Lady. I believe it is the same as the
one on your book."

"Do you think we have time to visit this man?"

Dino and Paolo conversed briefly in Italian. "Well, if
we are able to see all of the publishers, we might be able
to arrange it. His home is a little more than an hour from
here."

Suddenly this was more important than the book.
"Could you call and see if it can be arranged?"

Dino shrugged. "Of course." He returned shortly after telephoning. "You know, he knows of you and is aware
that the picture is on your book. He will be happy to have
us come, so we will go tomorrow afternoon. That gives us
today and tomorrow morning to take care of business if
you are not too tired. Then, after we return from our visit
with Pino, we will leave for our country home in Manasco."

We visited several publishers with no concrete results.
But I wasn't concerned. The book would be published, as
there was considerable interest by several of them. It was
just a matter of which one we chose. I was far more anxious to leave for our meeting with Pino Casagrande.

On the drive to the village where he lived, I asked Dino
what he thought of him. Dino laughed. "We have never
met him, so this is a first for us as well. Pino Casagrande
claims to be a visionary. According to reports, the Blessed
Mother appears to him several times a month, not daily as
it is with Marija and the others in Medjugorje. He has a
strong following, and sometimes, it is a little too contro-
versial for me."

I frowned, uncomfortable with what I was hearing. "Do
you believe he is a visionary, Dino?"

Dino laughed. "I will let you know after we meet him!"

As we approached the address given us, a tall, slender
man waved at us from a driveway. It was Pino. He was
gracious and humble as he ushered us in his apartment
and introduced us to his wife. I was impressed with this
man in his middle seventies, with thin, grey hair and a
quiet demeanor. As his wife served expresso, he began his
story, with Dino doing the translation.

He had first received a mystical picture in August, 1983,
but it was not of Our Lady. During an adoration service at
a nearby church, Pino took a Poloroid picture of the priest
as he raised the monstrance containing the host. To his
amazement, the picture revealed instead a beautiful face

of Jesus, and shortly after, he began having locutions from the Blessed Virgin.

In the ensuing years, he received many other mystical pictures, always taken with a Poloroid. In August, 1986, Pino received the picture that now appears on the cover of my book. He was taking a picture of the outside of a shrine, a long scenic shot of the church and the surrounding countryside. The breathtaking face of Our Lady was the result.

I listened, studying Pino as he related his story, as well as the faces of my two Italian friends. I had a feeling about this man the same as I did about Marija and the other Medjugorje visionaries. It was the same feeling received when meeting a few others in my travels around the world, who claimed this phenomenal gift. And of course, I had met others making the same claims and had not felt the discernment.

Pino suddenly stood up and went to a cabinet, pulling out several large photo albums. "He wants to show us some of the pictures that have been given to him over the years," Dino explained. We went through the albums, marveling at the array of photographs. Several pictured Jesus and Our Lady with tears of blood flowing; others showed the face of Jesus in the sacred host.

The albums were overflowing with loose pictures, many similar to those posted on the pages. Suddenly, Pino began shoving copies toward us. After several exchanges in Italian, Dino thanked him. "He wants us to have these pictures. He says he has asked our Blessed Mother not to give him any more pictures because they are a distraction from the importance of her messages. He doesn't need them anymore."

I was stunned at receiving such a precious gift. It was further evidence this man could indeed be a visionary of Our Lady. Never once did he attempt to convince us of his authenticity. His manner remained humble and quiet throughout the visit. It also registered when he stated he no longer needed the pictures. Like rosary chains turning to a golden color, and a spinning, pulsating sun, these were merely little signs along the way of conversion.

"Well . . ?" I left the question hanging as we headed back to Milan.

Dino waited a few moments, choosing his words carefully. "Whether he is a true visionary, I do not know. I will simply say, I am impressed." Paolo agreed.

Late that evening, we picked up Marija and Margaret and another couple at a large crossroad about an hour's drive from our destination at Manasco. The conversation was lively as we caught up on events before Dino suggested we pray a rosary. I was grateful for the opportunity to take my mind off the queasiness I felt as Paolo raced through the curves of the mountain roads.

Saturday was a beautiful day. We caught up on news of the war, with Marija listening intently to the television news each hour of the morning. That afternoon we went mushroom picking in the countryside in sunny, but crisply cool weather.

However, my mind was not on mushrooms. I was filled with anticipation at being present during the time of Marija's daily apparition with Gospa. We would attend Mass in a little church practically next door to the Lunetti's cottage, then return for the apparition. Dino laughed when I asked if we would have enough time. "My dear friend, this priest completes the Mass in less than fifteen minutes, so do not expect a spiritual Mass such as in Medjugorje. We will be back here in plenty of time!"

Fifteen minutes! I wondered how he could possibly do this. Nevertheless, I looked forward to the apparition. No matter how many times I had been present for this special grace, the excitement and awe remained with each opportunity.

We entered the tiny but beautiful chapel and I immediately felt the same sensation experienced when entering St. James Church in Medjugorje, even with the staccato pace of the liturgy. Margaret was next to me, with Marija to her right.

As the priest began the consecration of the gifts for Communion, I was suddenly flooded with emotion and fell to my knees, struggling to regain composure. I did not want to break down in front of Marija and Margaret, but the agony of not being able to receive the Holy Eucharist, mixed with a strange sensation of overwhelming joy and peace, finally won out. The tears came in streams.

I remembered little except for Margaret's arm around my shoulders as I opened my eyes. Mass was over, the church was empty, and the only people still there were the three of us, still kneeling. Marija turned to me, smiling. "Our Lady came to me in apparition during the consecration of the gifts!"

It was the most beautiful of all the experiences of being present during an apparition of Our Lady—even though I did not realize she was present! Marija explained that Our Lady appeared as she usually does in a brilliance of light, standing near the priest and saying nothing, just smiling and blessing us as she looked over the small gathering of celebrants. Now I understood the holiness felt in this minute chapel despite the haste of the priest in celebrating Holy Mass. Gospa was there and as always, wrapping us in her mantle of love.

24
The Greatest Gift

"Dear children, today I bless you in a special way with my motherly blessing and I intercede for you to God, for Him to give you the gift of the conversion of the heart. . . ."

That mantle of love would sustain me throughout the month of November as I left for the Far East on the second, and returned on the thirtieth, making it the longest tour of the entire mission. Never had I been away from Terri and the kids that long.

The tour took in all major cities in Australia, with Leon LeGrande again organizing all but Perth. Yolanda and Joe Nardizzi did the rest. From there it was on to Singapore under the guidance of Victor and Vivienne Wee, where we did a three-day retreat. Two more days were slated for Jakarta, Indonesia, new to the Medjugorje message, and finally, three days in New Zealand. As always, each stop was filled with stories of struggle and conversion. Two in particular, stood out.

Leon LeGrande, there to meet me in Sydney, where the tour began, was prepared to take me straight to the hotel for rest. But something unusual had happened dur-

ing the normally arduous 12,000-mile flight; I slept close
to eight hours, arriving refreshed and ready for a full day
of events. That was a rarity. "Well then, we'll grab a bite
and go directly to our meeting with the organizer of
tonight's talk."

"Fine, I'm in good shape. Let's go!"

He smiled. "There is a surprise waiting for you. Tanya
will be there. She wanted to see you right away!" I was
surprised. Tanya, an Australian teenager I met in
Medjugorje on my second pilgrimage in 1986, had suffered from drug addiction. She was only sixteen at the
time, yet had been in hospitals and treatment centers eight
times for overdosing. It was the same Tanya whose story I
had related at the girls' school in Trinidad.

This young girl had received every possible grace to
bring on conversion to God. With a Croatian mother and
Australian father, she was fluent in the language, and got
to know the visionaries personally, even staying a month
with Marija. But the drugs and alcohol continued to win
out.

Returning to Australia, her parents reunited after years
of separation, she become pregnant and had to marry. It
was a troubled marriage. Even the responsibility of motherhood, after she gave birth to a beautiful little girl, did
not help.

Tanya would call our home sporadically, seeking assurance I was still concerned for her. But on my first trip
to Australia, she had not been there, again a victim of her
addictions. I asked Leon how she was doing. "Better now,
but she is still struggling. The problem is, she won't help
herself. And until she realizes that only she can create the
necessary changes in her life, it will continue to be a
struggle." Leon took a deep sigh. "Nothing can really be
done for her until she decides she truly wants to change."

Unfortunately, the meeting with Tanya proved Leon

right. I was sincerely happy to see her, taking advantage of the opportunity as we talked and stressing the points Leon had mentioned, especially about wanting to change and do good. She assured me she would try harder. But she telephoned me several times during the tour saying she was going to take drugs again and imploring my help. "I can only pray for you, Tanya; you have to do the rest," I told her. As frustrating as it was, I would never give up praying and fasting for her full conversion.

Offsetting Tanya's struggles was an encouraging victory. While in Perth, at a Saturday morning prayer retreat, I was approached by a couple beaming broadly. "Do you remember us?" the woman asked softly.

How many times I had been asked that question. "I'm afraid I can't quite place you . . ."

"That's all right, you meet so many people in your travels," she replied. "We are John and Kathryn Gardner. We met you in Geraldton on your last visit and told you of our plans to leave the Catholic faith for a new church."

"Of course, now I remember!"

"Well, after what you said about the Eucharist, and the Blessed Mother, we returned to our church determined to find an answer. We are so grateful to you for your witness and advice. And, we remained Catholic and love the Church more than ever, thanks to a renewal in faith through Medjugorje!"

It was the highlight of many wonderful stories stretching from Australia to New Zealand.

On the return flight, I did not sleep as I had coming over. But I felt good spiritually. During daily and Sunday Masses throughout the tour, there seemed to be a new peace within me. The agony of not being able to receive the Eucharist was still there, but subdued now with quiet resignation that in God's time and way, it would soon be resolved.

Just before the Notre Dame conference in June of this year, I had sensed Our Lady was preparing me for the coming change. During my talk, I suddenly announced that I no longer wanted to be known as "that Lutheran Protestant" preaching the message of Medjugorje. It was my intention as well as my wife's, I told the audience, to fully convert to the Catholic faith at some point in the future. I went on to say our decision was a personal one, and would not deter me from continuing to bring the message of Medjugorje to people of all faiths.

Overall, people reacted positively. I thought of the number of times in the past five years I had been asked when I was going to become Catholic. Now, some questioned whether I would lose the uniqueness of a Protestant speaking about a perceived Catholic event. Protestants feared I would no longer reach out to other faiths. My only answer to both was that I was trying to be obedient to what God was asking of me.

Terri and the kids met me at the airport as I arrived home from Australia, late on Friday. It was emotional, and I vowed to never be gone that long again. "Boy, have I missed you guys! I'm worn out, and all I want to do is go home and sleep for two days straight!"

"How many times have I heard that?" Terri said, holding tightly to my hand.

"I know, but I'm thankful there's only one trip left and that's the New Orleans Conference on the first weekend in December. I might just sleep 'til then!"

"Oh, I don't think so," Terri smiled, squeezing my hand. "But I do want you to get some rest because we're going out tomorrow evening—just you and me. I have a surprise and it's going to be a special occasion!"

Special or not, the last thing I wanted was to go out. "Terri, I'm too tired to go anywhere. Let's wait a few days."

She was not deterred. "Sorry but we have to celebrate. This is very special!"

I finally relinquished, too exhausted to argue, wanting only to get some sleep and readjust to the twelve-hour time difference.

Saturday evening, we dined in a little Italian restaurant we hadn't been to since our dating days. This must be special, I thought as we were seated. "Okay, tell me."

"Not yet, I'm saving it for coffee and desert!" My wife was enjoying the suspense. Finally, as we sipped coffee, she opened her purse and handed me a letter. My heart leaped as I saw it was from the Tribunal office. Having completed counseling just before leaving for Australia, the counselor had immediately written their office with the results of nine months of weekly meetings. At last, the Tribunal was giving full clearance to enter the Church!

I was overjoyed, but in a quiet, peaceful way that had settled in over the past few months. Terri stared at me, mildly disappointed at my reaction. "I can't believe you're not jumping up and down. Do you realize we can be received into the Church before Christmas?"

Strangely, the actuality of that happening after five years of agonized waiting, was now anticlimatic. "You know, we've waited this long. With Christmas coming and so many things to do, I think we should wait until January, or even February. We'll arrange everything and announce it after the fact."

"Are you serious?"

"Yes I am." I smiled and shook my head. "It is strange, isn't it? I've had this dream of entering the Church in Medjugorje, with a glorious celebration. Now we can't because of the war. Maybe this is what Our Lady wants, a nice quiet ceremony with no fanfare."

We talked awhile and Terri finally agreed; waiting might be the best plan under the circumstances. "But let's pray about it after our Tuesday morning prayer meeting group," she quickly added.

It was nice to hear her suggest prayer for confirmation. There was a time when the last thing she would have done was to pray out loud with me or anyone. Medjugorje had changed that, just as it had changed our approach to everything concerning family life.

The timing was right. Each Tuesday morning following Mass, a small prayer group devoted to St. Therese, would meet for intercessory prayer. It was only fitting since St. Therese had been an important part of our entire Medjugorje experience, that we pray about this decision at this particular meeting. She truly was Our Lady's First Lieutenant, always involved in our major faith decisions, always doing her heaven on earth.

Immediately after the prayer meeting, Terri and I moved to the rear pews of the church, waiting for everyone to leave. Silently, we began to pray. I thanked Our Lady for leading us to her Son and His Church. "I guess this is the way you want it done, in a quiet, humble way like everything in your life was done. I'm just thankful that in a couple of months, I'll be able to receive your Son, Jesus in the Holy Eucharist. I don't mind waiting."

Abruptly, I heard very clearly within my heart: *"No, I am asking you to enter the Church in front of the people at New Orleans. It is for them!"*

Jerking upright from a bowed position, I said aloud, "No!" Surely this couldn't be! But the message was repeated. Tears began running down my cheeks. It was one of the clearest of her messages, and it was happening with my wife praying right next to me!

Terri, alarmed at my sudden reaction, put her hand on my shoulder. "What's the matter? Did you get an answer?"

"Oh, yes! I got an answer!" I told her about the message.

Her reaction was also immediate: "No way! You pray some more. I can't get up in front of all those people!"

Calming my wife while trying to regain my own composure, I assured her that if she did not want to go to New Orleans, arrangements could possibly be made to have her enter the Church at Myrtle Beach on the same day. But I knew I had to do it as the message indicated: in front of the people, and for the people; not just the people at the conference in New Orleans, but for all the people who had read my writings or listened to my talks. That was the purpose of the entire mission, to spread the good fruits of living the gospel message. Medjugorje was the vehicle; I was merely one of its instruments.

Moments later, Terri's trademark methodical reasoning returned. "You're right, this is what you have to do. It fits with everything else that's happened in the last five years. The whole purpose of going through the Tribunal process was to show obedience to God and His Church. By going through it, we agreed to be public witnesses to its validity." She gave a sardonic smile. "So, I'll see if Monsignor Kelly will arrange for me to enter at the 7:30 A.M. Mass. There shouldn't be too many people there at that time!"

Heading home, I was still tingling from the brief but powerful message from the Blessed Mother. It would have to be arranged in a minimum of time. And somehow, in the jumble of thoughts flying through my mind, I realized we would be entering the Church on a Marian feast day, the Feast of the Immaculate Conception. Terri was right; it all fit nicely into the *modus operandi* of Our Lady of Medjugorje!

I telephoned Mimi Kelly in New Orleans, telling her what had occurred and asking if it were possible to accomplish this during the conference. "I know this is only four days notice, but I'm asking if it can be done."

"Wayne," Mimi began in a quavering voice, "I wrote you a letter several months ago, asking this very thing: if you would consider entering the Church during the conference. I knew your coming into the Church had to be close, and hoped it would coincide with our conference." Giving in to her emotions, she continued: "But I tore the letter up, thinking it was too presumptuous on my part to even ask such a thing of you!"

It was the final sign of confirmation.

Within minutes, arrangement were made; we would tell no one at the conference until just before the final Mass, so as not to disturb other activities and speakers; retired Archbishop Phillip Hannon would conduct the confirmation, while Father Ken Roberts would do the Rite of Initiation.

Terri scheduled an early-morning meeting with Monsignor Robert Kelly, our local pastor who had assisted us through part of the tribunal process, praying beforehand that whatever he advised her, she would be obedient to that course. "Terri, I'll be happy to receive you into the church on Sunday, but . . . you and Wayne went through this together, and I think you should be with your husband for such an occasion."

She returned home, numbly stating she would go to New Orleans with me. "I just hope I survive the ceremony without passing out!"

Laughing, I put my arms around her. "That's nice of you, but you're saved. There are no available seats on the flight. I've already checked."

"You call them back. If this is what the Holy Spirit wants, a seat will be available!"

Amazingly, in thirty minutes we not only had a seat for her, but also for our children. This was a bonus, especially since my son Michael was also going. I had arranged that long before, hoping to expose him directly to the good fruits of Medjugorje, just as I had with Lisa a year ago. Now it would truly be a family affair.

The next few days including through Saturday, were agonizingly long and nerve-racking. For both of us. Terri was numb with anxiety at having to get up in front of 6,000 people, and I was due to speak on the same morning. I wondered how I would make it through the talk without becoming emotional, and was doing fine until I mentioned something about being Lutheran. Pausing, I suddenly realized this would be the last time I would speak about Medjugorje as a Lutheran. I conveyed this to the audience, not mentioning details. That did it. I could hardly finish the talk.

"You'll both be fine," Father Ken assured us as we went over preparations in the speakers' lounge just before Mass.

"I think everything is in order—all the paperwork has been handled, and we have gone over the ceremonies," Archbishop Phillip Hannon noted. "There is one question though, who are your sponsors?"

Terri and I looked at each other. "Well, I don't know—we planned for Marija and Ivan but of course they aren't here. Mimi's daughter Christina had agreed to stand in for Marija . . ."

"Well, I guess I'll have to be the other sponsor!" Father Ken laughed. And thus, it was settled. Christina Kelly would be one sponsor and Father Ken Roberts, the other. "I guess you know that makes me your Godfather!" he added, roaring with laughter.

One last touch was added: Kennedy, our son whose baptism had led us back to church and thus laid the groundwork for the mission, would serve as altar boy. I could stand it no longer. "Listen, let's go down to our seats now—I need to pray!"

As we were escorted to the front of the auditorium, I was grateful Michael was there to watch over Rebecca during the ceremony. Also, he had been deeply affected by the total events of the conference. Father Ken, just as he had done with Lisa, had taken him under his wing and spent extra time with him. Michael O'Brien, there to sing and give his witness, served as a good role model as well as someone close in age to hang out with. Settling into our seats, he blurted out, "Dad, this is great! I'm really glad to be here. Maybe one day . . . I'll be Catholic!" I gave him a hug and prayed silently to Our Lady that his emotions and desires would last beyond the excitement of the conference.

Closing my eyes, I tried to comprehend the enormity of what was about to happen to us. "Lord, Jesus," I muttered to myself, "I'm so happy . . ."

"Excuse me, Mr. Weible." I opened my eyes to a young conference volunteer standing in front of me. "There's a woman from Poland here who wants to speak to you a moment. I told her you were preparing for the Mass."

I took a deep breath. "I don't mind, let her come."

A diminutive woman timidly approached. "I apologize if I am bothering you but I need to ask you something important."

As had happened so many times, I felt that inner sense telling me this was important. "It's all right. How can I help you?"

Her face brightened. "I am Zofia Sordyl and I am from Poland, but I have been living in the United States twenty-seven years. I know you went to my homeland but gave only two talks. Would you return to Poland if I can arrange a tour for you to go to many other places?"

I didn't hesitate. "Yes, if that is possible, I'd like to go back." And then out of nowhere: "Listen, could you also arrange the tour to include Russia, the Ukraine in particular?"

She looked at me puzzled. "I don't know, but I will be happy to try and include the Ukraine." With that we exchanged addresses and telephone numbers, briefly discussing details.

As she exited our area, the conference emcee approached the podium, announcing Mass was about to commence. "But first, I have a very special announcement . . ." And with that, he told of our planned induction into the Church during the Mass.

After a moment of stunned silence, there was a thunder of applause and cheering from the 6,000 conference attendees as the Mass procession began. My heart was beating so fast I felt dizzy, sure I'd never make it through the ceremony. Terri didn't appear a whole lot better. But as we were called to the altar on stage, a calmness set in. It was as though I were walking in a dream, watching what was taking place around me, hearing with keen clarity each word of the Rite of Initiation, and Confirmation.

Following the ceremony, we returned to our seats. People were applauding again but it was hardly heard. I kept saying to myself, "I'm Catholic! I'm finally Catholic!"

Minutes later, I received Jesus in the Holy Eucharist for the first time as a confirmed member of the Roman Catholic Church. Returning to my seat, I knelt on the floor. "My Jesus, I'm truly ready to die of pure happiness."

His gentle words echoed in my heart: "Your work is just beginning."

"Yes, Lord, Your will be done."

It was the greatest peace, the greatest grace, the greatest gift.

25
New Witness

"Dear children, today also, I invite you to prayer. Only by prayer and fasting can war be stopped. Therefore, my dear little children, pray and by your life give witness that you are mine and that you belong to me, because Satan wishes in these turbulent days to seduce as many souls as possible. Therefore, I invite you to decide for God and He will protect you and show you what you should do and which path to take . . ."

From the outset, the early months of 1992 were a time of new witness as the holiness of The Day at the New Orleans Conference spilled into daily life. We had topped it off by renewing our wedding vows on December 21, with Father Garry Dilley as celebrant; and all of my children present. Each Mass was a rerun of that special day of entry into the Church. Everyone kept asking how it felt. Frankly, I was at a loss for words until Terri wrote a short letter intended for family members and close friends.

While she felt unable to stand in front of large audiences to give witness, her letter captured our deepest thoughts. It was powerful testimony, personifying the "feeling of Jesus within" at Holy Communion, especially the last part in which she wrote: "That first time of receiving the Holy Eucharist in New Orleans, and the first time in our local church, I did not feel any different. I was too busy listening for Jesus to speak to me, for fireworks to go

off in my mind. The third time was different. His presence inside of me was so strong. Yet, I knew it was only a
tiny, tiny presence. I now have a much clearer understanding of what is meant by the statement that one cannot feel
God's full presence and live . . . To feel what I felt in that
moment of the third Communion, it would have been nothing to stop wars or move mountains. There was no sense
of time, just that moment, with nothing before it and no
sense of future to come."

That feeling carried over as I began travel in the middle
of January, 1992, heading for Indiana and my first witness
as a Catholic convert.

I grabbed a handful of unopened letters and stuffed
them into my briefcase, hoping to catch up by answering
them during the tour. As I read the third letter during the
flight, I suddenly caught my breath, noticing it was from
the mother of Paul, the man with AIDS whom I had prayed
over in Medjugorje in August of last year.

After identifying who she was, she wrote: Paul died in
September, shortly after we returned from Medjugorje.
He died in peace and received the sacraments of the
Church. His time in Medjugorje brought great joy and he
believed.

I carefully folded the letter and returned it to the envelope, placing it in the stack to be answered. It was then I
noticed the address—Little River, South Carolina, about
fifteen miles north of Myrtle Beach. This mother had
brought her ailing son 4,500 miles away to Medjugorje,
and it is her "neighbor" who prays over him for healing! I
shook my head in amazement at how God works in what
we call His mysterious ways.

The first talk in Indiana was a noon engagement during the week. Once again the church was packed to the
rafters, with radio and television news reporters also
present. I gave Paul's story—including my reluctance at the

request of Our Lady to pray over him—as witness to the power of Medjugorje's grace. "You see," I said in concluding the story, "Paul was healed, but it was spiritual. He returned to the grace of the sacraments of this church. . . ."

I also spoke strongly—although nervously—on my conversion to the Catholic faith, noting that it was not by accident that the Blessed Virgin Mary chose Catholic children as visionaries. "Historically, the Church was established by Jesus and continues under the same sacraments," I intoned, "with all other branches of Christianity breaking away from the main body. They, in turn, have continued to break away until today, we have hundreds of separate Christian denominations. Our Lady is asking us to come together as one family under one shepherd!"

But it was also no accident she chose this Protestant to help spread the message of gospel renewal, I added. "She gave a message in January 1985, that sums up what I am attempting to convey. Listen carefully to her words: *'Those who are not Catholics, are no less creatures made in the image of God and destined to rejoin someday the House of the Father. Salvation is available to everyone, without exception. Only those who refuse God deliberately are condemned. To him who has been given little, little will be asked for; to those who have been given much, very much will be required. It is God alone, in His infinite justice, who determines the degree of responsibility and pronounces judgment.'*"

Smiling, I quickly added: "It would take a team of theologians to fully comprehend the enormity of that message! Yet, for us who have been touched by Medjugorje, I think it's quite clear; we are all the children of God, each with different responsibilities."

Reaction was predominantly positive. Several Protestants stated they understood what I was saying and why I had converted; they felt as I did about the Eucharist. Others felt called to remain in their faith to continue witnessing to the role of Mary in leading us to Jesus.

Still, hesitation to speak out on the Church lingered, until the third talk. Moving quickly to the foyer of the church following the talk, I prepared for an onslaught of people as they finished singing a closing hymn. A young couple, obviously touched by the talk, had followed me.

"We had to tell you," the woman began, "your book has changed our lives. We weren't attending church, but had decided to return to our Protestant roots and were scheduled to join a church next weekend. But now . . ." She paused; her husband smiled and finished her sentence. ". . . Now, we're going to see a priest and begin instructions into the Catholic faith. We just wanted to personally thank you."

As if further proof were needed of the new witness, it came in a double-dose as I traveled to Sacramento, California several months later. On the first evening, an unexpected addition to the program was announced just prior to my talk. My host introduced David Spencer, a man in his early 40s, sporting a full beard beneath penetrating eyes. He began a familiar witness: "My name is David Spencer, and about a year ago, I was in a fundamentalist church . . ."

I settled back as my host smiled at me, thinking it was simply another Protestant who had converted through the good fruits of Medjugorje—until he continued.

David Spencer began speaking of his hatred of the Catholic Church as he fervently attended his fundamental church. He hated it with a passion that concerned even his fellow fundamentalists. His self-proclaimed mission was to evangelize as many Catholics as possible out of their church into the "true Gospel-based church." He especially attacked the rosary, statues of the Blessed Virgin—and the Eucharist. "I would tell my fellow Protestants that these poor Catholics really believed this bread and wine of the Communion was the Body and Blood of Jesus, which of course, I thought was blasphemy."

One day, David related, he stopped at a Christian book store looking for literature to teach in his adult Sunday school class. Walking into the store, a book with a picture of the Blessed Virgin Mary on the cover caught his eye. He reacted in anger, questioning how such a book found its way into a Christian bookstore.

"I wanted to see what this book was all about but it was wrapped in plastic and I could only read the back cover. It told of Mary appearing to six young Croatian children in Yugoslavia. Being Serbian, I thought maybe she's supposed to be appearing to Serbian children as well. And then I discovered it was written by a Lutheran Protestant . . ." David paused and looked directly at me, making sure the audience understood it was my book!

He bought the book, mainly to find out more about "this new heresy," and to get it out of the store since it was the only copy. But, returning to his house, he flung it in a corner and forgot about it until forced to stay home a week with an eye injury from a work-related accident. "As I sat there, wondering what to do with all this spare time, I heard someone or something saying to me: 'Now you have time to read the book . . .' The only trouble was my eyes were watering so much, I could only read a little at a time."

But he continued reading, discovering that the message the Virgin Mary was bringing to these children, and to the world, was the Gospel message. Now he was hooked. He began to gather other Medjugorje material, including a video that showed the children giving witness. It was the same video that I had watched in the beginning of my Medjugorje experience!

"I would come to this part where Vicka was speaking," he said softly, "and the next thing I would be crying. I couldn't help it; I would play that part of the tape over and over, and each time I would cry. I knew this was real."

From there, David's experience was like many others; he kept hearing this gentle female voice telling him to pray. Finally, he asked who she was and Our Lady identified herself, asking David to live and spread her messages. He obeyed, and in the following months, this fervent anti-Catholic, Jewish, Serbian convert to fundamentalism, became a son of Mary.

It was a powerful introduction, and one more beautiful story of conversion wrought from Mary's ongoing appearances in the little village.

After the talk, there was a reception for meeting the people and signing books, a time I eagerly looked forward to because of the opportunity to share with those in need of prayer or special support. It was during these times I gave medals to individuals at what I felt was a prompting of Our Lady. A man approached, smiling somewhat sheepishly. "You probably don't remember me, . . ." he then turned and added, "or my wife."

"Well, you look familiar . . ."

"You gave me a medal a year ago in Baton Rouge, Louisiana. We've been transferred here now, but a lot has happened to us since then."

Surprisingly, I did remember them. "Yes, I gave you the medal and you insisted it wasn't for you but for your wife."

"That's right. I only came to the talk that night at her insistence. In fact, I didn't even like the Catholic Church or anything associated with it. I only attended for her sake because she was Catholic. I couldn't believe it when you said the medal was from the Blessed Virgin Mary and she wanted me to have it."

"And now, he's taking instruction to join the Church," his wife added quietly. "We wanted to let you know what that medal did for our family."

Quietly thanking them, I knew I would never again

hesitate to call all Christians to their historical church beginnings, the Holy Catholic and Apostolic Church of Jesus
Christ.

"There is a lady on the telephone who wants to talk to
you about going to Russia. She says she has called several
times. Do you want to speak to her or shall I take a message?"

I knew immediately it was Zofia Sordyl, the Polish lady
at the conference in New Orleans who asked me to return
to Poland. "No, I'll take it at my desk, thanks." I wasn't
aware of her previous attempts to reach me and now I was
anxious to find out what arrangements if any had been
made for me to go to Russia.

"Yes, we can get you to Russia," Zofia informed me. "I
am leaving in three weeks for St. Petersburg, where I will
be staying for the next five months. If you can give me a
date you can come, I will arrange everything for a tour of
Russia and Poland."

Fifteen minutes later, I had committed to three weeks
starting in late October. "I'm going to Russia! I'm finally
going to Russia!" I told Christina, who ran our small
Medjugorje center.

"That is wonderful, but right now you need to prepare for England, and you better pray we find someone
for the office soon. It is getting difficult to keep up with
the mail and your schedule."

"Don't worry, we will," I assured her, grabbing my airline tickets and schedule for the England tour, and dash-
ing out the door. My secretary had left on short notice,
and in the rush of things, Zofia's previous calls had gone
unanswered. Uttering a short prayer of thanks that I was
in the office when she called this time, I gave a slight shud-

der at the thought of almost missing a second opportunity to take the mission to the former Soviet Union. Immediately, Russia dominated my every thought, even as I boarded the international flight for Manchester, England.

Once again, there were stops throughout the United Kingdom. The most rewarding came as I returned to Wales, and a meeting with Geraldine Loftus and her family. This little girl whom I had prayed over a little more than a year ago, was doing well according to reports I had received. But I was anxious to see her and confirm for myself she was healed of the cancer that had threatened her life.

In the second week of the tour, I arrived at an ancient Franciscan church in Wales, for Sunday Mass, followed by my talk. I was assured by John and Rose Walsch, my hosts for both visits to Wales, that Geraldine and her family would be there.

Entering the overcrowded church, we discovered the only seating room left was in the choir section. I smiled as I began making my way through the crowd, happy that so many had come. Just as I approached the choir, I heard my name called softly. Turning around, Geraldine and her father were standing there. She ran into my arms and the tears began to flow.

What a joy to see this healthy little girl who was now eleven years old, with long, beautiful brown hair and rosy cheeks—and a smile that would melt ice. I could hardly contain my emotions or take my eyes off of her throughout the Mass.

During the talk, I asked Geraldine to come forward, having promised in advance she wouldn't have to say anything, telling the audience that this is what Medjugorje was really all about. "Here in your midst, in the healing of this child, is living proof that God exists and that He loves us, and is a merciful, healing God!"

I pointed out Geraldine's healing was reward for a family that accepted its crosses, having also adopted a mentally retarded little boy just prior to Geraldine's diagnosis of terminal cancer. They accepted God's will but never stopped asking for a healing of Geraldine, or her little brother; he was now progressing far beyond expectations. This was the living message of Medjugorje, and the result of thousands of prayers from those who knew of Geraldine's illness.

That afternoon, we returned to John and Rose's home, along with Geraldine and her family. I still could not take my eyes off her and wanted this time to last forever. Like others, I needed confirmations along the way to bolster my conversion journey. This was one of the best.

Rose approached us as we sat on the couch talking. "Excuse me, Wayne, I was wondering, would you like that coffee and dessert now?"

I burst out laughing. "Yes, I think it's a bit overdue!" Rose was referring to my last trip when we had rushed from her home following dinner for our unplanned visit to Geraldine, leaving our coffee and dessert on the table.

As the Loftus family departed late that evening, I didn't know if I would ever see Geraldine again. It really didn't matter; she would always be part of the good fruits of Medjugorje.

Usually by March or April, I would return to Medjugorje. It was a special time, marking the beginning of increased pilgrimages as the weather warmed. But March, 1992 was different. I would not be going, as only a handful dared go. The war was too intense.

But there was increased fervor in the talks around the

country. This was Satan's ways of stopping the grace of Medjugorje, I exhorted the audiences, enforcing more than ever the need to pray and fast. I was stunned by the message of Our Lady given on the 25th of March, to Marija: *"Dear children, today, as never before, I invite you to live my messages, and to put them into practice in your life. I have come to you to help you and therefore, I invite you to change your life because you have taken a path of misery, a path of ruin. When I told you to convert, pray, fast, be reconciled, you took these messages superficially. You started to live them and then you stopped because it was difficult for you. No, dear children, when something is good you have to persevere in the good and not think 'God does not see; He is not with me; He is not helping me.' And so, you have gone away from God and from me because of your miserable interests.*

"I wanted to create of you an oasis of peace, love and goodness. God wanted you with your love, and with His help to do miracles, and thus, give an example. Therefore, here is what I say to you: Satan is playing with you, and with your souls, and I cannot help you because you are far away from my heart.

"Therefore, pray! Live my messages! And then, you will see the miracles of God's love in your everyday life."

Here was the Gentle Woman, the mother of Jesus, pleading with us as any desperate mother would plead with her children to save them from harm. Just as in the messages prior to, and during the Gulf War, her words were pointed and blunt.

But unlike the Gulf War, few nations came to the rescue. There were no worldwide gatherings in prayer to prevent escalation, no conferences or allied meetings of outraged nations ready to defend the human rights of the people in these newly independent republics. And the reason was clear: no global economic interest; no oil or other valuable commodity; just the lives of the Croatian and Bosnian people. The only hope was prayer and fasting as Our Lady asked. And penance, as a few brave souls dared go to take relief and help where they could.

Even in the face of atrocities taking place in cities, towns, and villages across Croatia, Bosnia-Hercegovina joined its former Federation republics in declaring its independence. By April, the United States joined its European allies in belatedly recognizing Slovenia, Croatia, and Bosnia in hopes that the hostilities would cease. It was too late; the war had spread its holocaust into the regions of Bosnia.

Tragically, the apathy of democratic countries constantly espousing human rights had emboldened the aggressor Serbs. Especially the United States, the global symbol and example of democratic freedoms had, paradoxically, remained silent too long.

The people of Slovenia, Croatia, and Bosnia waited, sure the American defenders of freedom would come to their rescue. But our government had developed close ties with the Serb-dominated government of Yugoslavia, spurred by private investments in the billions under the guidance of a firm headed by a former high government official. Two key members of the administration, on leave from this same firm, were directly involved in foreign relations with Yugoslavia.

Thus, while it was a shock to those involved in Medjugorje, it came as no surprise to the "worldly" when our Secretary of State stated for all the world to hear, that these republics should stay together. Satan's weapon of greed would allow the holocaust to spread. Never had I felt such shame and embarrassment for my country.

Just as in Croatia, entire villages were destroyed and its residents massacred, including women and children. Medjugorje was empty of pilgrims again. There was no way I could go or recommend in good conscience, that anyone else go.

Croatia had already seen more than 250 Catholic churches, monasteries and convents severely damaged or destroyed. They were usually the first targets of the Serb insurgents and Federal Army. Now, Medjugorje itself was threatened. Thousands of Serb Federal troops and insurgents massed on the other side of the Neretva River, near Mostar, many of them criminals and renegades. The U.S. State Department issued strong warnings for would-be pilgrims to stay away.

Aircraft of the Federal Army dropped cluster bombs on Siroki Brijeg, the town to which Father Jozo Zovko had just recently been transferred. It was a special shrine for the Franciscans, the site of past horrible massacres of Franciscan priests. Now, they were trying again to kill this charismatic priest and destroy yet another shrine of Franciscan Catholicism.

The bombs hit the center of town at the foot of the hill on which the monastery was located. The attacking forces attempted to strike the church as well, but failed to cause more than limited damage to the outside of the building, and fortunately, Father Jozo and the others were not harmed. But more than 30 villagers, including children, were killed.

The city of Sarajevo was attacked and badly damaged, along with the airport; soon, it was crawling with Federal troops and Bosnian Serb insurgents; street fighting and sniper fire were seemingly everywhere. Within days emergency supply lines were stopped cold as the airport became a constant target of shelling from the surrounding mountains.

While the world's media focused on Sarajevo, the same horrible things were happening in Mostar, only seventeen miles from Medjugorje. The Catholic cathedral was hit with intensive damage done. Later, further attacks left it in ruins along with the bishop's house. Every building was hit by Serb shelling, including the new hospital, once under the administrative leadership of a Serb who now commanded the destruction from the hills. Refugee Moslems driven from their villages poured into the city, creating further problems.

And finally, Medjugorje was attacked by air. Bombs were dropped; miraculously, they would explode in the air or land in surrounding fields not detonated. But for the first time since the beginning of the apparitions, Saint James Church was closed and boarded for protection; the Blessed Sacrament was removed and placed in the basement of the rectory, where Mass was being held twice a day. It appeared as if Satan had finally succeeded in closing down the fount of grace. But his success would be short-lived.

Incredibly, small bands of pilgrims continued to journey to Medjugorje. They took food, medicine, clothing—and prayers—for the refugees and victims. My good friend, Father Svetozar Kraljevic was making constant trips into the war zones, and also throughout the Western world to raise funds and awareness of what was happening in his homeland. I was relieved to see him at a conference in late May.

"Yes, it is good if people continue to come," he said when I asked about conditions. "Medjugorje is still a place of peace, and Our Lady will guide you." Then, placing his hand on my shoulder, "And you should definitely come to see what is happening."

I was dismayed. "Father, I have absolutely no desire to return to Medjugorje at this time. I'm doing all I can to make people aware and to promote relief, but I don't personally feel called to go, and I cannot in good conscience tell others to go."

He smiled slightly. "Do not forget that Our Lady is still appearing each day. She continues to call us to come and pray. So now, you pray about it. I would like to see you come."

Frankly, there was little time open to go. It had been an extremely busy six months. And as promised, I would remain at home during the summer months with Terri and the kids. But Father Svet's words stayed with me, even as I focused on the upcoming trip to the former Soviet Union in October.

26
Russia

"Dear children, today, my call to you is that in your life you live love towards God and neighbor. Without love, dear children, you can do nothing . . ."

The summer of 1992 was uneventful—except for a family vacation to Italy in August, the hottest month of the year. The reason for the trip was two-fold: First, Paolo and Dino had succeeded in having my book published by one of the largest publishing houses in Italy. I needed to meet with the publisher and work out details for a spring tour to promote the book. Second, I hoped we might ferry across the Adriatic with Paolo for a quick visit to Medjugorje.

Father Svet continued his campaign of persuasion. Each time we spoke by telephone, he would again ask if and when I was coming. The war was raging, yet there seemed to be a small corridor free from all fighting, ranging from the northern tip of Croatia near Split, along the coast and inland to Medjugorje. It was like a contemporary parting of the Red Sea, allowing pilgrims to travel with relative confidence. "I think you and the family can come in safety," Father Svet assured me, when I told him of our tentative plans to ferry over from Italy. "Others from the United States are coming every day and there were many here for the anniversary."

Paolo was confident it would be safe. "I have made this trip many times with no problems." Thus, we planned to meet in Ancona, with Paolo driving us to Medjugorje, and back to the ferry several days later.

In the meantime, we stayed three days in Assisi, much to Terri's delight. It was a combination of joy and penance. There was plenty of time to see all of Assisi she had missed on our first journey to the home of St. Francis, but the price was sweltering nights in a tiny room at the convent where we stayed.

I called Paolo on the last evening in Assisi, checking plans for our rendezvous in Ancona. "Well, there is a slight change. The ferry departure has been delayed from noon until 5 P.M. I don't think it will cause any problems."

But I did. That meant we would not arrive in Medjugorje until well into the early morning hours, making it a tough trip for the kids and leaving us only a day and a half in Medjugorje. More importantly, I felt a warning bell going off. After talking to Terri about my concerns, I telephoned Paolo, cancelling our part of the trip. "I'm sorry, but I just feel we shouldn't go at this time . . ."

Disappointed, we returned home four days earlier than planned. Medjugorje would have to wait. Meanwhile, there were only a couple of tours before leaving for Russia in late October.

The frustration of not going to Medjugorje was soon lost in the excitement of the Russia tour. I was awed at the prospect of playing a role in the conversion of Russia. One day as I was driving home from the office, the thought struck me that in a few days, I would leave for the beginning of a five-country tour of Eastern Europe. It was so overwhelming, I had to pull to the side of the road for a few minutes to regain composure.

The family huddled together at the departure gate in the airport. This was it. We would be apart for three long weeks. Terri was quiet and sad. And for the first time in countless departures for speaking tours, I noticed tears in Kennedy's eyes. Of course, my twelve-year-old son denied it, saying it was caused from "yawning." Even Rebecca, normally hopping and skipping about with nonstop chatter, was somber and still. There was a lump in my throat, mixed with the excitement of a new adventure, as I boarded the plane for the twenty-hour flight to St. Petersburg, Russia. I was very much aware of the significance of the departure date, October 25—the anniversary day of Medjugorje.

As the plane descended toward the airport outside of St. Petersburg, there was just enough evening light left to see a rather desolate landscape. There were thin patches of early snow in little gullies where the sun was unable to penetrate. Structures and roadways were sparse until we passed over the city. Even then, the lights were dim and traffic only a trickle. It was surprising considering this city was home to six million Russians.

There was more surprise on entering a shabby, dingy building for customs. The entry process was swift and nonchalant. It was hard to imagine this was the Russia we feared for so long during the Cold War years. Exiting the building to stinging cold, I saw Zofia, faintly remembering her from our brief meeting in New Orleans; but she recognized me.

"So now, you are finally in Russia," she said, shaking my hand lightly. "Welcome! Here, let Stepan carry one of your bags." She shoved a bag at her Russian driver and grabbed the other, a large suitcase containing 3,000 rosaries given to me by Stas Majewski at the airport in New York just before my departure. Over my protests, Zofia struggled with the bag, following Stepan to a small, dilapidated automobile. It was immediately evident there was a strong determination housed in the frail frame of this Polish woman.

We journeyed into the city in near darkness, the headlights of Stepan's ancient automobile barely bright enough to see the road. It was an intensely dark night with no moon, adding a pale of uncertainty as I asked Zofia details of the tour. "Well, we have many problems now at the last minute," she began hesitantly.

"What do you mean?"

She sighed before answering. "You know, I have been here for five months now. I did not know anyone when I came and did not speak the language. Now, I have traveled everywhere by train arranging each conference. The telephones do not work very well and it takes hours to call contacts in the different countries. Each time details were arranged, they would call and tell me it was changed. It has been very difficult."

Suddenly thoughts of being even a small part of the conversion of Russia dimmed. Zofia continued the bleak news. The group that was going to assist her backed out at the last minute. "I only have Stepan and his wife Helena who live here, and some youth from the church." She paused and sighed deeply again. "Now, I am not sure we will have too many people for your two talks on Sunday here in St. Petersburg. Many of the young people I paid to distribute the posters and flyers announcing your talk threw them away or just did not put them out."

"Don't worry, Zofia. Whoever is intended to be there will come." Even as I said it, I sank into a feeling of doom. Maybe I made a mistake in coming.

"But don't you worry," she said, mustering up what

little optimism was left. "Poland is all set and I think the other stops will be fine." And then adding proudly: "And I have learned the language!"

"That's nice." I just wanted to go to bed and forget everything until tomorrow.

As always, things looked better after a night's rest, despite a cold, overcast morning. Stepan and Helena took us on a tour of the city and for a little shopping. St. Petersburg was at one time a beautiful city. Now, it was grimy. Every building seemed in need of repair and painting, while the roads were filled with potholes and huge cracks. It reminded me of a once-beautiful lady that had fallen on hard times.

Shopping like everything else was complicated. Items purchased had to be paid for at a central cashier before they could be wrapped and received from the original section of the stores. Prices were extremely high on some items and too low on others; the entire system made no sense.

We returned to Zofia's small apartment for a long conversation over coffee and sandwiches. I knew little about this woman who had single-handedly set up the tour. After some coaxing, she told me of wanting to become a nun as a teenager growing up in Poland, and being told by a priest that her calling was in the world. She married, came to the States, and for twenty-seven years had lived in a suburb of Detroit, Michigan. Planning retirement soon from work as an operating room nurse, the future became unsure when her husband, who worked for the U.S. government, died suddenly of a heart attack in April, 1991.

"But I accepted that as God's will," Zofia continued. "It is strange that you requested of me to also arrange a tour in Russia when I first asked you to return to Poland. My plans had always been to come here one day to work as a missionary for the Catholic Church by distributing literature and materials. When my husband died, I was prepared to do that."

It was incredible what she had accomplished in the five months she had been here. Cold, sleepless train journeys of 20 to 30 hours were common, with little or no food and drink. There had been no one to assist her. Yet in addition to Russia, she had arranged venues in Latvia, Lithuania, and the Ukraine; then on to Poland, for a tour in the eastern half of the country, including returns to Cracow and Warsaw.

I marveled as she laid out our travels plans. "Zofia, what you have accomplished is unbelievable. But why didn't you call me and just cancel the tour when you discovered you had no help?"

"That is another story," she said with a mysterious smile.

I returned her smile. "Well, we have all day!"

"After my husband died, I resigned from my work and began planning to come to Russia. That is when my best friend, Veronica, told me that you were going to be speaking at a conference in New Orleans, and she felt something important was going to happen. Both of us heard you speak before in Detroit. We began to follow your work, and we read your books and listened to your tapes.

"So you decided to come?"

"Yes—at the last minute." Zofia folded and unfolded her hands nervously. "You have to understand that I have never experienced anything like what happened next. Saturday morning of the conference, when I was waking up, I heard Our Lady speaking to me, saying, *"Bring Wayne to Poland, as a birthday gift for me."*

I was not surprised at her receiving such a message, but puzzled at the last part. "A birthday gift? But her birthday was in September."

"Yes, I know," Zofia nodded. "But, you must understand that it was Our Lady and that is what she said! Well, I tried to see you Saturday afternoon but there were too many people around you. I asked one of the conference people if they would arrange for me to see you. He told me to come to the front of the auditorium just before the start of Mass on Sunday, and of course, that is what I did. And then right after our meeting, I find out you are entering the Church during the Mass! So right away Veronica and I knew that was the important thing that was going to happen."

Sitting back in her chair, she added, "And now, you are here. So, even if we do not have many people tomorrow for your two talks, you are meant to be here—and so am I."

I could hardly argue with that reasoning.

That evening, another friend of Zofia's came by the apartment. He knew of my work and would be meeting us later in Lublin, Poland, where he lived. He talked of working for the church for fifteen years by secretly training seminarians from throughout the former Soviet Union in Lublin, and then returning them to their native countries as underground priests.

I was still feeling the effects of jet lag, and only after "Ksiadz (Polish word for Father) Marian" as Zofia called him, mentioned something about confession, did I ask him, "Are you a priest?"

"Yes, of course."

"But you're dressed in a suit and tie."

Father Marian nodded. "Yes, I can understand now why you did not know. You see, my assignment is directly from the Vatican. I have worked quietly during these years because of the political conditions."

Suddenly, I was wide awake—and feeling a little sheepish at expecting so much on this tour. After listening to his stories of the underground church for the next hour, I asked him, "Father Marian, would you hear my confession?"

Preparing for bed after Father Marian Radwan had left, I prayed to be able to accept whatever God wanted of me in this land. My being a glorious part of the conversion of Russia was no longer important. If only a handful of Russians attended the talks, so be it.

Sunday, after early Mass in a tiny room serving as one of only three Roman Catholic Churches in St. Petersburg, I waited at Zofia's apartment for Stepan to come for me, packing my bags since we would be leaving late that night for Latvia by train. Zofia and Helena had gone to the conference hall immediately after church to oversee preparations. There would be two talks—in the early afternoon, and evening. Prior to the talks, a video titled, "Marian Apparitions of the 20th Century" would be shown. It had been dubbed in Russian and would serve as an introduction to the events in Medjugorje.

The quiet time was a blessing. I prayed my rosary, praying for success throughout the tour, success based on conversions to Jesus, not on numbers of people present. I marveled at the work Zofia had accomplished in such a short tenure. Not only had she arranged the entire tour, but had managed to have 50,000 copies of my articles printed in Russian, having distributed thousands in St. Petersburg. She was just one little woman, and not nearly as frail as I had imagined. A strong mixture of determination and stubbornness had allowed her to accomplish her goals.

Thus, as I rode to the site of the first talk, recalling that Zofia said this would be the first Christian event held in this famous concert hall since the beginning of the Revolution, I prepared myself for the worst.

Although Stepan spoke no English, I clearly understood his excitement as we approached the concert hall. There was a line of people at least five wide, running from the entrance to around the corner and down the entire block! Somehow, word had spread and Zofia's estimation of only one or two hundred people had swelled to thousands.

Entering at the rear of the concert hall, I found Zofia engaged in intense conversation with a swarthy Russian man. "Zofia, have you seen the line of people coming in? It's incredible! There are thousands!"

"Yes, but this man refuses to turn on the microphones or the lights unless I pay him additional money."

I was incredulous. The crowd size did not phase her, only the last-minute demands of the theater manager. "But Zofia, look at the people coming in. This is wonderful!"

There was a near riot as copies of my articles ran out, followed shortly by all 3,000 rosaries, which were supposed to be used throughout the tour. And the concert hall was filled to standing room only with more than 2,000 Russians. It was repeated in the evening with a total of more than 4,500 people learning of the miracle of Medjugorje. No matter what occurred the rest of the tour, this made the entire trip worth it.

I ended the evening talk by telling the audience in a highly animated state, "Do you realize that you, the Russian people, through your total conversion, will be the greatest glory of God? That is what the mother of Jesus said at Fatima, and now at Medjugorje!" The crowd stood and cheered for more than a full minute, sending chills throughout my body.

But as always, Satan was also there. Just as I prepared to exit the stage, a group calling themselves Disciples of the Church of the Mother of God, came on stage, uninvited. Dressed in long robes with large crosses around their necks, they had come backstage earlier to speak to me and had stayed. The leader grabbed my arm pulling me back to the microphone. "Please, we want to make a presentation to you."

Having been forewarned of the activities of this group, I refused adamantly, pulling away and leaving the stage after telling the audience through my translator that these people were not associated with our presentation. They were taking advantage of an opportunity to propagandize their cult, which worshiped the Virgin Mary as a goddess. It was neither Catholic nor Orthodox, but formed out of extremism, with a doctrine that was the very essence of what many non-Catholics accuse Catholics of in their devotion and veneration of Mary.

"But what can we do?" Zofia asked, beside herself at this last-minute intrusion. "They will not leave!"

"Tell the stage manager to cut off the mikes and stage lights. Then let's get out of here!"

It was clearly a warning that Satan would be present to disrupt and destroy what he could throughout the tour. But I wasn't going to let this one incident ruin a tremendously spiritual evening.

The mood was euphoric as we drove toward the train station for an overnight journey to Riga, Latvia. Suddenly, Zofia exclaimed, "Oh, I wanted you to ride on the metro (subway) system before we leave. It is a very good system."

I gave her a light hug. "Listen, don't worry about that. This has been a tremendous evening!"

"But you must see this system." And with that she spoke to Stepan in Russian. "Stepan will drop us at the next station where we can ride the metro for several blocks. He will pick us up at the next station."

"Whatever you say," I answered, happily resigned to allowing her this extra little pleasure.

We dashed down marble steps for a good five hundred feet to a clean, well-lighted platform. It was a stark paradox to the poor conditions of the city streets. Within minutes our metro arrived, and we grabbed seats near the door for the short ride. Casually glancing around, I did a double-take as a young man sitting next to me was reading a copy of my articles in Russian! "Zofia, look at this," I whispered.

I couldn't contain myself. I tapped the young man on the shoulder, and turned the tabloid to my picture on the front page, pointing to it and then to myself. He was perplexed for a moment and then it registered. Just then, we arrived at our station stop and got off, waving to the young man who kept staring at the tabloid and then at us, as the metro car pulled away! Shaking my head in wonder, I asked Zofia, "What are the chances of us randomly deciding to ride the metro in the middle of St. Petersburg, only to sit next to this young man reading my articles about Medjugorje?" We both knew it was a special sign that the message of Medjugorje had arrived in Russia.

Another surprise awaited us at the train station; Father Marian was there. "I wanted to make sure everything was all right," he explained as we made our way down the long platform. I was glad for his presence and the opportunity to see him again.

"This is my car," Zofia said as we reached the mid point of the long train, "I have arranged a first class sleeper for you. Ksiadz Marian will assist you. I will meet you in the morning when we arrive." I began to protest. "It is no use, everything has been arranged," she said, disappearing into her car.

"Ah, here is your car." Father Marian hoisted my bags into the doorway and we made our way to the proper compartment. I opened the door and was taken aback by the sight of a woman who would be my traveling companion. She was in her mid-thirties and already settled in the lower of the two bunks in the cramped, narrow compartment. Father Marian, after speaking to the woman, stated, "I told her you were an American and asked her to assist you if necessary." He seemed totally unconcerned that I would have to share the compartment for the night's journey with a woman.

The only thing "first class" about the compartment was the name. I struggled to load my luggage on one end of the upper bunk, the only place available. The cramped quarters and presence of the woman made sleep near impossible. Slipping down from the bunk, I motioned to the woman that I would be just outside the compartment. Shaking her head vigorously, she indicated I should stay, but I couldn't stand it any longer; I had to get out and stretch my legs.

The clickity-clack of the wheels and the dark, eerie landscape barely visible through the train windows presented a setting straight out of an old Russian spy movie. I stood there for nearly half an hour, until two men squeezed by me, staring and looking as unsavory as any casting director could ask for. I immediately returned to my cramped bunk, sensing it wasn't too safe in the corridor.

And finally, I dozed off—only to be suddenly awakened a short while later by hard banging on the compartment door and shouts in Russian. The woman responded and then quickly opened the door. Two Russian soldiers burst in, loudly demanding our passports. After several seconds of staring at my passport and visa papers, one of them frowned at me and mumbled, "Problem!"

I was petrified. The woman began arguing with the soldiers who finally tossed my passport on the bunk but kept the visa. "Wait a minute, I need the visa!" But with a cold glare, they left slamming the door. Immediately, the woman locked it and placed the safety chain in its slot.

Again I lay there trying to calm down when suddenly, the door opened quietly, stopped only by the chain lock. Someone was attempting to enter our compartment—and it wasn't soldiers! The woman yelled something sharp in Russian, and the door slowly closed without a sound from outside. My heart began to pound as I realized someone was trying to rob us, in all probability the two men who passed me earlier in the corridor and noticed this naive American standing there.

After several hours, exhaustion from the night's ordeal brought a fitful sleep, again harshly interrupted with knocking on the door. But this time, they were Latvian soldiers, and it was daylight; right behind them was Zofia. "Oh, wow, am I glad to see you! What a night!" After relating the events of the evening, I took Zofia by the shoulders. "Look, we're not going to separate again. I don't know what would have happened if it hadn't been for this woman!"

"This is the only train trip. We will not be separated again." And with that, she opened a bag containing juice, bread sticks, and homemade Polish dried sausages, which we promptly shared with the woman. Only then did I realize that we had been on the train for fourteen hours without food or drink. Enjoying the food as much as I would an expensive gourmet meal, I felt a renewed respect for the travails Zofia undertook to arrange this tour.

Riga, Latvia, was a welcome sight. We departed the train to bright sunshine, offsetting the biting cold. Immediately we were welcomed by a several people from the group that arranged the talk and I was taken to my hotel, free until the evening talk.

Literally as well as figuratively, the dark Russian night was replaced by the bright daylight of Latvia, which was beautiful. Empty, unrepaired streets and unpainted buildings were replaced by old but well-kept buildings and bustling traffic of vehicles and people. The stores were busy and loaded with food and merchandise.

A major difference, explaining the stark contrast to Russia, is that the people of the Baltic states never lost their faith in God. Even though discouraged and harassed by the Russians, they continued to live their faith, often in secrecy. Thus, today, with newfound freedom, they were prospering, while the Russians, without God, floundered.

At the talk there were as many Lutherans present as Catholics, as the two religions dominated the republic. And again, the people did not want the evening to end. I discovered later they had never seen or heard of a lay person speaking about the Gospel. A lone man approached as we prepared to leave the church. After speaking to him, my translator replies, "This man is a Lutheran."

"That's wonderful. Tell him I was Lutheran for many years."

"But you do not understand—he is a Lutheran pastor!"

I prepared for debate, thinking that is why he approached us. "He tells me that he has been seeking a relationship with the Virgin Mary all of his life, but has had difficulty due to his church theology, his congregation, and his family. But something strange happened tonight."

The stranger continued talking, his voice quavering. It took my translator a moment to digest the man's statement. "Well, this is beautiful. He says that tonight, he came home and was preparing for a quiet evening when he heard a voice inside telling him to come to this church. It was so strong, he immediately came. He did not know anything about a talk being held here this evening, or about Medjugorje, or you. But after listening, he feels at last that closeness to the Virgin Mary."

I was deeply touched, and promised to leave him a picture of the statue of Our Lady from Father Jozo's church in Tihaljina, and a medal blessed during the time of an apparition, at the hotel desk where he could pick it up in the morning.

At last, we arrived in the Ukraine, the country I most wanted to visit! Kiev was a beautiful and holy city. Driving from the airport, I could see the signs of struggle under the oppression of Communism in its structures and in the faces of the people. The buildings were not nearly as impressive in design, but they were clean and in good condition. Prosperity wasn't as noticeable as it was in Latvia, but it was clearly better off than St. Petersburg. The reason was the same: a people who never lost their faith in God.

Talks were planned for this and one other city in the Ukraine. At both venues, I told the people they have suffered a crucifixion, just as Jesus did. The Ukraine Catholics truly represent a people who have undergone decades of redemptive suffering. As I related this, asking if they could forgive their Russian oppressors, there was a loud chorus of yes!

From there, we traveled to Vilnius, Lithuania, the last stop in the former Soviet Union, before journeying on to Poland. The church again was full and the talk, extended by people not wanting to leave.

Sunday, November 1, was All Saints' Day. We arrived at a beautiful church for early morning Mass, and an impromptu talk afterwards. The day before, we had visited the church at the urging of our translator. "This is one of the most beautiful churches in all of Lithuania. You really should see it," he had related.

While there, he introduced us to the young associate priest, who immediately began asking questions about Medjugorje. After awhile, he asked, "I wonder, if I can arrange it, would it be possible for you to speak after the early Mass tomorrow?"

Zofia looked at me with a look I was beginning to recognize, a plea to say yes to anything these people requested for the sake of conversion. This time, it was easy. "I'll be happy to speak, Father. We have to attend Mass and this is a wonderful place."

And arrange it, he did! On a bitterly cold morning,

the church was filled. We entered the sacristy, looking for the associate, but instead, found the pastor. He was not pleased. As soon as Zofia told him who we were, he exploded in a tirade of words. The translator listened attentively and then said. "I am very sorry, but he says it is impossible because of time to have a talk."

Just then the associate arrived and once again the pastor began an angry tirade. "Please accept my apologies," the young priest explained, "But yesterday, he gave his permission to have the talk. Now, for some unexplained reason, he says he cannot allow it."

"It is okay, Father. We are just happy to be here."

When the associate announced there would be no talk, a rumble ran through the crowd. An angry rumble. Many had arisen in the very early hours to endure long, freezing rides on public transportation to come.

Following Mass, there was a rush of people into the sacristy engulfing the pastor. It didn't take a translator to know they were extremely angry and did not hesitate to let the pastor know it. I felt sorry for him, but knew that his denial of the talk was done out of pride, and this was Our Lady's way of letting him know he had made a mistake.

We left that afternoon for Poland, having completed what I felt was a triumphant tour of Russia, and the other countries of the former Soviet Union. It would last well beyond the exhaustive seven days of bringing the story of Medjugorje to these people. I was anxious to return sometime in the future to complete the triumph.

Sleeping the entire morning, I arose in time to pack for a six-hour automobile journey to a city called Turon, our first stop in Poland. We would be there for an hour-long radio show on a station called Radio Maria.

Exhausted and suffering a mild letdown after riding the high of the Russian tour, I was grateful the radio show was the only venue of the day. But I asked again anyway. "Are you sure the radio show is all that we have to do tonight?"

"Yes, and then you will be free to rest until the next day." Zofia had taken note of my mood and chose to allow me the quiet time needed to rejuvenate the mind and spirit. The pensive mood of the journey was broken only by prayers of the rosary.

We arrived in Turon, but after searching and asking directions, we could not locate the building that housed the radio station. Irritation was beginning to set in. Zofia glanced at her watch. "Don't worry, we will find it; we still have a little time before the show."

After several more inquiries, we arrived at a small wooden building. "This is the radio station?" I was expecting something more professional.

We were greeted by an ebullient, bouncy priest, the founder of the station. He escorted us along with a local translator to a small kitchen in the basement of the building, seating us at a table laden with sandwiches and drink. "Zofia, I don't want to eat now. I was hoping for a good meal in peace at the hotel after the radio show."

Zofia gave me that look. "Please, they are so excited about you being here, can you eat just a little?"

Reluctantly, I took a sandwich. While we ate, the priest quickly told the history of the station, how he felt called to start it at the request of Our Lady. "And you know," Zofia interjected, "the station went on the air December 8, 1991, the same day you entered the church, and the day I asked you to come back to Poland as a birthday gift for Our Blessed Mother. . . ." She was doing all she could to change my dour mood.

The show began as I briefly told my story of learning

about Medjugorje, and then details of her messages to the world. That was followed by call-in questions. From the beginning, my irritation grew as the translator was slow and unsure of himself. During a short break, I whispered to Zofia, "Listen, this guy doesn't know how to translate. Why don't you take over, or at least jump in and help?"

"He will do okay. He just needs a little more time to adjust."

But time didn't help and soon Zofia was forced to assist him. The show was finally over. "Thank goodness, that's done. I can't wait to get to the hotel."

Again Zofia gave me her look. "I know you are tired, but Father insists we accompany him to Mass. They are going to broadcast it live and there are thousands who will be listening. Please say yes."

"No way, Zofia! Tell him thank you for asking but we went to Mass this morning and I am very tired after the long day."

"But the listeners are expecting you to make a few comments about Medjugorje after the Mass. It has already been announced. And . . . he has made plans to take us to dinner afterward."

I struggled to restrain my anger, knowing this priest would not give up. "Okay, okay. Tell him I'll go to Mass and do the broadcast, but no dinner!"

Zofia was almost afraid to continue. With a nervous little laugh, she added, "Oh, my, I know this is difficult for you but he wants you to return after dinner to the station to take caller's questions for two hours." The last words became slower and quieter as she turned her hands up in resignation at being caught in the middle.

I began shaking my head furiously. "Absolutely not!"

"Please—for Our Lady?"

That did me in. Slumping in the chair and staring at the wall, I let out a deep, tired sigh. "All right, Zofia, I give up. But I'm only coming back for half an hour of questions—no more!"

Zofia smiled lightly and gave me a reassuring pat as she related my words to the priest. He clapped his hands excitedly and hustled everyone off to the waiting automobiles.

I excused myself to recompose in the washroom. The second I closed the door, I heard Our Lady's voice, clearly and resonantly: "How can you say no, when you know it is I who is asking?"

Startled and filled with discernment that I was saying no to her "birthday gift," I dropped to my knees. "Oh Blessed Mary, I'm sorry."

Sliding into the backseat next to Zofia, I mumbled, "I'm sorry for being so rude. Please tell the priest I'll do whatever he wishes." Later, I told her of Our Lady's message in the wash room.

Of course, it was a spirit-filled evening. The Mass was magnificent, the talk uniquely inspired. And the dinner was delicious. We returned to Radio Maria for more than two hours of questions.

At a little past midnight, I sank into my hotel bed, spent—and happily humbled.

A bright new day—and new attitude—dawned as we departed for a long drive to Czestachowa, the beautiful shrine of the Black Madonna. This second visit to the shrine included an additional bonus of staying there for the night, since the next talk was in a city still three hours journey from there.

It was the presidential election day in the U.S. Our rosary prayers during the long drive were fervent intercessory prayer that the people would vote based on the laws of God, and not man. For me, it was a one-issue campaign: pro-life or pro-choice for abortion.

Another blessing came as we arrived in time to celebrate Mass in front of the Icon again. But this was different from the first time; now I was Catholic! It was a beautiful way to end the day of travel.

The tour was greeted at every stop with thousands, as the articles and book had been translated and were available at each talk. After a night in a city named Bielsko Biala, we arrived in Cracow, my favorite Polish city. And Zofia Oxzkowskaczkowska, whom I immediately named "Zofia Two," joined us for the remainder of the tour to serve as translator.

After a restful day of touring and return to the Divine Mercy Chapel, the ancient church that was site of the evening's talk was beyond crowded. People were in the streets surrounding the church. "It is because of your book," my translator Zofia relates. "It is very popular!"

There was a near riot afterwards, as people literally stormed the sacristy, wanting books signed, or to grab my hand. The priests pleaded with the crowd, reminding them that Mass would begin shortly. Thirty minutes later, order was restored when the priest announced that I would remain as long as necessary to sign books and speak to the people.

After Mass, we were escorted to an area in the front of the church. The priests placed a large, oval-shaped table into the doorway, and people lined up outside in extreme cold and misting rain, singing and praying the rosary as they waited in penance to have a book signed or simply to say thank you for coming to Cracow. I felt as if I was on the edge of heaven as the singing grew in volume.

Both Zofias, standing nearby began to laugh. "What is it?" I asked, taking a brief respite from signing.

Zofia Two pointed to the table. "The priest just told

us this table on which you are signing was often used by Pope John Paul II as a Ping-Pong table, when he was assigned to this church for several years!"

Two and a half hours later, we left one of the most heart-touching stops of the entire mission.

From there, it was on to Tarnobrzej, a large industrial city; and then to Lublin and a rendezvous with Father Marian. "I have been hearing great things about the tour," he smiled, as we sipped hot coffee in his tiny kitchen.

After a quick tour of a new dorm named after the Pope, and constructed for students from Eastern Europe, Father Marian pulled me aside. "I am very grateful for all you are doing and I want you to know I am submitting a full report of your mission in Russia and Poland that will be given directly to the Holy Father."

I started to thank him. "Wait, there is more I wish to say." He lowered his voice and spoke slowly to emphasize the importance of what he was about to say. "I have never asked for any special favors from the Holy Father's office, but I will attempt to arrange for you to attend a private Mass with the Pope while you are on tour in Italy."

I was speechless. Father Marian knew from our discussions in St. Petersburg, I would be going to Italy later in the spring for a tour and book promotion. I hugged him in silence, whispering my thanks, hoping this long-held dream of someday meeting the Pope might be coming true. "Just let me know the dates and I will see what I can do," he said just before we left.

Finally, we arrived in Warsaw for one more talk, and then departure for home. It was difficult and emotional saying goodbye to Zofia. She would be staying in Poland for a few more days before joining the other Zofia on a short pilgrimage to Medjugorje.

There was no way to properly thank her for what she had done in arranging this tour. "I can only ask Our Lady to give you a much-needed rest in Medjugorje."

"Well, I have one more thing to ask you," she responded, giving me that look again.

Smiling, I returned her look with one of mock consternation. "Okay, what is it now?"

"There is still so much to be done in these countries. Will you come back next year if I can arrange it?"

I hugged her tightly. "You can count on it!"

27
Still a Place of Peace

"Dear children, today, like never before, I invite you to pray for peace; peace in your heart, peace in your family, and peace in the whole world. Because Satan wants war. He does not want peace. He wants to destroy all that is good. Therefore, dear children, pray, pray, pray!"

The plane lurched sharply as it passed through a thick bank of clouds. I awoke with a start, having dozed and daydreamed the majority of the nine-hour flight from the States. We were minutes from landing in Split, and in a few hours, I would be back in the little village of Medjugorje for the first time since the Fall of 1991.

I was anxious to see Medjugorje as it was now in January, 1993, to see how in the 18 months since my last visit, this satanic war had altered it. Pilgrims had continued to go, if but a handful. Surrounding cities and villages had suffered heavily in damage and casualties, yet Medjugorje remained unscathed, like a cool spot in the middle of a raging inferno of flames. It was still a place of peace.

Father Svetozar had convinced me to return, and was waiting at the airport to drive us to the village. He had remained an important information link to Medjugorje for me during the war-imposed hiatus as we shared speaking time at conferences and retreats.

As the airliner touched down on the tarmac, I thought of the visionaries. I wouldn't see Marija, Ivan, or Jakov; they were traveling in different countries, witnessing to the fruits of Our Lady's daily visits to them. Marija was in South America, Ivan in Australia, and Jakov, shy and adverse to speaking in public, was nevertheless in Italy, doing the same. Only Vicka remained in the village, doing what she had been doing for eleven and a half years: serving as Gospa's special ambassador to the pilgrims who still came to the village.

Ivanka and Mirjana were married and mothers of little children. Although they no longer saw Gospa daily, they were still actively involved in living and spreading the messages. Each had received the tenth of ten secrets of future events Our Lady had stated she would give to each visionary; the others had nine. It had been this way since early in 1987.

Our Lady appeared to Ivanka each year on the anniversary day of the apparitions, and to Mirjana on her birthday in March; however, for more than a year, she had been appearing to her at least once a month, preparing her for the future events, the ultimate conclusion to her visits on earth.

These "children" as people still referred to them, were now young adults; Jakov, only 10 at the time the apparitions began, was 22, with plans to marry an Italian girl in the spring. And Marija and Paolo were certain to marry within the year. The teenage visionaries had grown up, but their lives remained basically simple, spiritual reflections of Our Lady's daily appearance to them.

Lugging my baggage through customs, I was quick to spot Father Svet in the awaiting crowd. "So, you have finally returned!" He grabbed me in a hearty hug and pounded my back.

"Yes, and I have something for you. Here is your cross!"

I handed him the cross he had asked me to bring, the same one I had reluctantly carried when attempting to come to Medjugorje just a month before. "I'm afraid it's a little more banged up from the flight."

The cross, with burns and scratches and the corpus broken in several places, had come from Father Svet's church in Mostar, which had been destroyed. "That is all right," he said, taking the cross, "like the damage to the Church here, it can be repaired."

We were on our way, after a quick stop to visit a priest who was coordinating relief efforts in Split. I left a cash donation, given by people from my hometown, Myrtle Beach, people who had been to, or had been touched by Medjugorje.

As we left the city limits of Split, my Franciscan friend updated me on the most recent events of the war. Mostar and the surrounding areas were now inundated with Moslem refugees and trouble was flaring. "This is a big problem because there are so many without homes. Now, they are fighting against the Croatians, running them out of their homes just as the Serbs did to them. This is very sad because the Croatians have helped them all during the war. So, not only is there war with the Serbs, but also now between Croatians and Moslems."

He suddenly changed the conversation. "You know, you look tired, more than usual; and you must be hungry. Would you like to stop for a meal? I know a very good restaurant just a little way further up the road."

I smiled at him. "You don't miss anything, do you? Yes, I'm a little more weary than usual these days. Too many trips in too short a time frame. But yes, a restaurant sounds great—I'm starved!"

We pulled into a dirt parking area at the side of a building with a small sign advertising Northern Italian food. It didn't look like much from the outside, but inside was warm atmosphere, pleasant live music, and some of the best Italian food I have ever tasted. Afterward we enjoyed rich coffee. Father Svet leaned back in his chair, relaxed and seemingly in no hurry. "Tell me now about your family. How is everyone doing?"

"They're all fine. Terri and the little ones send their love. She wishes she could have come with me. And Lisa has been dating a young man I feel certain she will marry. They met while working with youth at the church; Tom is a good Catholic, very devout in his faith."

"And what about your son, Steve?"

Taking a deep breath, I wondered if Father Svet was able to read my mind. Relations with Steve were at an all-time low. "Well, there's good news and bad news. The good news is, he's still in college and doing well. But he has yet to do anything about his faith. Just before coming here, we had a terrible argument. So at the moment, we aren't on very good terms." I went on to give Father Svet the details, leaving nothing out.

He listened attentively. "I know it has been difficult for you with this son, but you must reconcile with him and continue to assist him in finding God. He needs your help and love more than the others."

"I know," I sighed, "and what made it worse, the argument occurred on the weekend his brother Michael was married. At least, Michael's doing better. Marriage should help him mature."

I appreciated Father Svet's concern for my family. It was more than passing interest as he had met all of my older children except Angela. He knew of their struggles with faith—especially those struggles of Steve.

Back on the road, it took longer than anticipated to reach Medjugorje, due to military checkpoints and detours around new danger spots, centered in the newly inhabited enclaves of Moslem refugees. There had been trouble within twelve miles of Medjugorje, just a few hours before our arrival at this checkpoint, thus, we were forced to detour, causing us to arrive in the village well past midnight.

I collapsed in one of the small pilgrim rooms at Marija's brother, Andrija's house, and was asleep instantly. Rest was essential, as there was so much to do and only five short days to accomplish it. Father Svet would be taking me to Mostar in the afternoon to tour the war devastation and visit old friends. Also, I planned to visit Father Jozo, at Siroki Brijeg. That would take the better part of a day.

Mostly though, I desired simply to be a pilgrim on this trip, to climb Krizevic and Podbrdo, and generally be alone for quiet meditation. I hoped to do that after a couple of days since Father Svet was leaving for the States the following day to speak at a war relief fund raising benefit in New York City.

I strode happily along the familiar pathway toward St. James Church for English Mass, refreshed somewhat after a few hours sleep, and enjoying the warm rays of sunshine on a chilly morning. Arriving, I was dismayed. No one was there! A woman entered and headed for the altar area. "Excuse me, is there no English Mass?"

"Yes, but it is in the little room there on the right."

I followed, and slipped quietly against the back wall of the little room that had served as the original apparition room for the visionaries. Now, pilgrims groups used it for special occasions, as the apparitions occurred in the bell tower of the church. This morning, the little chapel was filled with about twenty-five English and Italian pilgrims, with an Italian priest as celebrant of the Mass.

Even in this confined area, it was Mass at Medjugorje as I remembered. There was such a sense of the presence of the Queen of Peace, who had come to the visionaries so many times in this room. Other than the lack of large

crowds, I felt very much like the pilgrim who had first
come here in 1986.

As the service ended, I held the door open, thinking
the priest was heading for the sacristy on the other side of
the altar; instead, he smiled, took me by the arm and led
me to the front. "My dear friends, I am happy to see Wayne
Weible here in Medjugorje. I am sure you know about his
work and his book." And then turning to me, "I am here
with a pilgrimage of forty people from Naples, and other
parts of Italy. We would be honored if you would join us
for an early lunch and speak to our group."

"Well, I would be honored," I stammered, taken aback
at this unexpected exposure. So much for peace and quiet
on this trip! I was also surprised Italians knew of my mission.

"Oh, we know you well from your book," the priest
responded. "It is very popular in Italy! We are also aware
you are coming to Naples in two months."

It was a pleasant luncheon ending with a short talk,
leaving just enough time to meet with Father Svet for our
trip to Mostar. In closing, I told them, "The beauty of coming to Medjugorje in 1993, here in the midst of war, is that
we are called to continue living and spreading the message even in the face of these horrible events. It helps to
understand the words of Jesus in Holy Scripture, when
He says: 'The last shall be first, and the first shall be last.'
Though some of you are finding Medjugorje for the first
time, under these circumstances, you are as much a part
of Medjugorje, as those who came first!" I then added with
a laugh: "And you know how Italians love to be first!"

Hurrying toward the convent where Father Svet lived,
I smiled, thinking about the Italians. They were zealous
supporters of Medjugorje and had come in droves in the
early days. Their reputation for wanting to be first was
well earned. Somehow, they managed to always be in the

front whether it be Holy Mass or the line at the gift shop.

I remembered an incident concerning Italians which had occurred at Medjugorje a couple of years ago. After giving a talk in the outside rotunda, people began asking for autographs and soon formed a short line. A small group of Italian women listening intently nearby, quickly jumped in the front of the line. I signed autographs for several of them when the next in line asked, "Are you Ivan or Jakov?"

I laughed and answered, "Neither one, I'm an American."

With that, she snatched the paper away, giving me an indignant looked as the group hastily left!

A more somber mood set in as we entered the outskirts of the devastated city of Mostar. "There, you can see the cathedral and the bishop's home are completely destroyed; and that apartment building was bombed killing many women and children." Father Svet described each horror in a monotone, as one resigned to the reality of war. "And that little park which used to be filled with families and children playing, is now a cemetery."

We walked through the ruins of Sts. Peter and Paul Catholic Church and monastery, the Franciscan center. "You see the bullet holes in the doors of the friar's rooms and the complete destruction of the church, and now you can understand that the priests and nuns, the churches, monasteries and convents are always the first targets of this war."

I could only nod. As we were leaving the ruins of what was the sanctuary of the church, I noticed a stained glass window depicting the Virgin Mary holding the baby Jesus. For some inexplicable reason, it had not been shattered in the shelling. Father Svet pointed out that there were only two holes in the glass, one in the head of the baby Jesus, and the other in the heart of the mother. "You can see the entire suffering of our Church represented in that scene."

We traveled a few blocks further to a convent for a short meeting with Sister Janja Boras, a Franciscan nun who had served in Medjugorje parish as close friend and spiritual guide to the visionaries for more than five years. "I can only tell you that we pray each day as if it is going to be our last day. We continue to pray for peace—even for those who are doing this to us."

Later, we paid a surprise visit to Father Svet's cousin, Jozo Kraljevic, whom Father had introduced me to several years ago. We had become close friends and I had stayed with his family several times. Jozo was well educated and extremely fluent in English, having taught it in the university. He also served as translator for many Medjugorje videos. When I asked about his wife, Slavka, and fifteen-year old son, Tony, he turned his hands up. "What can I say? Like so many living here, they have suffered from the war. They are living with Slavka's brother in the mountains where it is safe." Jozo added that Tony would probably never be the same. "He is quiet and always nervous now, and keeps to himself most of the time. But there are many children like him. That is the fruit of this war."

"We must go—it is not good to be here in the evening," Father Svet said, moving toward the door as we said our good-byes to Jozo, promising to stay in touch by telephone.

As we maneuvered the steep curves on the inclining road leading away from the city, the muffled thump of shells could be heard. "Yes, they are still active," Father Svet retorted when I asked about the shelling, thinking it had stopped with the recent signing of the latest cease fire. "They usually fire several shells each evening just to let the people know they are still present in the hills."

The entire war scene was forever embedded in my mind as I stared down at the city from the elevation of the mountain road. Standing out as a grim reminder was a huge crater in the side of a relatively new hospital building. Father Svet related that the former administrator was a Serb, who was now commanding the shelling of his former hospital and its clinic from the hills.

On the day before my departure for home, Jozo drove me to Siroki Brejig, to see Father Jozo, with a brief stop to see Slavka and Tony and deliver gifts Terri had sent to them. My heart was filled with emotion and joy as Slavka's eyes brightened when she received the gifts. She scurried about trying to find something to give in return, but there was nothing. "Please tell her she does not need to give us anything other than the pleasure of seeing her again." I told Jozo. I was glad they were in the hills away from the daily shelling. Jozo was strong and stoic; but his family suffered the effects of the fighting like so many others in this country.

There was more joy as we met with Father Jozo and Anka for two hours. He had come to the United States last summer, shuttling between New York and Washington, D.C., in an effort to bring the case of the Bosnian people to members of our government. He had met with senators and congressmen, with Anka along as translator, but had accomplished little. Now he told of the last minute meeting with several members of the legislature, the state department, and a representative of the president.

"We had talked and discussed many things for a long time," Anka translated. "Finally at the end, just before we were to leave to catch our flight home, one of the senators said, 'Father Jozo, can we just spend a few minutes in prayer; it seems to be the only answer to this problem.' When he said that, I knew I had to return and tell my people this was the real answer to stopping the war. It is the only answer!"

I asked him about not being able to see the president personally. "He sent a representative," Father Jozo responded through Anka's translation. "He refused to meet with me. I sent a message to him that when he is no longer president, he should come and see for himself our suffering." It was indeed a prophetic message.

What about the new president? Did Father Jozo think he would do anything more to help the Bosnian and Croatian people? He looked at me for a long time. "I see the White House now splattered with blood—and with mud."

It was a reference not to the war in his homeland, but the war of abortion raging throughout the world, with a new president vowing to make abortion an even stronger law of the land.

As I was leaving, Father Jozo blessed me and said, "You must continue to be a prophet of steel."

Late that night, I walked alone along the road below Podbrdo, where the children first saw Gospa, in June, 1981. I thought of the few days I had been here, of the things I saw, and of the words of Father Svet and Father Jozo. It had been a busy five days with no time to simply be quiet and pray as a pilgrim.

I prayed the rosary, offering a special intention for all the people of Bosnia, including the insurgent Serbs, to find the peace that could only come from God. In these nearly twelve years, Our Lady had asked continually for prayer, fasting and penance; it wasn't just motherly love and concern. It was the only way to bring the war to an end, and it was the only real answer Father Jozo had found in his efforts in the States.

After packing, I had about 40 minutes before leaving for Split. At a sudden urge, I scrambled up Podbrdo and knelt breathless and sweating in front of the spot where Gospa had first appeared to the six children in June, 1981. It was just a few minutes of prayer; but in those minutes, everything I had felt in the past 17 trips to Medjugorje, seemed to flash before me. I was thankful to Father Svet for steadfastly urging me to come and see the Medjugorje of today. And, to Our Lady for confirming it.

I would return home to spread a renewed message that Medjugorje remained a place of prayer, fasting, and penance; now, more than ever, we needed to live these messages. And people needed to come in pilgrimage. It was still a place of hope and peace.

28
Italy

"In my messages, I recommend to everyone, and to the Holy Father in particular, to spread the message which I have received from my Son here at Medjugorje. I wish to entrust to the Pope, the word with which I came here: 'MIR' [peace], which he must spread everywhere . . ."

Three weeks later, I was in Monza, Italy, enjoying dinner with Paolo and his parents—and Marija, who had come for a short visit. It was the start of a fifteen-day book promotion and speaking tour, traveling from the northern part of Italy, to the south and back to Naples, before ending in Rome. I was anxious to relate to the Italian people that Medjugorje and its message was alive and well.

Paolo and Dino had done a masterful job, working with prayer groups throughout the country and coordinating venues with the book publisher. "Paolo will drive you to most meetings and serve as translator," Dino commented as we went over logistics of the tour. "And of course, all of us will be with you for the talks here and in nearby cities."

That meant Marija would be in the audience, which made me a little nervous. "No, no, I am on holiday," she said smiling and shaking her head when I suggested she might want to share speaking duties. "But I will be listening carefully and taking notes!"

It was a relaxing evening, amply spiced with light teasing and laughter. Never had I seen Paolo and Marija so happy and at ease together. All concerns were now past; they were simply two people in love and had announced their engagement. While a date had not been set, they would likely marry within the year.

"That's great news," I responded, when told of their plans. "And I also have some potential good news." I related the promise of my Polish priest-friend, Father Marian Radwan, to attempt arrangement of a private Mass for me with the Pope. "He has given me the name and number of Father Stephano, at the Vatican, and I'm supposed to fax him tomorrow." Hesitating, I added, "I'm going to ask him if he will include all of you as well!"

"That is wonderful," Dino said softly, "It would be a great gift. But please, do not lose the opportunity yourself if we cannot be included."

I assured him it could probably be worked out as I had already asked Father Marian to include them if possible.

Paolo shrugged and smiled. "Well, we will pray and see what happens!"

The next morning, Ash Wednesday, I typed a fax to Father Stephano. "I know this is the beginning of Lent and a time of sacrifice," I prayed silently after completing the fax, "I pray this request will be approved for all of us." I promised to pray more, fast more, and be completely open to the workings of the Holy Spirit throughout the tour.

That afternoon, I joined Marija, Dino and Millie at a hospital two blocks from their apartment to attend Mass and visit a retired, elderly priest, hospitalized due to problems with arteries and veins in his legs. Watching Marija with him, I marveled how loving and attentive she was with those who suffer. While she disdained public speaking, having her picture taken and signing autographs, she was Our Lady's special emissary when it came to the sick, suffering, and disadvantaged. I had seen it time and again.

Later that evening, in a little village at the northern-most edge of Lake Como, I gave my first talk to an Italian audience, struggling somewhat with the translation. And when I gave the listeners the Virgin Mary's special bless-ing at the end, no one raised their arms.

"You must understand, Italians have a different church attitude than Americans. They are very reserved when it comes to things related to faith," Dino explained late that night when we returned. "I have some news for you that is not promising," he added. "Father Stephano telephoned in answer to your fax, and stated he would do what he could to arrange space for Mass with the Pope. The Holy Father will be on retreat for the entire week. The only time possible is Monday morning, March 8."

"That's the day before I fly home from Rome. It would work out fine!" I began to get excited.

"One moment, my friend, there is more. He feels it may be too late since the Holy Father will not return until Friday evening, and, he is not sure he can obtain extra passes for us."

"It will work. I just know it!"

"Well, in any case, he asks that we call him late on the Friday evening before your departure to see if it can be arranged."

In spite of the news, my optimism was running high, refueled the next day, the 25th, as Marija received the monthly message from Gospa during her apparition. Twice now I had been present for this particular event. Each was strong confirmation of Our Lady's presence. It was pure grace to actually see Marija in a state of ecstasy receive the message, write it down, and then telephone it to Father Slavko in Medjugorje.

I asked Paolo if I could copy the message for my notes.

"Yes, but please realize that it is not the final translation until Father Slavko reviews it to make certain of its proper translation from Croatian to English."

This obedience under the guidance of a priest only added to the confirmation. But ever the journalist, I wanted the message in its raw state for comparison later with the English translation.

The message was beautiful: *"Dear children, today, I bless you with my motherly blessing and invite you all to conversion. I wish that each of you decides himself for a change of life and that each of you works more in the Church, not through words and thoughts but through example, so that your life may be a joyful testimony for Jesus. You cannot say that you are converted, because your life must become a daily conversion. In order to understand what you have to do, little children, pray and God will give you what you concretely have to do, and where you have to change. I am with you and place you all under my mantle."*

It was the right tone for the beginning of Lent. And, since she had mentioned again her special blessing, it strengthened my resolve to continue giving it at the talks.

That evening in Milan, Marija was present as I read the message she had received from Our Lady that day in the course of my talk. On the way home, she said, "My compliment for your talk. You have helped me in my conversion by your comments about the Holy Eucharist." She said it with quiet humility, highlighting the need to continue each day on the road to conversion, as Gospa had stated in the message.

"This was much better than your first two talks," Dino chimed in. "You were much more relaxed and very much filled with the Holy Spirit."

I was beginning to feel more at home with these people. "Yes, it seems a little easier, and did you see the people raise their arms to receive Mary's special blessing? Some of them were on their knees!"

The following evening was even better, if that was possible. We traveled to Romanengno, about two hours from Monza, to a packed church, and this time, Marija unexpectedly gave a personal witness I would never forget.

She had been hesitant in joining us for the trip to Romanengno, finally coming at Paolo's insistence. Their good friend Luciano, the local connection for arranging the talk, was active in Medjugorje, presently organizing large food, clothing and medicine shipments of relief for Bosnian refugees. Handicapped and confined to a wheelchair, he was an enthusiastic man with tireless energy, defying normal expectations, much less those of one handicapped. And he absolutely loved Marija.

Paolo was noticeably upset with Marija's hesitance, knowing Luciano would want to see her. I smiled to myself, enjoying the normalcy of their relationship. It was good to know their love experienced little tests like any other couple.

The evening began with a rosary in a large church filled to overflowing again. Marija had agreed to participate in leading the prayers with me. After the first two decades, I prayed the next in Croatian as a special gift for her. Her smile as I finished was a special moment.

But there was more. Following my talk, in which I spoke deeply about my love for the Holy Eucharist, Marija suddenly approached the microphone. She told how she knew of my suffering many times in her presence while attending Mass, mentioning specifically the experience at Manasco, telling them, "I felt so sorry for him that he could not receive, and I tried to hide him from others seeing his pain. It also made me think of how precious the Eucharist is to us as Catholics."

I was overwhelmed and deeply touched by this unexpected revelation, as Paolo translated her words. He hugged her in obvious conciliation as she returned to her seat.

Luciano had prepared a huge, four-course banquet at his home following the activities. "You may as well relax as we will be here for a long time," Dino said as the first course was served.

Luciano was a gracious host, bubbling over with excitement and thanking us constantly for coming to Romanengo. Late into the night we wined and dined, listening with rapt attention as Marija, now totally open and animated, spoke for nearly an hour about the early days of Medjugorje's apparitions. We arrived in Monza in the wee hours of the morning totally spent and stuffed to the gills.

Toughing it out after a few hours of sleep, Paolo and I flew to Rome at mid-morning for a special talk at a large conference. It was a charismatic gathering, not familiar with Medjugorje, and somewhat reserved in Marian devotion. The priest in charge was apprehensive about my witness, asking that I limit it to half an hour. But the Spirit took over and the talk took more than an hour.

I started to apologize to the priest, but his attitude had changed completely. I had talked about Mary being the bride of the Holy Spirit and thus being the "first charismatic." That had struck his heart in a special way. After a lengthy personal discourse, he asked us to come forward so that he could pray over the two of us before our departure for the airport and a late return to Monza.

The next three days passed swiftly, each marked by long drives, chronic late starts for the talks, and a near obligatory dinner afterwards. I felt near the point of total exhaustion but somehow, there was always just enough strength at the start of each talk. Venues were scattered over long distances as we traveled first to Trento, followed by a long snowy drive to Udine where we stayed the night. Then, we were up early for a return to Monza and an appointment with Rusconi publishers, followed by a long magazine interview. From there it was on to Genoa for two more talks.

"You can relax and rest as we have the entire day off, Paolo commented as we began the drive to Monza in the early morning hours. "Then we will go to Mount Blanco for a little skiing. It will be a good break."

I could only nod in agreement, grateful for the opportunity to revive mind and body, beginning with the drive as I slept almost the entire way, as we arrived home at 3 A.M.

"There has been a slight change in plans," Paolo began apologetically as we sat around the table after lunch. "I have an important interview this evening, so we cannot leave for Mount Blanco until after the interview."

It did not surprise me; plans were always changing on this tour. "That's okay with me. I can use the extra rest, and maybe we can do a little shopping later."

"Yes, we can do that, so we will go around 2 P.M." Somehow, when that time rolled around and we still had not left, I wasn't surprised!

As it turned out, Paolo was late in returning from his interview, and we didn't leave for the mountains and skiing until after 9 P.M. We arrived at the home of Raphaella, a mutual friend, well after midnight. And as always, we had to eat and talk for another two hours. I slept little and it showed on the slopes. However, it was more than lack of sleep. I knew the grind of not just this tour, but the cavalcade of tours over the past months was finally taking its toll.

We left earlier than planned, leaving Marija to spend a few extra days with Raphaella. It was back to work with a late talk that evening. By the time we returned to Monza, I felt like a zombie. When Paolo asked if I was all right, I brushed it off. "I'm just a little tired—nothing rest won't cure."

"Well, I am afraid there is going to be little rest for the remainder of the tour. We leave early Friday morning for L'Aquila."

It turned out to be the longest auto trip of the tour, long even driving at high speed on the autostrada. Dino was with us and was able to relieve Paolo at driving, but he was no slower. Even at such speeds, it was more than seven hours before we reached L'Aquila, as it was located in the central mountains of Italy approximately 185 kilometers southeast of Rome.

L'Aquila was beautiful, but very cold. We stayed in a monastery and I met a deeply spiritual priest, Father Angelo, who was actively involved in stopping abortion in Italy. He took us to a special cemetery where a small monument had been erected to the unborn. Father Angelo was also pushing for enforcement of a law that all human remains must be buried, which was raising havoc with the clinics and proving successful as a peaceful, dignified way in slowing and stopping the deaths of many of the unborn babies. The trip to L'Aquila was worth it just in meeting and spending time with this holy priest.

That evening, I made the call that had been on my mind the entire tour; I called Father Stephano at the Vatican, checking on the availability of space for us at the private Mass with the Pope. "I am very sorry, but I still am unable to give you a response. Please telephone me again tomorrow morning." My hopes began to fade. I called again Saturday morning; still no news, he related; please call again that evening.

The final stop of the tour was Naples, with a Friday evening talk in a small community on the outskirts of the city, followed by an early Saturday evening talk in the inner city; we would then leave Sunday evening for Rome, where Dino and Paolo would drop me at the same hotel where I had stayed with the Australian group. I was to fly home Tuesday morning and they would return to Monza.

Telephoning Father Stephano at the Vatican again Saturday, just before the talk, nothing had changed. "Well, that's it," I thought, "It isn't going to happen."

Still, I was at peace. It had been a tremendous tour and we had been able to speak to thousands about the message of Medjugorje. The response had been exceptional, causing me to develop a new respect for the Italian people. Their indefatigable energy, acceptance and resulting participation in the spreading of the Medjugorje message was something special. Maybe there would be other opportunities in the future to meet the Holy Father.

Sunday morning as we prepared to leave for Mass, Dino approached me. "Our hosts want to ask you if you would consider stopping at the home of a young man who is dying of cancer. They want you to pray over him. His parents were at your talk last night and asked you if you might consider doing this."

I readily agreed, no longer fearing such encounters. In fact, I was grateful for the opportunity.

Arriving at the home of the young man, named Genaro, I discovered he and his parents spoke fluent English. He was at peace with his disease and able to talk about it freely. Thin and jaundiced, Genaro's deep brown eyes shone as he spoke softly of his belief and trust. "Of course I want to live," he said, "but it is up to God and I accept that."

Suddenly, his mother interrupted. "But why does this have to happen to my son?" she wailed, breaking into tears. "He has always been a good boy, never in trouble and always in church each week. He is a good Christian. Why does God do this to us?"

She covered her face with her hands. "Oh, I am sorry

to be so angry with God but what can I do? I cannot seem to pray anymore!"

I went to the distraught woman. It was evident it was she, not her son, who needed prayer. Our meeting had been planned for only a few minutes, but it stretched into an hour. Words flowed effortlessly, just as they did in the talks. We talked about redemptive suffering and of how fortunate they were to have a son like Genaro.

How rewarding to have had the opportunity to meet this family and to pray over their son. Arriving at the Mass just as the priest was coming up the aisle, I prayed fervently, dedicating the Mass to Genaro and his entire family, asking specifically for his healing. I felt a warmth and knew the opportunity to use the healing gifts of the Holy Spirit was probably the greatest grace I could have received during this tour. Mass with the Holy Father no longer seemed important.

Just before lunch, Paolo, who had telephoned home to talk to Marija, rushed into the room. He paused, smiling widely and hardly able to contain himself. "Listen! I have very good news! Father Stephano telephoned our home a little while ago. It has been arranged for all three of us to attend holy Mass with the Pope on Monday morning!"

My heart was about to burst! I knew instantly this was a pure gift from Our Lady. "Bravo!" Dino roared, clapping his hands as Paolo and I embraced in celebration. I hardly remembered eating lunch!

At 6:45 A.M. Monday, we stood shivering outside the huge doors of the Vatican, leading to the living quarters of the Pope. None of us had gotten more than three hours sleep, having arrived in Rome after midnight. We were still so high with excitement, we decided to go out and celebrate with a late-night dinner, finding a quaint all-night restaurant near our hotel.

My heart raced as the Swiss guard opened the doors and ushered us inside, leading us to the small private chapel where the leader of the Church celebrated Mass each morning. The Pope was seated in a large chair in the middle of the chapel, deep in meditation. Approximately twenty-five other people were there as well, including a Gregorian choir from Austria, which was singing a low, steady chant, adding to the drama of the moment.

I sat just a few feet away, awed at being so close to John Paul II. And yet, I felt very much as though I were attending a regular morning daily Mass. I joined my prayers to his, praying also for my family, for the entire Medjugorje family—and especially for Genaro's healing.

After a long meditative silence, the Pope arose and approached the altar, surprising us by announcing that the Mass would be in English. He turned to the altar and began, and soon I was lost in the liturgy. Only when we were moving forward to receive Jesus in Holy Eucharist, did it register that I would be receiving Communion directly from the hand of Christ's Vicar on earth. "Please, Blessed Mary," I prayed silently as I stood in front of the Pope, "Let my eyes remain on Jesus!"

As we sat in meditation another thirty minutes after Mass, I realized that even though this was the Pope, he was simply another priest during these precious moments, giving us the greatest gift of all: the Body and Blood of our Lord, Jesus. To a degree, it was like every Mass; no more holy—no less holy.

We were then led into a large reception area to meet with Pope John Paul for a few minutes. I had brought two copies of *Medjugorje: The Message*, one in Polish and the other in Italian, to present to him. Suddenly, he was standing in front of me. "Here, Holy Father, I would like to present my book to you. . . ." There was so much more I wanted to say, but the words wouldn't come.

"Ah, Medjugorje!" he said slowly, smiling. "Have you been there recently?"

I relaxed immediately, feeling completely at ease. "Yes, Holy Father, I have."

"But have you been there during the war?"

"Yes, Holy Father. I was there in January, just two months ago."

He smiled again. "Good. That is good!" And he moved on to Paolo, who was next in line.

It was over so fast. So very fast. As we crossed St. Peter's Square after leaving the living quarters, I felt a momentary letdown. But just as quickly, the realization of the grace we had been given to be with the Pope, filled me with gratitude. Now, we were once again part of the throng of people walking through the square.

The memory of the nearly two hours shared with this Pope, handpicked by Our Lady for these times, would last forever. It was a crowning moment of the entire mission.

29
Return to Russia

"Dear children, I thank you for your prayers and for the love you show toward me. I invite you to decide to pray for my intentions . . . I am your mother, little children, and I do not want Satan to deceive you, for he wants to lead you the wrong way. But, he cannot if you do not permit him. . . ."

Returning home, there remained a heavy schedule of international trips to Puerto Rico, Honduras, and Mexico. Spaced between these were short tours in the States, and by the middle of May, my spiritual, physical and mental faculties were at maximum burnout. Summer of '93 would have to be a time of recuperation.

The burnout was so complete, I seriously contemplated ending the mission, including cancellation of an upcoming return to Russia in August. The last thing I wanted was to continue activities beyond the time Our Lady desired. If that meant giving up returning to the former Soviet Union, then so be it.

The turn of the war in Bosnia added to my depression. Muslims and Croats were fighting as fiercely against each other as they had as allies; and, they were still fighting the Serbs. War, destruction, and death spread in towns and villages all around Medjugorje. The only bright spot in an otherwise gloomy scenario was that the village was still untouched. Although usually without water, electricity and other daily amenities, it remained a holy place of refuge, recently discovered by the native faithful from throughout Bosnia and Croatia. Incredibly, pilgrims from many other countries also continued to come.

"I'd say you're overreacting and more in need of rest than you think," Terri said as we strolled along the beach, discussing the possibility that perhaps Our Lady was ready for me to conclude the speaking mission. "How many times have I cautioned that you cannot continue at this pace? It's simply caught up with you."

I stared into the ocean. "You're probably right, but I don't ever want to do this for personal reasons. If Our Lady wants me to stop now and stay home for the rest of my life, I'm more than willing to do that."

"That's the right attitude and I agree. But as much as we'd like to have you home, I don't think your mission is completed. Think of all the work Zofia Sordyl has done for your return to Russia; you can't just cancel out on that. And there are other places you still need to take the message."

Terri continued, pointing out needs and offering suggestions for better coordination of events. Again, she was right; especially about Russia. Zofia had been in St. Petersburg for more than two months arranging the second tour of the former Soviet Union. She had arranged venues in St. Petersburg, Moscow, Kiev, Rostov, and Odessa, as well as several smaller areas. My books had been translated and published primarily for the tour, along with a plethora of related materials.

I sighed deeply. "Yes, I'll have to make that trip, at least. But I need to really pray before making a decision to continue beyond that."

Confirmation was not long in coming. Clearly, I was

to carry on the mission. However, there was also the discernment that pride played too large a part in trying to do too much, even though it was for God. Humility in realizing limitations, along with common sense, was more valuable to the mission than extra stops along the way.

I smiled in recalling a story about Marija, sure that its recollection at this critical time was not coincidence. Our Lady had asked Marija to fast twice a week for a special intention; Marija, in her desire to please Gospa, fasted three times a week instead of the asked-for two times. By the end of the third week, she was ill. Our Lady gently reprimanded her, reminding her to do in obedience only what she was asked to do.

By the end of June, I was buoyed by the swiftness of physical recovery. Plus, the news from Medjugorje was encouraging. Fighting between the Croats and Muslims had all but stopped, with ongoing negotiations toward a permanent cease-fire; in fact, the entire war was burning down to embers with most of the actual fighting confined to areas along the Bosnian-Serb border.

Pilgrims came by the droves for the 12th anniversary, with estimates ranging from twenty to thirty thousand present on the 25th. Jakov, the little 10-year-old visionary of 1981, was now married and settled in the village with his Italian bride. Both Ivanka and Mirjana were expecting babies, and Marija had announced a wedding date of September 8, the official feast of Our Lady's birth.

Thus, we arranged for Terri to fly to Milan a few days before the wedding, where I would join her on completion of the Russian tour.

By the end of August, things were back to normal. I was anxious to resume Our Lady's mission with great expectations—hardly prepared for what was to come. . . .

"At last, they let you in! What was the problem?" Zofia greeted me at the doorway of the small arrival terminal at St. Petersburg Airport, wondering why I had been delayed by the Russian customs officials.

"Just the usual annoyances! Since the airline changed the schedule for my flight and I'm arriving a day earlier than originally planned, the visa, which had already been processed is not official until tomorrow, which is in three hours," I said, looking at my watch. "The customs official wanted me to wait until midnight, but after a lengthy discussion they reluctantly decided to let me in."

"And everything has gone wrong here in these last days." Zofia shook her head. "There is a fuel shortage for airplanes and your schedule is centered around the dates I could get airline tickets. And I have had little help. . . ."

"Wait a minute," I laughed, "I've heard this story before!" I refused to be discouraged, sure that this tour would be a triumphant continuation of the last one.

Despite steady rain, the following day brought nothing to discourage my optimism. A young television journalist from Odessa, where we would end the tour, had traveled to St. Petersburg to film the entire tour for a documentary to be shown in the future. We did some filming for him, plus a short radio interview. Overall, it was a quiet, restful day.

There was another good sign; the first talk was on the 25th, just as it was last time in St. Petersburg. I carried an air of expectant confidence—until we arrived at the auditorium.

There were less than 700 present, a far cry from the 4,000 in attendance last year. While the majority of those present were enthusiastic, there was heckling and some of the questions after the talk were less than friendly.

Zofia was disappointed. "I am sorry, but I told you, there have been many problems. Cults of all faiths have come into all of these countries, causing great confusion among the people. There is even one lady from Ukraine, who claims to be the reincarnation of both Jesus and the Blessed Mother, and she has many followers. Some people think our tour is part of her cult. It is terrible!"

I had seen the posters of this woman. They were everywhere, placed high on buildings and light poles, making it difficult to remove them. Additionally, there was a priest of questionable credentials, who inexplicably did everything possible to discourage his parishioners from attending my talk. "I still do not believe he is an authentic priest," Zofia said. "It is known that he worked with the KGB."

"Well, I'm sure the talk in Moscow will be better." That was our next stop, the one I looked forward to the most, not having been able to speak there on the last tour.

But it wasn't. We arrived at the airport in Moscow to the usual mass confusion that seems part of the flying experience in Russia. It was worse now due to the acute fuel shortage. A man approached us. "This is Vladislav," Zofia said, introducing us. "He will be our driver and assistant while we are here."

Vladislav spoke in halting English, but was well educated. He was a devout Christian who had become interested in Medjugorje, and was part of a Moscow prayer group. His wife taught English and thus, he had also learned, adding, "But since I do not have opportunities to use it, I am not very good."

As we journeyed to the hotel in his small car, I asked him about the present attitude of the people, pointing out the differences from last year. "Yes, at that time, we were experiencing freedom for the first time. Everyone thought life would become better right away but it did not happen. There have been food shortages and much unemployment, and now this shortage of gasoline, which makes it difficult to find fuel for our automobiles."

He worked as an engineer after completing his studies at the university, but only earned the equivalent of thirty dollars a month. "And I have a wife and new baby, so it is very hard."

When asked about the political, social and spiritual life, he was pessimistic. The government was in total confusion with infighting between the president and the parliament. No one seemed to be in charge—except a new Russian Mafia, a criminal element that had swiftly taken control. Everything sold was controlled by them; even the small stands and kiosks that had sprung up everywhere. There was also corruption at all levels of government, he added.

As though to prove the point, we were suddenly stopped on the highway by a policeman, who fined Vladislav three thousand rubles (about three dollars) for having a dent in the rear fender of his car. "Now this policeman will put the money in his pocket," Vladislav wryly pointed out. "That is the way the system works with everything these days."

My hotel was a huge structure that had been used by Olympic athletes at one time. As we pulled to the front, Zofia gave Vladislav the amount of the fine, insisting he take it as he was transporting us at the time. "Yes, please accept it," I urged him. "Also, I would very much like to see Red Square on the way to the talk if you can take us."

"But you only have time to check in and have dinner before the conference," Vladislav said.

"That is all right," Zofia interjected. "We will have to come back through Moscow in four days. I would like to hire you to pick us up and take us to the other airport, and since we have four hours before our flight to Rostov, perhaps then we could visit Red Square and some of the other historic spots of Moscow."

"Yes, of course I will be happy to drive you again."
Vladislav then smiled broadly. "And if you would permit
me, I would like to take you to my apartment to meet my
wife and have coffee with us!"

It was agreed. I checked in, grabbed a quick meal and
we were off to the talk, which had a turnout of only 300
people. I was getting discouraged. Back in the lobby of
the hotel, I went over a large map of Russia with Zofia,
trying to pinpoint exactly where we were going. "After three
days in the Ukraine, we go there, to Rostov," she said, pointing to a distant city on the coast of the Black Sea. "And
then on to Minsk, in Belarus, and finally to Odessa."

"But why go way over there?" I asked, pointing to
Rostov. For some reason, I had an uneasy feeling about
going there.

"Oh, but they are wonderful people and they need
you there. The priest is so excited that you are coming!"

I could only utter a weak "okay." But the ominous feeling remained.

As we left the next morning for Kiev, Ukraine, I was
filled with doubts as to why I had even come. I wanted to
be a continuing part in the conversion of Russia, but this
was a far cry from what I had expected after the first trip.
Possibly it was the wrong time of year; and the political
unrest didn't help. Adding to the confusion of the people,
every religious cult possible was invading the country, creating a religious war for converts. The Parliament had even
passed a law that would forbid foreign religions from coming into Russia without a specific invitation. It would include Catholics, even though the Church had been here
for hundreds of years.

Something was definitely wrong. It wasn't just small
crowds and inconveniences of travel. Inside, I felt an un-
easiness that I had experienced only a few times in the
hundreds of tours in the past six years; it was a feeling of

evil. I felt Satan's presence trying to destroy the work of conversion.

"Yes, but you cannot get discouraged," Zofia stated as we discussed the first days of disappointments. "We are here for Our Lady and she will take care of us!" I smiled and patted her hand, saying nothing. Zofia had that solid, blind faith that many have found through Medjugorje. She had worked hard only to watch plans crumble beyond her control. "These people need our help," she continued. "You have seen their churches and the need for repairs."

I truly hoped Kiev's talks would be better—for her sake. It was Sunday and we attended Mass in a once-beautiful church that was under almost total reconstruction. In fact, it was the Cathedral of Kiev. Mass was held amid scaffolding and work tools. Everything was covered with dust. In spite of the surroundings, it was a beautiful service.

This church and others I had seen created a graphic picture of the faith in Russia . The rebuilding appeared to be an almost impossible task. St. Petersburg only had three Catholic churches for more than a million Catholics. There were only a few more in Kiev, a onetime Catholic stronghold. I had to wonder how Russia could ever be converted without churches? But then, our God was the God of the impossible.

The talk in Kiev was the lowest point yet. Two churches had feuded over which location would host the talk. The result was a boycott by the loser, and less than a hundred people in attendance. Thoroughly demoralized, I returned to the hotel in a steady drizzle of rain that continued throughout the night and into the next day. My mood worsened when attempts to reach Terri by telephone failed for the fifth day in a row.

We were scheduled to go to Zeitomir next, about two hour's drive from Kiev. It had been the highlight of the tour last year and I looked forward to returning. I sat in the lobby of the hotel dressed and waiting for Zofia and the driver. The minute she walked in the door, I knew something was wrong.

"I am so sorry! The materials advertising your talk never arrived in Zeitomir and there has been no publicity . . . we had to cancel the talk."

I was crushed. Surely, this was the nadir of the entire tour. "How?" I asked, totally frustrated. "How could the materials not reach the city? I mean after last year—" I stopped in mid-sentence and began pacing. Turning to Zofia, I took her by the hand and led her to the small couch in a corner of the lobby. "Listen, I know you've worked hard, but this is not accomplishing much. Maybe we should just cancel the remainder of the tour."

"Oh, no, please!" She gripped my hand. "Please, we must complete this. The people in Zinnetsa and Rostov, and Odessa—they are so excited! It will be fine, I know it. If just one soul is touched. . . ."

The magic words again. "Okay, okay. It's just that Rostov is so far and with this fuel shortage and all; but we'll tough it out to the bitter end."

That evening, after having stayed in my bleak hotel room all day with little to do because of the rain, I finally reached Terri. Being able to tell her of all of the woes of the tour served as good medicine. And the next day, things seemed to get back on track as we journeyed to Zinnetsa.

Here Franciscans were in charge and it was an entirely different setting. A joyous, enthusiastic assemblage of villagers sang beautiful hymns with great gusto, reminding me of Medjugorje itself. I spoke for two hours and took another to answer questions. The priests insisted we stay for dinner, which we gladly accepted, realizing we had eaten little during the day of travel. We arrived at the hotel after midnight, but it didn't matter to me, or to Zofia. The day had been a success!

As if to signal things were better, we were unexpectedly placed in business class on a new Russian airline, called Transeara, as we left for the four-hour layover and change of airports in Moscow, before flying to Rostov. "This is not what I purchased," Zofia whispered as we settled into roomy seats at the front of the plane.

"I'm not complaining," I grinned.

Zofia was beaming. "See how Our Lady is taking care of us. This is a good sign for the rest of the tour!" Little did we know it would be the only point of light in a day that would turn into almost total darkness.

We enjoyed a nice breakfast and a relaxing flight to Moscow, happy to see Vladislav awaiting us as we entered the Moscow terminal. "There is just one little problem," he stated, loading our bags into the small trunk of his car. "I was not able to buy gasoline this morning, so we will have to wait in the line. It should not take long."

But it did; we waited in line for almost two hours before Vladislav was able to purchase a spare tank from someone in the front of the line. It was enough to take care of the day's driving as we headed for the city, but our time before the connecting flight at the other airport was now less than two and a half hours. "Maybe we better skip the sight-seeing and visit and go directly to the airport," I suggested to Vladislav.

"Please, we go to my home for only ten minutes. My wife has prepared some fresh pastries for you." Reluctantly, we agreed; it was a mistake. We suddenly found ourselves in a horrible traffic jam in the middle of Moscow, something rare according to Vladislav. As time ticked away, I urged him to go directly to the airport. "Please," he pleaded. "Just five minutes. We are close!"

On arrival at his apartment building, there was less than a hour before our flight. "Vladislav, tell your wife to come with us. We don't have time for coffee—hurry!"

We waited an excruciating ten minutes, with no sign of our driver. Zofia began to panic. "We must go now! Why isn't he here?" Finally he came, without his wife, as the baby was sleeping and she could not leave. "Hurry! Hurry!" Zofia was fairly yelling at him.

Reentering the traffic clog, it became worse. Zofia kept yelling at Vladislav, telling him not to let anyone in front of him and to drive fast. It was an impossibility. I gently eased Zofia back into the seat. "Zofia, please, sit back and calm down. There's nothing he can do now. I think it's too late and we're going to miss the flight." Strangely, I felt a great calm that this was confirmation we were not supposed to go to Rostov at all.

"But we must make it! These people are counting on you." She then added bitterly, "You didn't want to go there and now see what has happened!" I had never seen her so upset. "Oh, no," she moaned, "Satan is having a good laugh at us. He is responsible for this horrible traffic!"

I placed my hand firmly on her arm. "Zofia, listen! Maybe this isn't Satan. Maybe it's Our Lady. I told you I haven't felt comfortable going to Rostov from the beginning. It's not a matter of not wanting to go, but because of these inner feelings."

Resigned that we were in all probability going to miss our flight, Zofia sunk into the seat. "I'm sorry, it's just that these people need you."

"I know, but possibly this isn't the right time. Besides, you know how Aeroflot Airlines is. They might be late with the flight. If so, that's a sign we're meant to go."

The minute we arrived at the terminal, Zofia jumped out and ran for the building, calling out to us, "I will check quickly to see if we can make the flight."

"We'll meet you at the entrance of the terminal," I yelled back, hoping she heard me. We unloaded the baggage and entered into pure chaos as people were everywhere; there was hardly room to stand next to our baggage, and the noise was deafening. We waited an hour and a half, with no sign of Zofia. After Vladislav had made several excursions through the melee of people looking for her, I suddenly sighted her near one of the ticket counters. "Zofia! Over here!"

The look on her face and the tears that began running down her face as she came running over, said it all. "I thought you would follow me to the counter," she said. "When you were nowhere to be found, I thought you had been kidnapped!"

I put my arms around her and hugged her. "It's okay. Everything's fine now. We'll just go on to Minsk. At least we'll be there early and there will be time to rest."

Vladislav interjected quickly, "But you can catch the next flight to Rostov and—"

"No, Vladislav, take us back to the other airport so we can go to Minsk." There was no way we were going on to Rostov now. Zofia worried we would not be able to change our tickets. I assured her that even if we didn't fly to Minsk tonight, we could stay in the airport and make arrangements the next day.

It was a shock when we arrived at a different terminal building from where we had arrived that morning. This terminal was new, clean and sparse in the number of passengers, a far cry from the chaotic crowds of the other airport. "This is a special place where visiting dignitaries and business leaders arrive," Vladislav told us.

The stress of the day was finally over and a calm, like that which follows huge storms, set in. We were able to get tickets for a 10:30 P.M. flight to Minsk. Vladislav departed for his home only after being assured we would call if anything went wrong.

I spotted a small coffee shop at the far end of the terminal, with several tables in the front. "Zofia, let's go and have a nice cup of coffee and see if we can find something to eat."

Through the rush of the day, we had not eaten since the small meal on our early morning flight. Zofia, always prepared, had some Polish sausages and a few stale pretzels. "And," she added, "I have this little bottle of wine they gave me in business class this morning."

It was the finest meal of the entire tour! I couldn't believe how good stale pretzels and cold sausage could taste when the stomach was empty!

True to the form of the day, we almost missed our flight to Minsk, as Zofia was on the telephone trying to get in touch with our contacts to inform them we were arriving. Late into the night, we landed at a beautiful— and empty—airport, where Zofia was finally able reach our contacts. They came an hour later, immediately telling Zofia they had been trying to contact us for several days to tell us not to go to Rostov, because there were no flights back out from there!

The bottom line was we would have been stranded in Rostov for an unknown number of days. Once again, we had been rescued by Our Lady.

I slept until noon, having informed Zofia to please leave me in peace until the next day. After a wonderful meal, I strolled the streets of Minsk, unable to find a Catholic church for Mass, but relieved and happy to have quiet time. On returning to the hotel late in the afternoon, I passed an unusual sight, a crowd of mostly senior citizens kneeling on the sidewalk in front of a large building, praying the rosary. Close by was a small kiosk with many religious articles in the windows, including copies of my articles in Russian!

Later when Zofia telephoned my room, I agreed to have lunch with one of the priests the next day. "He wishes to show you his church which is still not open for holy

Mass yet. We will pick you up at noon."

Once again, as I had witnessed everywhere we had been on the tour, the church building was in shambles and undergoing extensive refurbishment. Weaving our way through construction and scaffolding, we entered a long room which served as kitchen, conference room, and sanctuary for Mass. "It is the only part of the church we can use right now," the priest explained through the interpreter.

Inquiring about the people I had seen praying on the sidewalk the day before, the priest told me that they were part of his parish, and they were praying in front of a building that used to be the cathedral. "Now, it is a sport palace for youth," he explained. "Every morning and evening, we conduct Mass on the sidewalk, and the young people come out and insult and push the worshipers around, but they continue to come. They have vowed to worship and pray the rosary there daily until the government returns the building to the Church."

"You actually conduct Mass there twice a day?"

"Yes, and I invite you to join us this evening just before your talk at the auditorium," he added.

That floored me as we sat down to a light meal of hard bread and borsch soup. Here, in a city of three million people with a third of them Catholic, there were literally no Catholic churches; the only Masses were on the sidewalk in front of the old cathedral building and here in this tiny room! It was all so—hopeless. I wondered again what I was doing here.

Suddenly, as I stared into my cup of coffee, I felt Our Lady's presence and her message filled my heart: *"My dear son, you are here not just to spread my message given at Medjugorje, but to see the condition of the Church in Russia; to see and feel and experience how these children of mine live everyday of their lives. I am asking you to help them to build their churches so they can find my Son . . ."*

It all became immediately clear. "Zofia, please tell the translator I have something important to tell the priest," I said excitedly. And with that, I related what had just been given to me by Our Lady, adding, "Father, when I return to the United States, I am going to raise funds to help your church, and also the churches in Moscow, Kiev, and Zinnetsa. I promise, you will soon have help for your churches!"

There was a loud, happy cheer from the twenty or so people in the room as the message was repeated for them. Zofia was beside herself. "The instant you began telling this, I felt confirmation in my heart that this is why you were sent here!"

The priest suddenly asked, "And will you return again to speak in our new churches?"

I hadn't counted on that. I didn't want to ever see this country again after these past days; but I heard myself answering that I would indeed return in the future.

Even though there was peace in now knowing the reason for the tour, the struggles were not over. Satan had not finished sifting us.

We returned to Kiev airport where we met the driver who would take us to Odessa, the last stop on the tour. It was a gruelling nine-hour automobile ride over extremely rough and dangerous roads. But we prayed the rosary with fervor nearly the entire way, arriving just before the talk. Again the crowd was limited and restless as the translator, who spoke nearly perfect English, simply could not translate.

"Well, at least you will be able to fly back to Kiev in the morning for your flight to Poland," our contact told me. "And we have a room for you at the best hotel in Odessa."

I was ushered into an old, dilapidated "famous" hotel, and shown to my room. The bed was swayed in the middle and as the door closed, a cockroach scurried across the warped floor boards. A small television sat on a rickety table in a corner, but it did not work. Laughing, I said out loud, "Okay, Blessed Mary, you want me to continue doing penance!" With that I got undressed, grabbed my rosary and sank into the narrow bed and fell asleep, praying the Glorious mysteries!

And of course, the flight was cancelled on arrival at the airport the next morning; thus, another tortuous drive back to Kiev. Along the way, we had three flat tires, nearly wrecking on the first, as the driver was traveling at over seventy-five miles per hour. Hitting the outskirts of Kiev with the last of the spare tires shredding, we hailed a passing taxi. It was in worse mechanical shape than the car we had just left, and got us to the airport barely in time for our flight to Warsaw, Poland.

It was difficult saying good-bye to Zofia at the airport the following morning as I left for Milan, Italy. She would remain in Warsaw for a few days before returning to St. Petersburg. "There is still a lot of material to be distributed," she said. "And when I return to my home in Michigan, we will arrange for your return trip here."

I grimaced, giving her a skeptical look.

"Remember, you promised a priest you would return!"

I laughed and waved as I passed through customs. "Yes, Zofia, I'll come back—but not right away!"

As the airplane lifted off for Milan, I opened my small Bible at random, feeling an urge to do so. My eyes fell on Romans 8:31: "In view of all of this, what can we say? If God is for us, who can be against us?"

Looking back at the obstacles and hardships of this second Russian tour, it seemed as if I had passed through the eye of a needle. But after reading this little passage of

Scripture, I realized everything that had happened had a reason. I was simply having to live a part of the Medjugorje message, just as these people did every day of their lives.

"Thank you, Blessed Mother," I murmured, aware now this was just another of the "small hovels" along the way of the mission. Strangely, I did look forward to returning again, knowing that indeed, God would be with me through the presence of His mother.

30
A New Awakening

"I invite you all to awaken your hearts to love. Go into nature and look how nature is awakening and it will be a help for you to open your hearts to the love of God, the Creator. I desire you to awaken love in your families so that where there is unrest and hatred, love will reign. . . . Do not forget that I am with you and I am helping you with my prayer that God may give you the strength to love."

"I'm so happy to be here!" I said it several times as Terri and I dined with Marija, Paolo, and his parents in their apartment in Monza.

"They must not have fed you in Russia, the way you're eating," Terri said with an amused smile as I took a second helping of pasta. There was some truth in that; during the rush of each day, the luxury of full meals was rare. And there had been little to drink. I felt dehydrated.

"Let him eat," Paolo laughed. "He is in Italy now! We want him well for the wedding!"

The day of the wedding arrived, welcomed by a light drizzle of rain. Approximately 100 people coming from all corners of the world were in attendance. Father Slavko Barbaric had journeyed from Medjugorje to concelebrate and represent the parish of Medjugorje. His trip became an ordeal when their vehicle broke an axle near the Italian border in the early morning hours of the wedding day. He caught a ride to the outskirts of town, took a bus into the center of the city and finally a taxi to the church, arriving 20 minutes before the ceremony. Unruffled as always, he beamed with happiness as the fourth Medjugorje visionary solemnly exchanged vows in the sacrament of marriage.

At the conclusion of the Mass, Marija suddenly went to her knees and began to pray, with Paolo quickly kneeling beside her: Our Lady was coming in apparition! She appeared to Marija for more than two minutes, blessing all in attendance, and giving a personal message to the newlyweds.

It was breathtaking, a perfect ending to an already beautiful and holy event.

Although the war was reduced to isolated skirmishes, the tragedy of innocents becoming victims continued, including the first American death. A young woman from Michigan, Colette Webster, who had traveled on five separate truck convoys of relief aid from England to Bosnia, was shot and killed by sniper fire in Mostar.

Colette had worked with the British Medjugorje Appeal, a relief program founded and operated by Bernard Ellis, an English Jew converted to Catholicism through Medjugorje. The Appeal had done a tremendous job, taking aid to all victims of the war, regardless of ethnicity. Colette, touched especially by the plight of refugee children, later began to work independently at Mostar General Hospital and clinic. It was while working with the children in late September, that she was hit by sniper fire and died.

In an earlier video made by ABC-TV during one of the convoy journeys, Colette was asked by the interviewer why she was there, and what she could do to help these children. She replied simply, "You just have to love them; it doesn't matter whether you speak their language or not, just love them and they will know that you really care."

This courageous woman, only 27, was not the only Medjugorje pilgrim to die in this satanic war. There were others from Italy, France, England, and Germany. Without their bravery, along with millions of dollars in contributions and direct help from former pilgrims to Medjugorje, the people of Croatia and Bosnia would have suffered even greater hardship. And those who died in this service were truly modern-day martyrs, whose mission was to give the ultimate gift of love, in response to Our Lady's plea.

Exhorting audiences to pray and fast for peace "like never before" as Gospa was asking more urgently with each monthly message through Marija, I also began the task of raising funds for the Russian churches. Donations poured in. By February 1994, we had raised over $50,000. The initial plan was to give five churches $10,000 each for construction and refurbishment. The funds would be worth at least ten times that amount with current exchange rates, and with the parishioners of the churches doing the actual work. Thousands of individuals were responding to the call to help others find the path of conversion.

Zofia, having returned to her home in Detroit, began making arrangements for a May return to Russia. We would personally deliver the donations to the parishes in need because there was no safe way to handle the transactions through the banks; too many were controlled or infiltrated by the Russian Mafia. Thus, it would be necessary to hand carry the donations in hard currency, which could also be dangerous if discovered. "I will be happy to take some of the donations when I go to Minsk in March," Zofia related in a telephone conversation. "You can bring the rest when you come in May."

"I guess that means I'm going to return sooner than I anticipated," I said with a wry smile as we decided on the actual date and time I would be there.

First, though, there would be another pilgrimage to Medjugorje.

It had been more than a year since my last trip; while I had no plans to return at this time, Our Lady did. Once again, I experienced the indescribable feeling of Our Lady unexpectedly speaking to my heart: "I am asking you to bring a pilgrimage to Medjugorje. If you do, others will follow."

Traveling to Medjugorje with a group of pilgrims was not my favorite way to go. I preferred to go alone. However, I had learned in these years of mission to simply say . . . yes. My going with a large group was a way of priming the pump, to induce others to come by letting them see it was safe. She needed them to come and pray as they had in the years before the war. She needed our help. Plans began immediately for a pilgrimage in April, 1994.

The few pilgrimages that had been making the journey in the last two years averaged around fifteen to twenty people, or less, except for the anniversary in June. Thinking we might take as many as fifty to seventy-five people, I promoted the trip in my talks and through our Medjugorje newsletter. By early March, 152 people had registered, the maximum number of seats available from Croatian airlines. A special charter flight was necessary with the overflow following on a regularly scheduled flight. Another two hundred people would have joined us if seats had been obtainable.

I was awed at the response, but not surprised. Again, feeling Our Lady's urging, I asked my son Steve to join the group. "But just as when I offered to put you in school," I told him, "you're going to have to do the preparations, such as obtaining your passport and arranging time off from work."

"It's good he's going," Terri stated when I informed her I had invited Steve, "as long as you're aware that he basically sees this as a chance for a free vacation."

I nodded. "That's probably true, but regardless of his reason, I know I'm supposed to take him; the rest is up to Our Lady!"

I fully believed that. Steve was the last of my older children to respond to my constant efforts to bring them to acceptance of Medjugorje's grace. My daughters were doing fine; Lisa now as a Catholic, and Angela as a Baptist, both actively involved in their faiths. Even Michael, now the proud father of a baby boy, was attending Mass on occasion and attempting to live more in tune with the ways of God. While he still had not followed up on his promise to take instructions in Catholicism, he sought out a priest and personally drove him to the hospital to have their new baby blessed.

As though to give full confirmation that she was calling us in a special way, the message given to Marija on the 25th of February seemed particularly pointed for those going on this pilgrimage: *"My dear children, today, I thank you for your prayers. You all have helped me so that this war may finish as soon as possible. I am close to you and I pray for each one of you and I beg you: pray! pray! pray! Only through prayer we can defeat evil and protect all that which Satan wants to destroy in your life. I am your mother and I love you all the same, and I intercede for you before God. Thank you for responding to my call!"*

We arrived at the village in the late evening, and although fatigued from the long journey, the majority were at the church for the evening Croatian Mass, mixed with the large crowd of Croatians and Bosnians. It had been a relatively calm journey, with no problems outside of one piece of baggage lost. Surprisingly, many of the pilgrims were first-timers to Medjugorje. They had come despite warnings from concerned family and friends, many not knowing exactly why they had come.

The next morning for the English Mass, Saint James Church was nearly full, and Communion hosts had to be broken into pieces to accommodate the unexpected crowd. "This is wonderful," one of the priests commented. "Except for the anniversary, there have not been this many English-speaking pilgrims here in nearly two years!"

Later, I gave a talk in the outside altar rotunda, very much aware my son was in the audience listening. I was deliberately staying away from him, wanting this experience to be fully his without interference or influence from me. He was as quiet as I had seen him in some time. He climbed Podbrdo and Krizevic with the other pilgrims, and felt particularly drawn to climb Krizevic several times more.

I settled on a bench on the lawn of the church the following evening, praying the rosary in preparation of Gospa's apparition. There were women huddled in deep conversation next to me; as soon as the apparition ended, one of the women turned to me. "Excuse me, could we speak to you a moment?"

"Of course, how can I help?"

"We met you at the airport; I'm Jan, and this is Susan. You just have to hear her story. I know you constantly hear conversion stories but this one is . . ."

"It's all right," I smiled, touching her arm. "I don't mind."

"I don't know why I am here or even how I got here," she began. I smiled, shaking my head. How many times had I heard this statement since our departure; I asked her to continue.

Susan (not her real name) told me her life had been "a

real mess" just a year ago, when something happened that frightened her into taking a long, hard look at herself. "I was heavily into drugs—mostly cocaine. It got so bad, I lost everything, my family, my job. Eventually . . . I turned to prostitution to finance my habit." She paused, taking a deep breath.

"Almost exactly a year ago, I was picked up by a man one evening, a huge man, who went wild after sniffing too much cocaine. He became enraged and began taking it out on me. We were in his car when he just flipped out and started shouting and cursing me. Suddenly, he pulled out a gun, and shoving me to the floorboard of the car, he put the gun to my head and said he was going to kill me."

Susan spoke in a low monotone. I wondered how she could have possibly reached such a point in her life. She was in her middle thirties, slender, attractive—and intelligent. The look in her eyes was the only indication of what she had gone through. They were large, hauntingly sad brown eyes, now filled with pain as she related her story.

"I stayed on the floorboard of that car for six hours," she continued. "And he kept on cursing me and telling me he was going to kill me. It was as if I saw my whole life in that horrible time, and finally, I didn't care anymore. I pushed the gun away, got out of the car and began walking away, telling him if he was going to kill me, he better do it now. I was shaking, knowing I was going to die any second. But instead, he just closed the car door and drove away. I don't know how long I stood there, but something deep inside of me told me to go and see a priest."

In the following months, Susan learned about Medjugorje and as she put it, "felt I had to go, somehow. I was raised Catholic and knew of the Virgin Mary, but it all got lost in my teenage years. I learned of this trip through a friend, and felt I had to come. Now, here I am, wondering how I deserve to be here after all I've done."

Jan was right; it was one of the most incredible experiences I had heard since becoming involved with Medjugorje. And I knew Susan's new friend Jan was there to assist her in understanding why she was in Medjugorje. We talked a long time. Susan related an incident that had occurred yesterday evening after the Croatian Mass, "which let me know the struggle wasn't over."

Standing on the front steps of Saint James Church after Mass, waiting for Jan, two Croatian men approached her and very directly asked her to sleep with them saying, "We have never had an American woman."

Susan gave a little laugh. "I couldn't believe this was happening here in this place. I guess that told me Satan wasn't going to give up easily. Anyway, I asked them if they realized where they were standing while making such a proposal. They just smiled and then left."

I walked slowly along the pathway, thinking about the story I had heard this evening. Many others on the pilgrimage had made similar remarks wondering why they were here, each with a personal story of struggle before feeling the urge to come. The obvious conclusion was Medjugorje continued to be a place of miraculous conversions. I hoped my son would also give in to this unique grace.

Two days later as the pilgrimage journeyed to Siroki Brijeg to listen to Father Jozo, I saw the beginning signs in Steve. He was hollow-eyed, gaunt, unshaven—and very quiet. We sat together on the bus, the first real time spent together outside of Mass. After awhile, he looked over, shaking his head. "This place . . ."

I smiled and slipped an arm around his neck. "Yeah, it's really special, isn't it."

His eyes moistened. "You know, Terri was right. I came here mainly because I wanted to see this part of Europe, but—I really didn't expect it to hit me like this. I mean, these people on the tour are great and they've really been good to me. I didn't think I could ever have anything in common with people that, that. . . ."

"That were Christians?"

"Yeah," Steve grinned, a little embarrassed.

We talked the entire way to Siroki Brijeg; I fought my emotions, not wanting to get hopes too high. But I knew: Medjugorje was beginning to conquer my son.

Later, when Father Jozo went through the crowd praying over people, Steve went down. So did Susan. Several minutes later, as Jan helped her to her feet, she was overcome and ran out of the church. I followed after her, leaving Steve with some members of our group. Seeing me, Susan's tears increased. "It's all wonderful, but it's just too much. I don't think I can take all of this at one time. I need to go home and sort things out . . ."

I put my arms around her, holding her for a few moments. "Susan, you are home. You belong to Jesus now!"

Two days later, I prepared to leave Medjugorje a day earlier than the rest of the group. I was going to Monza, for a short visit with Marija and Paulo, and his family. Unfortunately, Paolo was away on business. It was the 25th day of April—message day. Once again, I would be fortunate to be with Marija as she received Our Lady's message given to all her children.

Again, the message was special: *"Dear children, today, I invite all of you to decide to pray for my intention. Little children, I invite all of you to help me realize my plan through this parish. Now, in a special way, little children, I invite you to decide to go the way of holiness. Only then will you be close to me. I love you and want to lead you all with me to paradise. But, if you do not pray and if you are not humble and obedient to the messages I am giving you, I cannot help you. . . ."*

I lay in bed that night thinking about the pilgrimage,

my recent trips to Russia, and this latest message. It was everything she had said to us so many times in the nearly thirteen years of daily appearances to the visionaries. Yet, she continued to come, always exhorting us in a gentle, motherly way to turn to her Son.

I knew our pilgrimage would be the beginning of a new awakening to the grace of Medjugorje. People would come again in large numbers. They would come, wondering what they were doing there, and by end of their pilgrimage, they would know the answer.

My mission was just one tiny part of Our Lady's plan. But it was a beautiful part. Through no merit of my own, I had been given the grace of hearing Gospa, the mother of Jesus, speak to my heart. And in response by the gift of free will, to then touch hearts and bring healing to body and soul to millions throughout the world.

Over the years since the prophecy message given at Trinidad, I had indeed taken the message into hundreds of grand castles and small hovels. The fruits had been consistently good. And my family was definitely now an active part of the entire mission.

Just as she had predicted of the mission, the little mustard seed had surely grown into a beautiful oak tree. As I fell asleep, I prayed it would never end.

Epilogue

So much good fruit had come from the mission. With only speaking engagements and our monthly newsletter, which reached at maximum a little more than ten thousand readers, we managed to raise in excess of $125,000 for Jaime Jaramillo's children of the sewers.

And now, to be able to give $85,000 to refurbish Catholic churches throughout the former Soviet Union—it was overwhelming. The third trip to Russia took place in May, when I carried the balance of the donations. Zofia had preceded me again to arrange the schedule. We were able to take the donations directly to the priests and bishops of no less than thirteen individual churches, far above the original estimate of helping only five churches. Additionally, we were able to fund a strong prayer group which established a Medjugorje center in Minsk. From that center, Zofia would continue her mission of distributing materials, now having a base and group to assist in these projects. Medjugorje's message would continue to renew the Gospel of Jesus to these special children of Mary.

Highlights of the return were twofold; in Kiev, where work on the cathedral had stopped due to exhaustion of funds, our donations enabled the priest to complete the work in time for a special celebration. Holy Mass would now be celebrated in the refurbished sanctuary, rather than in the small, cramped sacristy as it had been for years.

Even greater, the old cathedral in Minsk, which the Communists had taken and made into a sport hall for youth, was unexpectedly returned to the Church shortly after my visit in August, 1993—a grace attributed to our prayers, according to the bishop. It made headlines throughout Eastern Europe. The people of Minsk simply rejoiced by participating fervently in the Holy Mass now held *inside* the building. For years they had come every morning and evening to attend Mass and pray the rosary on the sidewalk in front of the building. I spoke in the returned Cathedral of Minsk to an overflow crowd that spilled onto the very sidewalk that had served as their only sanctuary for years.

The three trips to Russia in the past 19 months were the most dramatic of entire mission. The first was filled with great expectations; the second was akin to passing through the eye of a needle; and the third—simply triumph. I knew I would return in the future.

In June, we traveled to Medjugorje to celebrate the thirteenth anniversary of the apparitions, joining thousands of pilgrims from around the world. Just as Our Lady had stated, Medjugorje had regained its reputation as the most popular Marian shrine, with large numbers of pilgrims continuing to visit throughout the remainder of the year. The pump had definitely been primed, and the fount of grace was flowing as in the early years.

The return of the Medjugorje pilgrims had a wonderful new twist: now, more than ever before, non-Catholics were coming, a definite contrast to the days of my first pilgrimage in May 1986, when I was the only Protestant pilgrim in Medjugorje. Protestants were now praying rosaries along with Catholics, bringing new fuel to the quest for Christian unity. And truly remarkable was the work of Bernard Ellis, a converted Jew who founded the Medjugorje Appeal in London, England, responsible for millions of dollars in aid to war victims.

Ironically, although the Madonna speaks Croatian in her daily appearances to the visionaries of Medjugorje, only now were a larger number of the people of Croatia, and Bosnia-Hercegovina, sincerely listening. Only now, after the consequences of horrible war; only now, in desperate need of peace and reconciliation. Even Orthodox Serbians were coming. As one good friend put it, "Now, one cannot tell a Thursday from a Sunday; the crowds are so big and people are coming from all areas of former Yugoslavia. Some are walking, others by buses, but they now come and pray for peace."

And their prayers were working. The war was confined to clashes near the Bosnian-Serb border, with occasional flares still in Sarajevo and Mostar. Ethnic cleansing by the Serbs continued, until all areas held by them were devoid of Croatians and Muslims. Sniper fire still interrupted the weak peace efforts of the United Nations, but overall, the war was coming to a conclusion just as Our Lady promised with the assistance of prayer, fasting, and penance.

The governments of the surrounding European nations and of the United States had done little, reluctant to the bitter end to defend the democratic rights they so strongly cherished themselves. The new administration's policy was to simply walk, uncommitted. Yet, in October, 1994, when Iraq once again threatened to cross the border of Kuwait, they were there immediately with strong diplomacy, propaganda, and massive military strength at the ready. Once again, the material world was far more valuable than the civil and religious freedom of people.

On this thirteenth anniversary, more than 50,000 pilgrims swelled the grounds of Saint James Church. So much had changed; but so much was still the same. Enlarged homes to house pilgrims were full again, as were the restaurants and souvenir stands. Surges of crowds carrying banners were everywhere, climbing Podbrdo and Krizevac; they processed through the streets with more than 5,000 participating in a peace march from twelve miles away, in sweltering heat. Masses were continuous. Lines of confessors stayed long throughout the day.

Finally the moment came when Our Lady appeared to Marija with the monthly message, as always, soul-touching: *"Dear children, today I rejoice in my heart in seeing you all present here. I bless you and I call you all to decide to live my messages which I give you here. I desire, little children, to guide you all to Jesus because He is your salvation. Therefore, little children, the more you pray, the more you will be mine and of my Son, Jesus. I bless you all with my motherly blessing and I thank you for having responded to my call."*

I wept with joy, happy that Terri, Kennedy, and Rebecca were there with me to hear the message, so simple, yet so profound; because Lisa, Angela, Mike, and Steve were now on the spiritual pathway, listening and attempting to live the messages. And because other members of our family were also now listening. There was special joy over Lisa, who was now fulfilling the prophecy of Our Lady, by witnessing at conferences of her own spiritual conversion—including having had an abortion.

It had come as a shock to her when she unexpectedly gave the first real witness about her abortion at the conference in Irvine, California, in November, 1992. I had asked her repeatedly to do it, but the pain and fear held her back. We prayed together just before her talk, for her to receive the strength needed from the Holy Spirit to do what Our Lady was asking. Abandoning her notes, and through a steady stream of tears, she related the painful story, touching deeply the hearts of those in attendance. Word of her witness spread, and in the next two years, the story was told at conferences throughout the country.

I was also happy because Marija was there with Paolo. Even though eight months pregnant, she actively took part in the events and gave talks with the other visionaries. In July, she gave birth to a son, and with Ivan's October wedding, all but Vicka had celebrated the sacrament of marriage. They are raising families, going on with life, living each day in accordance with the grace given by Gospa's presence.

There was one more reason I was especially grateful on this anniversary. Following the head-on automobile crash, Father Jim Watters was given little or no chance of ever recovering memory and motor skills so that he could function again as a priest. He was now serving in a small church in North Carolina, limited, but able to carry out most of his priestly duties. It was pure miracle.

Mostly, I was filled with the peace, love, and grace of Jesus, knowing that Our Lady, Queen of Peace, would continue coming in apparition until every possible soul could be reached and given an opportunity to allow her to lead them to her Son.

In September, 1994, after the now mandatory three months of rest during the summer and several early conferences, I left for a week-long tour of Central American countries, Guatemala and El Salvador. It was another grueling day of air travel, leaving home early and arriving in Guatemala City thirteen hours later.

Typically, my bag was lost, and the flight arrived late. I was traveling in casual clothes and was somewhat disheveled and in need of a good bath and rest, but as always, there was no time. "They are waiting for you at the church," my host said, anxiously. "We will pick up your bag in the morning."

We hastily drove through congested traffic in a rather poor area of the city, arriving finally at a large church which thundered with singing from a crowd swelled to standing room only. As I was escorted up the aisle of the church, the people broke into applause. They knew of this one-time Protestant who was now a member of the Catholic Church; and they knew of Medjugorje's apparitions. The book had preceded me, as well as the tabloid of my original Medjugorje columns. And many people from the area had made pilgrimages to the village.

Suddenly, the weariness of the trip was forgotten. I spoke for more than an hour, interrupted often by applause as they eagerly soaked in every detail of Medjugorje and its message of Gospel renewal. The talk was followed by Holy Mass celebrated by the local bishop. Afterward, there was more singing. It seemed no one wanted to leave.

Well after midnight, some eighteen hours after departing my home in Myrtle Beach, I wearily sank into a small bed in a shabby hotel not far from the church. Three soldiers stood guard in the lobby, armed with automatic weapons, giving rise to apprehensions, and yet defining clearly what I was doing here. In the meantime, others of the sponsoring prayer group had scurried about finding toiletries, clean clothes, and a pair of pajamas for their guest.

Smiling, feeling secure in such surroundings, knowing my God and His mother were there with me, I took my rosary in hand and began praying in thanksgiving.

There was still much to be done. The mission *would* continue.